no one awaiting me

two brothers defy death
during the Holocaust in Romania

UNIVERSITY OF
CALGARY
PRESS

JOIL ALPERN

Jewish Heritage

© 2001 Joil Alpern. All rights reserved.

University of Calgary Press
2500 University Drive N.W.
Calgary, Alberta, Canada T2N 1N4

The Jewish Heritage Project
150 Franklin Street
New York, NY 10013
U.S.A.

National Library of Canada Cataloguing in Publication Data

Alpern, Joil, 1930-
 No one awaiting me

(Legacies shared book series, ISSN 1498-2358 ; 5)
 Includes bibliographical references and index.
 ISBN 1-55238-071-8 (bound) -- ISBN 1-55238-061-0 (pbk.) University of Calgary Press
 ISBN 0-9660440-6-1 (bound) -- ISBN 0-9660440-7-X (pbk.) Jewish Heritage Project
 1. Alpern, Joil, 1930- 2. Holocaust, Jewish (1939-1945)--Personal narratives. 3. Jews--Romania-
-Biography. I. Title.
 DS135.R73A46 2001   940.53'18'092   C2001-911271-8

The Canada Council for the Arts
Le Conseil des Arts du Canada

Canada We acknowledge the financial support of the Government of Canada through the
Book Publishing Industry Development Program (BPIDP) for our publishing activities.

Jewish Heritage gratefully acknowledges the support of: Patricia and David Hauben, Trustees, the
Lowe II Foundation; the Literature Program of the National Endowment for the Arts, Cliff
Becker (Director), Amy Stolls (Program Officer); the Literature Program of the New York State
Council on the Arts, Kathleen Masterson (Director), and the assistance of the staff of the United
States Holocaust Memorial Museum, including Martin Goldman (Director of Survivor Affairs),
Genya Markon (Curator of Collections), and Christopher Sims (Photo Archivist).

This book is printed on acid-free paper.

Printed and bound in Canada by AGMV Marquis.
Interior book design by Alberta Graphics.
Cover design by Sona Khosla.
Cover image: © Raymond Gehman / CORBIS / Magma.

CONTENTS

Acknowledgements

My thanks to Benton Arnovitz, Director of Academic Publications at the United States Holocaust Memorial Museum for directing me to Alan Adelson, Executive Director of the Jewish Heritage Project in New York. Mr. Adelson has been instrumental in bringing this book to the light of print. His invaluable assistance and commitment to the project are sincerely appreciated. Thanks also to Molly Magid Hoagland and Alan Anderson for their proficiency in editing.

I would like to thank Sharon Chisvin for her expressions of confidence in the manuscript during its early stages. To our friends Howard and Sandra Collerman, I wish to express my thanks for their keen interest and ongoing encouragement. Thanks also to my nieces Lisa and Pamela Reiss for their computer expertise. To my wife Ida, who assisted with the writing and editing of the book, as well as doing all the typing, my sincerest and heartfelt thanks. Without her help and perseverance this book would not have been written.

Dedications

In memory of my parents
Isaac and Rosa Alpern
and
sister and brothers
Molly, Shimon, and Avrum

Introduction

by Alan Adelson and Heather Coleman

Joil Alpern made his way from an orphan's nightmare during the Holocaust in middle Europe to the peaceful prairies of Canada where he lives today as a cattle dealer. He remains so haunted by the horrors that drove him to write this moving account that the doleful faces of the powerless livestock he has sorted for shipment to market bring back memories of the helplessness of so many from his community and his own rigid fear as he and his fellow Jews were force-marched under the threat of death. The author's understated courage and faith, and his determination to focus on the positive aspects of life, not only enabled him to survive as a youth but also to muster the stamina to face the nightmares he left behind. The result is a memoir which is a remarkably inspiring reading experience for anyone willing to consider the conflict which remains between the finest and most constructive values of humankind and the vicious, destructive capacities of our species as well.

An obviously direct individual, Mr. Alpern seems to have adopted the Canadian prairie tradition of wasting no words and allowing no indulgence in self-pity. He has been scrupulous in restricting his memoir to his own experiences and has been unflinching in re-opening the wounds inflicted on him as a boy to render his story with an acuity and authenticity rarely encountered in such works.

No One Awaiting Me brings to the light of print a little-told but numerically significant phase of the war against the Jews. The story begins in 1930s Romania where Joil Alpern spent a joyous childhood, despite the anti-Semitism which began intensifying well before war broke out in June of 1941. The story moves quickly to "Transnistria" – literally, "across the Dniester" – an artificial geographic entity in south-

---

About the authors:

Alan Adelson is the Executive Director of the Jewish Heritage Project in New York. He is the producer and co-director with Kathryn Taverna of the film "Lodz Ghetto" and is the author of a forthcoming family history of the Einsteins.

Heather J. Coleman teaches in the Department of History and is co-ordinator of Central and East European Studies in the Faculty of Communication and Culture at the University of Calgary.

western Ukraine chosen by Romania's genocidal planners as a "dumping ground for Jews" from the provinces of Bukovina and Bessarabia. The murderous Nazis would accomplish the extermination of these Jews, Alpern writes, "by allowing them to perish from cold, starvation and disease, rather than be murdered outright.... It was just as cruel and, in the end, just as effective."

Bukovina, a small province in northeastern Romania, was repeatedly victimized in a series of military campaigns over the years. In August of 1939, Hitler and Stalin shocked the world by signing a non-aggression pact in which each side pledged to remain neutral if the other went to war. Unknown at the time were secret clauses to the treaty which divided the region between them into two spheres of influence. This gave Germany a free hand in western Poland and granted the Soviets rule over Latvia, Estonia, Lithuania, Finland, eastern Poland, and Bessarabia. Hitler invaded Poland from the west in September of 1939, and the Soviets advanced to take the territories designated for them. Although Bukovina had not been part of the original secret agreement on spheres of interest, in the summer of 1940, the Soviets decided that they wanted it too. By June 1940, faced with an ultimatum from the Soviet Union, Romania gave in and ceded Bessarabia and northern Bukovina. So Joil Alpern and his family experienced a year of Soviet rule. But in June of 1941, Hitler broke his non-aggression promise, invading the USSR. The Romanian Army joined in the invasion, regaining control of Bukovina and Bessarabia and beginning the era of brutal deportations which proved so tragic for the Alpern family and the vast majority of the Jews of the region. Romania's opportunism was evident in its vicious handling of the "Jewish problem."

"Complete ethnic liberation" and the "purification of our lineage" is what Mihai Antonescu, the vice president of the Romanian Council of Ministers, promised a conference of administrative inspectors and military prosecutors in July of 1941. His listeners were bound for service in Bessarabia and Bukovina. "The act of ethnic cleansing will involve removal or isolation of all Jews in labor camps from which they will no longer exert their nefarious influence."[1]

The Nazis' racial policies and their military pursuit of the war were not as separate from one another as has often been described. From its

---

[1] Quoted in Radu Ioanid, *The Holocaust in Romania: The Destruction of Jews and Gypsies Under the Antonescu Regime, 1940-1944,* Chicago, 2000, pp. 91-2.

very conception, the German campaign on the Eastern Front had a strong racial component. The Nazis had long asserted the need for "living space" for the German people in the less populous east. Their plan was to force the "subhuman" Slavs in the region to serve the allegedly superior Aryan race, while the Jews were to be eliminated altogether. Working towards a common cause, Hitler and Marshal Ion Antonescu, Romania's military dictator, agreed that the 40,000 square kilometres between the Dniester and Bug rivers, which was designated Transnistria, would be administered by the Romanians under German oversight. Jews would be deported into the region, and their energy exploited in labour camps. But this political arrangement was by no means protective of those Jews. In fact, Transnistria became Romania's killing field. Joil Alpern gives us a rare eyewitness account of this relatively unknown chapter within the history of the Holocaust. In the summer of 1941, tens of thousands of Jews perished as German and Romanian troops reconquered northern Bukovina and Bessarabia from the Soviets. Like the Alperns, most of those who remained were first forced into internment camps or ghettos and then, between October, 1941, and January, 1942, they were deported to Transnistria.

Although its own participation in the attempt to annihilate Europe's Jews is still relatively unrecognized, Romania's voluntary involvement in the large-scale massacre of Jews in the Holocaust was second only to Germany's. In the first six months of the German and Romanian occupation of Transnistria, German mobile killing units and Romanian troops annihilated some eighty percent of the Jews native to the region. Of the estimated 160,000 Jews deported to Transnistria – Bukovinians, including Joil Alpern's family, Bessarabians and Jews from the Dorohoi district – two-thirds died. The Romanian Jews who survived the intentionally genocidal "death marches" into the area were then herded into ghettos and camps, and some, like the Alperns, housed in pig barns and cow sheds. Many were then worked to exhaustion. Historian Radu Ioanid has described the genocidal strategy as a cynical policy of subjecting the Jews to the so-called "*natural* process of extermination through famine and disease."[2] But the Antonescu government's attack against the Jews lacked the systematic complexity practised by the Germans.

The death toll in the first winter of that occupation was staggering. Joil and Avrum lost their sister, a brother and both parents during those

---

[2] Ioanid, p. 205.

harsh months. In what Dalia Ofer has called "A Special Case of Genocide,"[3] between thirty and fifty percent of all the Jews deported to Transnistria perished from typhus, exhaustion, hunger and exposure in the winter of 1941–42. Of the 51,000 who survived by 1944, 5,000 were orphans, including Joil and his brother Avrum.

Young Joil was among the very few who emerged from that horror of death marches and deadly internment to take it upon himself, like Melville's Ishmael, to bear witness to the destruction. But he accomplishes much more in this remarkable memoir. Alpern details the passionate struggle he and his little brother Avrum waged to fulfill their youthful drive to live. The brothers endured a series of agonizing losses as one family member after another perished in the mud of Transnistria, in the filth of a pig barn, in their family members' arms. Theirs is a story of triumph to outlive the most oppressive existence mankind could devise. That plight destroyed the dignity and sapped the will to live of most who fell within its stifling hold. To fight back was to risk probable death. Fleeing was a deadly gamble in its own right. Yet the two orphans endured. They wandered together from danger to refuge and into new dangers again. Always, Joil's most pressing concern was how to protect little Avrum – to share a precious raw potato, to situate him safely in the pig barn while Joil goes out to forage for food, even to stand between his trembling brother and a soldier's gun. While never acknowledging such sentiment, it is clearly the love Joil and Avrum shared with one another which proved to be so powerful a force that the brothers were able to survive.

Even those who steep themselves in the literature of the Holocaust – the writings of those about to perish, and those who made it through – will never get beyond the terrible awe invoked by the phenomenon of the extinguishing of so many lives while others are inexplicably left alive. There is not an iota of self-congratulation in Joil Alpern's attitude towards his own survival. The perils he faced *obviously* could have taken him time and again during those years when he and his people were the object of the most complex and concerted effort ever mounted to destroy a single people. He confronted brutal soldiers, hardened Nazi sympathizers, and cruel acts of nature with the same consistent determi-

---

3 Ofer, "The Holocaust in Transnistria: A Special Case of Genocide," in *The Holocaust in the Soviet Union: Studies and Sources on the Destruction of the Jews in the Nazi-Occupied Territories of the USSR, 1941-1945*, eds. Lucjan Dobroszycki and Jeffrey Gurock, Armonk, 1993, p. 143.

nation to survive. But we read not only about the depths of human cruelty but also about the inextinguishable qualities of human kindness. We thrill at the small gestures of those who have little toward those who have nothing: a piece of bread and a few kind words, a bit of unsalted butter to help heal a blistered hand, and a night spent in comfort and security around a fire. We ponder with our author how such acts of goodness could emerge amid such suffering and cruelty.

Endurance became a goal in its own right for Joil and Avrum. That war within a war, undertaken by a party of elite which ruled over one of Europe's strongest industrial nations, was accomplished with the extensive co-operation of Germany's population, and other nations' pervasive refusal to acknowledge the murderous crusade. But in Transnistria under the Romanians, a greater chance of survival existed. While the Jewish populations in Romania beyond Bukovina and Bessarabia suffered economic and social persecution, they gained some protection as a result of the government's indecisiveness and its lack of full-scale commitment to the genocide. They could even co-ordinate some assistance for their less fortunate brethren in Transnistria.

Against this background, only one alternative remained for the beleaguered youths: if they could endure, they would accomplish a personal triumph even against the pervasive backdrop of death and defeat from which they sought to separate themselves. Progressively, the memoir becomes a remarkably inspiring and thoughtful experience for any reader who is willing to consider the never-ending conflict between the finest and most constructive drives of humankind, and the murderously destructive capacities of our species.

As a child struggling to win such a contest against hardened adults, Joil Alpern had to rely purely on his instincts and strength of will. Therein lies this memoir's remarkable inspiration. The publication of this book half a century later is the fulfillment of that struggle. Yet Mr. Alpern finds no cause for celebration. He writes with admirable honesty of the terrible sense of anti-climax and loneliness he felt on liberation. As the title he has chosen for the book states so poignantly, he had no one awaiting him.

The memoir is distinguished as well by Joil Alpern's prodigious capacity to remember with the most immediate detail and authenticity the horrors he witnessed. These episodes are rendered in an unschooled, honest voice, chilling in its starkness and immediacy. The truth of the story pulses with the lives of those being subjected to suffering and depravity, beatings, hunger and exhaustion elevated to the level of epidemic disease. Joil and Avrum are reduced, with their fellow Jews, to eating grass. They emerge victorious from these nightmarish days – only to be parted forever by yet another cruel turn of fate.

Romania's Jews had a higher survival rate from the Holocaust than any other European country. But the chauvinistic efforts by some Romanians to congratulate themselves for offering safe haven to the Jews are far from accurate and attempt to brush aside the extermination of a quarter of a million Romanian Jews. Joil Alpern's book constitutes one of the few first-person accounts of the Holocaust in Transnistria and will stand against such efforts to gloss over an indelibly dark chapter in Romanian history.

With his own characteristically positive outlook, Joil Alpern has written this statement of why he devoted many difficult years to the compiling of his written testimony:

"This book was written to bring to light the stories of those Holocaust victims who lie buried and almost forgotten in a land filled with unmarked graves…. By piecing together shards of memory, I have been able to recreate the story of my family's past, the story of my youth and the little-known story of the Jews of Transnistria. In so doing, I have also been given the opportunity to retell the universal story of the triumph of hope over despair."

THE BEGINNING

I was born in 1930 in Storojinet, a city in northern Bukovina, Romania, and my earliest memories are of happy occasions. I remember the tailor and the shoemaker coming to our house to take my measurements as well as those of my brothers and sister. I must have been six years old, because I had just started first grade. It was customary to receive new clothes for the High Holidays in the fall, as well as for Passover in the spring.

The holidays were joyous times. Attired in our new clothing, we walked proudly to synagogue with our parents. But we quickly tired of sitting quietly in the synagogue and went out to play and show off our new clothes. My friends and I behaved well, not that it was in our nature to be model kids, but the clothing acted as a restraint from vigorous activity. After the service, we would go home to a family gathering with traditional holiday food: gefilte fish or boiled carp as appetizer; chicken soup; roast chicken and beef with horseradish or applesauce, noodle kugel or a flaky-pastry potato roll; and for dessert fruit compote, along with cake and dainties. My parents kept kosher and followed all the Jewish customs. They were not Orthodox, however, and as children we were allowed to play with other kids on the Sabbath, kicking around a rubber ball soccer-style, playing hopscotch and other games.

Chanukah was another exciting time. Traditionally, parents and relatives gave children Chanukah gelt – money – as gifts. We also got dreidles, four-sided toys marked on each side with a different Hebrew letter, each standing for an abbreviation of the miracle that happened in the Temple in Jerusalem. These dreidles revolved like spinning tops and were used as a children's game of chance. We spent many evenings during the eight-day holiday spinning these dreidles and, depending on which letter turned up, determining the winner.

Our family consisted of my parents, Isaac and Rosa Alpern, my older brother Shimon, my older sister Molly, myself, and my younger brother Avrum. My father, who was in his mid-thirties, was a contractor for a large sawmill in nearby Berhomet, which was surrounded by vast forests of fine timber. The sawmill, the main employer in town, was owned by a

Jewish man by the name of Josel Rudich. The timber was harvested and transported on flatbed cars over narrow rail lines to the sawmill. There it was cut into planks, primarily for export. It was a seasonal business and my father hired workers, most of whom were Gentile, according to need. He treated them with respect, which created good working relationships.

My mother was a housewife who was kept busy looking after her four active youngsters. Father enjoyed eating meat dishes, but we kids preferred home-made pastas and dairy meals; consequently, Mother spent a lot of time in the kitchen. Each afternoon, as soon as I came home from school, I immediately went to the stove to see what was cooking, a habit that has remained with me to this day. Purim was especially memorable for someone with a sweet tooth; I couldn't wait to sample the delicacies that came out of the oven.

The first scolding I can remember took place one day when I returned from our German neighbour's house where I had gone to play with my schoolmate. After playing for a while, I found myself alone with her in the room where the Christmas tree was set up, the customary branches laden with chocolates and nuts. She asked me to kiss her.

"Sure," I said, "as long as I can pick some chocolates off the tree."

After kissing her, I filled my pockets and went straight home. I proudly showed them to my brothers, and my mother overheard our conversation.

"Where did you get them?" she asked.

"At Ingrid's," I said.

"Take them back right now and apologize," she said sternly.

"But Mother, they belong to me. I kissed her for them." She grabbed my arm and led me to the door. On my return, I was reprimanded, accompanied by some spanking. I was ashamed to take the chocolate back and didn't walk into their house again for a long time.

As the years slowly progressed, we children never lacked for happy times. Summer vacations and family functions were events that we all looked forward to. My parents came from large families, and we frequently visited relatives during the summer, particularly those in Berhomet where my paternal grandparents, aunts, uncles and many cousins lived. My maternal grandmother lived in Storojinet. These relatives and others also came to visit us. We were constantly active swimming, picnicking, picking berries, and playing games until we were exhausted. Winter also had its attractions – skating, tobogganing, and building snowmen and tunnels in the snow.

I even enjoyed going back to school in the fall. In addition to attending public school, where classes were conducted in Romanian, I went to Hebrew school in the afternoon. I also learned to write in German, which was widely spoken throughout Bukovina. We spoke Yiddish and German at home. Due to territorial changes resulting from being conquered by different countries, Bukovina was a multi-ethnic province: Romanians, Jews, Germans, and Ukrainians made up the majority of the population. I liked my studies and was particularly interested in mathematics and geography. I liked to watch Shimon do his geography homework and play around with plasticine to create topographic details on a map. He patiently explained what he was doing, and he also taught me to tell time. There was a huge tower in the city with an enormous clock that could be seen from a distance as it rang out the time on the hour. I impressed my friends by being able to tell them what time it was just before the bells rang.

My siblings and I generally got along well, except for the odd squabble. Occasionally, we all went to see a matinee movie, even though they had subtitles which changed too quickly for me to follow. One that stands out in my mind featured curly-haired Shirley Temple. Even more impressive was seeing a black actor in that movie; I had never seen a black person in real life. I did not believe he was real and argued about it with Shimon.

I was a mischievous kid who liked to play pranks. In the winter, some friends and I would hide and throw snowballs at passers-by. We had a good laugh when they turned around and couldn't see anyone. Sometimes, we found discarded flashlight batteries and, after dismantling them, wrapped them up to look like rolls of coins. We'd plant them on the sidewalk, then watch people's reactions as they picked them up.

Shimon was six years older than me and had a more mature mind. I was interested when he joined Betar, a Zionist organization dedicated to regaining Palestine. Dad, a firm believer in Zionism, was pleased with his choice. When Shimon first joined the organization, he talked with enthusiasm about its ideals and goals. He told us how much fun he had learning Israeli songs and dances, listening to speakers, and participating in various recreational activities, including ping-pong and soccer.

The soccer and ping-pong appealed to me as well, and I begged him to take me along. I must have been eight at the time, and I made friends on my first visit. I was attracted by the sports activities and the attitude displayed by the leaders. After that, I started going with Shimon whenever he went. In addition to playing sports and games, we were taught about the history of Judaism and the meaning of Zionism. Jews have regarded Palestine as their homeland since biblical times and hoped one day to return from the Diaspora. Great emphasis was placed on the importance of emigrating to Palestine when we were old enough to help reclaim and build our homeland. I gradually learned that other Jewish youth in our town belonged to one of several Zionist organizations with different approaches to the goal of reclaiming Palestine.

That summer, I attended a two-week Betar summer camp. It was held in a large, clean barn that was rented from a farmer. About thirty of us kids, ranging in age from eight to fifteen, slept on straw that we covered with blankets. To give us a sense of belonging, the counsellors encouraged us to participate in the preparation of meals: carrying pails of water, chopping wood, peeling potatoes, cleaning vegetables. Most of the food was bought from the farmer.

We were awakened early each morning and taken for a hike. After breakfast we participated in various sports. We took a nap after lunch and then listened to speakers who emphasized the importance of having our own country, especially at a time when Europe was being engulfed by fascism. Each evening, we gathered around a campfire, singing Hebrew songs. At the end of the two weeks, I was imbued with Zionism. I left with a strong desire to move to Palestine one day.

✳

Through the mid-1930s, we children had not a care in the world; we thought only about having fun. Gradually, however, the environment began to change. By the latter half of that decade, we began to feel the effects of anti-Semitism in Romania, as did the Jews in most other European countries.[1] Out of a total population of eighteen million people, there were approximately 800,000 Jews living in Romania at that time. Romania's Jewish population was the third largest in Europe.

I was too young to understand the politics of the day, but my parents followed every development with growing concern. A professor from the University of Iasi, by the name of A. C. Cuza, was the leader of one of the most anti-Semitic political parties in Romania. In 1937, he joined forces with Octavian Goga, a leader of another anti-Semitic group, and with King Carol's approval, they formed a government in December. Even though this government did not last long, its oppressive policies toward Jews were continued by successive leaders.[2] Along with Corneliu Codreanu, the leader of the Garda de Fier (Iron Guard), these three parties constituted a powerful force that inflamed the population against the Jews with anti-Semitic slogans and speeches.

Relations between Jews and fascists became more strained; people who previously had shown no animus toward us were revealed to be fascist sympathizers. Jews felt hatred directed against them and were sometimes beaten on the streets. Life became more restrictive, particularly for Orthodox Jews whose appearance and attire made plain their identity. Zionist organizations were targeted for persecution.

One day, while I was playing ping-pong at the Betar club, members of the Iron Guard stormed in and smashed everything in sight. They beat many of us and warned us that if we came back again, the consequences would be more severe. The children were allowed to go home, but the adults were kept back for interrogation and were released later with bloody noses and black eyes. At the public school I attended, fights often broke out between Jews and non-Jews. Non-Jewish students no longer held back their hatred and did not hesitate to insult us or pick a fight. We were frequently told to move to where we belonged – Palestine. Most fights broke out during recess between students from different classes. They would start with a deliberate push and an insult, lasting until the bell rang or a teacher intervened.

Tension was at its highest when we had our weekly class on religion. Students gathered in different rooms, according to their religion. The Jewish students were instructed by a rabbi, the Christian students by a priest. This division gave the agitators an opportunity to congregate, and they took full advantage of this to promote fights. Some Christian students did not exhibit any hatred toward us, nor did they try to break up the fights; they watched from the sidelines. When we walked home from school, we went in groups to discourage students who had intentions of provoking fights with us. When fights did break out, however, we were not punching bags; we fought back as hard as we could.

Nationalism became so strong in the late 1930s that a decree was issued stating that people had to speak only Romanian in all public places, as well as in stores; they would be fined if caught speaking another language.

As the political situation deteriorated, Dad decided that we should move to Berhomet, where he worked. He was well known in the area and felt it would be safer than Storojinet. In addition, he no longer would have to commute the thirty kilometres between the two communities.

I remember very well the day when Cuza, the anti-Semitic political leader, came to our town to make a speech. Jews were forewarned that fascists from surrounding villages were going to gather in our town to hear his speech and celebrate the occasion. We were told to stay inside our homes.

That evening, we were having supper in our new home in Berhomet when we heard singing. As the voices came closer, we recognized the songs of the fascists. A short while later, men knocked on our door and windows and called for my father by name to open the door. My father looked through the cracks in the shutters, but it was dark outside, and he could not make out who they were. The knocks grew louder, and the men demanded that my father open the door. Dad told us all to leave the kitchen and go into the bedroom. I hid under the kitchen table to see what he would do. He grabbed an axe and opened the door. He was a tall, strong man who was determined to protect his family.

When Dad opened the door, the kitchen filled with his employees. They all seemed happy and a bit drunk, and some of them embraced him. They were fond of him, and, even though they knew he was Jewish, they said they had come to take him to hear Cuza speak. My mother came out of the bedroom; she cried and pleaded with those men she knew to let Father remain at home. They promised Mother that they would bring him back unharmed after the speech. Having no choice, he got dressed and went with them to hear a condemnation of the Romanian Jewish population. My mother stayed up, worrying about Dad. Sometime during the night, they brought him back unharmed.

Jews developed a keen interest in politics as the threat to their well-being increased. They listened closely to their radios and scanned the stations for any bit of information from the outside world. Signals were weak, and the words faded in and out. Sometimes we could hear Hitler himself ranting at the top of his lungs against the Jews. The applause was frequent, long and deafening. Every word he uttered gave us the jitters. We couldn't just wave off his words; we knew they might be shaping our very future.

My father used to get a weekly German-language paper from Switzerland. It contained articles from all over Europe and was presumed to be unbiased. One of these articles described the horror of "Kristallnacht," the night of November 9, 1938, when Nazis in Germany rampaged and looted Jewish homes and stores. Windows were broken and glass littered the streets in cities and towns. Synagogues were burned, and Jews were killed at will.

My father feared that a similar tragedy could occur in Romania. Since it was difficult for Jews to get visas for Palestine, he made plans to emigrate to Bolivia, where a few Jewish families from our town had already gone. These emigrants had sent letters back to their relatives saying that conditions were favourable. We almost sold our home, but my grandparents and my parents' siblings discouraged us from leaving as we were a large close-knit family with strong ties to each other. Even though my father anticipated difficult times, it did not take much persuasion to convince him to remain so as to keep the family together. This unwillingness to separate was typical of most Jewish families.

✳

I was introduced to politics at an early age. Dad was my idol and I spent a lot of time with him. I would listen closely to the political discussions he had with friends and neighbours who often gathered at our house. I could not fail to understand the prevalence and importance of anti-Semitism in every facet of daily life.

On the way home from school, my friends and I would read the anti-Semitic newspaper headlines that were posted at the newsstands. If a headline interested me, I used part of my weekly candy allowance to buy a paper. I wanted to see what they were writing about the Jews. Even though I did not understand all the words, I understood the message. Every page would have an article or caricature condemning Jews and blaming them for everything. My parents forbade me to buy this paper, so I had to read it on the street or in the park. They did not want me to be subjected to false propaganda, nor did they want to burden me with unnecessary worry at such a young age.

Distressing news reached us one day. In December 1937, the Romanian government issued a decree that would strip a large percentage of the nation's Jews of their citizenship and threaten some with deportation.[3] This seemed like a morbid joke to us: To where would they be deported? It was doubtful if any country would accept more than a few Jews.

Even the British government's 1939 "White Paper," its policy statement regarding Jewish immigration to Palestine, recommended that only a limited number of Jews be allowed to enter Palestine.[4] Of course, Palestine did not belong to England. After the First World War, the League of Nations gave England a mandate to be the custodian over Palestine. The Balfour Declaration stipulated that the country eventually was to be turned over to the Jewish people.

Meanwhile, Jews were already trying to escape from Europe to Palestine, but the British government stuck to its quota – 15,000 Jews

per year for a five-year period. This figure was a minute fraction of the population of seven or more million Jews in Europe. Only a few countries outside the European continent allowed a small trickle of Jews to enter them and find a safe haven. It turned out that the fate of the Jewish people was sealed: They were marked for total destruction.

The British government's policy prompted Zionist leaders, the most outspoken of whom was Ze'ev Jabotinsky, head of the Betar movement and well-known to European Jewry as a fighter for a Jewish homeland, to organize a movement to smuggle Jews out of Europe by boat. Another Jewish organization in Palestine, the Haganah, also tried to smuggle Jews out of Europe to safety.

The British government, however, succeeded in putting pressure on countries with port facilities to stop these illegal departures. This intervention choked off the single effective escape route and kept us corralled within easy reach of the Nazis. It felt like another turn in the vise that would eventually crush us all to death. Ironically, the vow to kill off the Jews was the only promise that Hitler kept while he was in power. Treaties that he had signed with countries under the glare of world publicity, and hailed as a victory by some free countries, were all ignored or broken within a short period of signing.

On the diplomatic front, shocking events were unfolding rapidly. New alliances were formed between Germany and the Soviet Union, two enemies with opposing ideologies. On August 23, 1939, Hitler and Stalin agreed to a non-aggression treaty between their two countries at a time when stability in Europe was threatened by Hitler. The pact contained a secret codicil giving the eastern part of Poland to the USSR as a reward for not intervening on Poland's behalf. On September 1, 1939, Hitler attacked Poland and conquered that country in less than a month. Then Soviet troops moved in as pre-arranged.

Germany found another useful ally in Romania – useful because the Ploiesti region had an abundant supply of oil, an essential commodity for waging war. Romania also had a large army and shared a border with the southwestern Ukraine. This border was to be a good starting point for a *blitzkrieg* on the southern Soviet flank.[5]

In 1940, even though Romania was an ally of Hitler, Stalin was able to make a second secret deal with Germany. The deal was that the Soviet Union would issue a 48-hour ultimatum to Romania ordering it to cede the province of Bessarabia (which bordered the Ukraine, and which Romania had annexed from the Soviet Union in 1918) and the northern portion of Bukovina (which adjoined Bessarabia). With all the turmoil in Europe, the USSR wanted a deeper buffer zone to be in a better strategic position to defend its southwestern border from attack. Hitler agreed not to oppose the Soviets in this plan. When the ultimatum was issued, Romania was forced to comply, because, without German help, it was not strong enough to fight the USSR. Germany did not oppose this arrangement because it benefited from commercial transactions with the Soviet Union; Germany also needed time to consolidate its conquests in Europe and to build its armies to full strength so it could launch the surprise *blitzkrieg* against the Soviets. Germany's plan was to use its fast-moving mechanized units, which had been successful to this point, to conquer the USSR quickly the following year before the severe winter set in. Hitler thought – mistakenly – that this strategy would allow him to avoid becoming bogged down in a long war in a vast, frigid and hostile country.

When the Soviet ultimatum was issued to Romania, many Jewish soldiers were serving in the Romanian army. As the Romanian army retreated from northern Bukovina and Bessarabia, many of these Jewish soldiers were beaten by their former compatriots, and some were killed. The Jews had become scapegoats – easy targets for the soldiers to blame and release their anger at having to retreat. One of the Jewish soldiers was Simon Hoffer, an uncle of mine. He was stationed in Czernowitz, the capital of Bukovina, but was fortunate during this troubled period to be on leave visiting a friend. His leave may have saved his life; others were not so lucky. As the Romanians retreated to a northern Bukovina town called Ciudeiu, they encountered two horse-drawn wagons carrying Jews on their way to Storojinet, a nearby city. The retreating soldiers shot them all in cold blood.

As the Romanian army withdrew, the Red Army moved in with troops and heavy armour. We were to live under the Soviet regime for a year until the war broke out.

I had just completed grade four and was to have started grade five in the fall. However, because the Soviets believed that their educational system was superior to Romania's, all students were ordered to remain in the same grade and repeat the year. Another reason for repeating the year was that we all had to learn the Russian and Ukrainian languages and the Cyrillic alphabet. One advantage was that sports were encouraged in the school system and we had easy access to facilities. In addition to soccer and ping-pong, I developed an interest in gymnastics.

Under Soviet rule, northern Bukovina became a police state. We literally had to adjust overnight to a strict and regimented communist system about which we knew little. Nobody could own any private business, no matter how small. All enterprises were nationalized by the Soviet government and inefficiently managed, resulting in frequent shortages. Sometimes whole families were removed by the Soviet police during the night for mysterious "political reasons." Rumours that they were sent to Siberia created much fear in the whole population.

During the evening of June 21, 1941, a large number of Soviet troops moved rapidly through our town. This was unusual; we had seen few military movements before. My father turned on the radio to listen to the news but we heard nothing. Many foreign stations had been jammed. He decided to go outside to see what was happening, and I went with him. Jewish neighbours huddled together, discussing the situation. They could not understand why the Soviet soldiers, along with their tanks and heavy armour, were retreating in haste. After being outside for a while, we went back into the house. My sister, my brothers and I went to bed. My parents, along with some relatives and neighbours, were in the kitchen drinking tea and discussing this grave situation.

On the morning of June 22, 1941, we were awakened and told that German and Romanian forces had attacked the Soviet Union and that war had begun. Jewish neighbours and some of our relatives gathered again in great agitation accompanied by fear and even panic. They discussed the lack of information and the sudden withdrawal of the Soviet army. They had no idea what to do, where to turn, or what fate awaited them.

The Soviet tanks and heavy armour shook the ground underneath us late into the night; by morning not a single soldier was in sight. A blanket of silence covered the streets, except for the occasional person scurrying by. The first tragic news reached us later that day when Uncle Schlomcu and Aunt Betty came to join us. They had heard that a pogrom (organized massacre and looting) had taken place in a Polish border town called Kuty, not far away, and that most of the Jews there had been killed. My father was especially concerned because his younger sister Schaendel and her family lived in Kuty. He was able to confirm through different channels that the massacre indeed had occurred. He also heard that savage murderers from our neighbouring area were moving toward our town.

Despite the Russo-German non-aggression treaty, Romania had joined forces with Germany in a surprise attack on the Soviet Union, known as Operation Barbarossa. Romanian forces quickly recaptured Bessarabia and northern Bukovina, the provinces they had been forced to cede to the USSR the previous year. Along with German forces, they were now advancing into the Ukraine republic of the Soviet Union. The Germans gave Romania part of southwestern Ukraine as a reward for their participation in the war as a German ally. This part of the Ukraine, situated between the Bug River and the Dniester River, was renamed Transnistria (for "across the Dniester") by the Romanians.[6]

During the initial onslaught of Operation Barbarossa, many thousands of Romanian Jews were massacred in cities and towns. Including those who were subsequently deported from Bessarabia and Bukovina to Transnistria, some 272,000 perished.[7] Approximately 50,000 Jews remained alive in Transnistria when the Soviet army liberated them in April 1944. I was one of them.

LEAVING HOME, JUNE 1941

June 22, 1941, was the beginning of a new chapter in my family's life. That was the day that rumour and hearsay turned into tragic reality. It marked the beginning of a process of upheaval and cruelty that destroyed my family. June 22 was the day the Nazis arrived. Their sudden invasion caught us all by surprise and, even before we saw a shadow of them, terrified us all. I saw many frightened people running to the forest to hide from the Nazis. Until that day, we Jews had considered ourselves equal members of the community and had only read or heard about the brutality against the Jews in Germany and in the Nazi-occupied countries. This day was the first time we experienced first-hand what we had heard about and feared. Some of us still hoped it would all blow over in a couple of days and that our lives would return to normal. This was not to happen.

As the sun slowly descended below the horizon and darkness set in, our lives began to unravel. Like most Jewish people in our town, my family decided to go into hiding in the thick, hilly forests nearby to get out of harm's way. Families gathered separately to lessen the chances of being spotted when they marched off to the forest. As we walked aimlessly into that dark night filled with terror and mystery, our brains were numb with unanswered questions and fear of the unknown. We did not know what the next day would bring, or if there would be a next day for us.

As we set off, Dad took the lead and placed Mother behind us to ensure that we all stayed together and did not wander off in the dark. We were told not to talk and to follow each other along the grassy strip next to the gravel road. The grass would help muffle the noise of our footsteps. Other members of our extended family followed at a distance. We soon left the road, walking on uncharted grassy terrain leading to the forest. After a long walk, which caused some bruised knees as we stumbled in the dark, we finally reached the forest, where we waited for the other family members. Together we wandered into a wall of darkness; seeing each other was just as difficult as foreseeing the future. We finally picked a resting place, exhausted and emotionally drained.

It was late when we bedded down for the night. Some people had blankets to spread on the ground while others lay in the clothing they wore. Parents made sure that their children slept between them so the youngsters would not wander off during the night.

This was the first time that I had no plans for the following day. It was summertime, we were out of school, and my friends and I had always arranged the night before to go swimming, play soccer or just to get together and laze around. Those times of making plans were now gone. I was scared and confused; my childhood was being taken away from me, literally overnight.

When we got up in the morning, families huddled together and discussed our grave situation; most of them were pessimistic. The children were subdued. Some were too young to understand what was happening; for them, it was an outing. I sat quietly, listening with interest to the adult discussion. The only thing that brightened our lives was the sun shining through the trees.

My parents were very concerned about my sister Molly; her appendix had been removed two weeks before, and she had not yet fully recovered. As it was summer, the adults decided not to make a fire for cooking lest the smoke reveal our hide-out to the Nazis. Dad knew that one of his Gentile employees lived on a small piece of secluded land at the edge of the forest, so he went to see if he could get some hot soup and milk for Molly. He returned later, to our great relief, with a lot of food, a couple of blankets and a few pillows. His employee wanted us to come and stay with him until my father thought it would be safe to return home. Since the weather was pleasant and warm, Dad decided we should not separate from the rest of the family, which included his parents, siblings and cousins, as well as some members of my mother's family. However, Dad said that if Molly's condition did not improve by evening we would have to go stay with the employee.

By evening, Molly felt better so we all remained. Food was not a problem because most people had brought some with them and we all shared with each other. The main concern of the families was that they did not know what was happening around them and to their properties since they left home. They were all in distress; tears started to appear on the faces of some adults who did not try to conceal them from us children. The little ones asked why their mothers were crying. Most of the time, the adults sat around in groups, discussing the political situation and wondering what was going to happen next. They could not decide whether to stay or return home; they had no idea what the military authorities and the local population had in store for us. It was an exhausting guessing game, with their families' lives at stake.

Disturbing news reached us one day when Uncle Moishe returned with food given to him by a Christian friend. The friend told him that Jewish homes in Berhomet had been ransacked and a Jewish barber's son had been killed. Apparently, not all Jews had gone into hiding. It was very difficult for the adults to accept that such things were happening. They thought they had had good relations with their Christian neighbours, all the way back to their kindergarten years. It was a relatively small town where many people knew each other by their first names and, regardless of religion, interacted in all facets of life.

For us children, the days in the forest were long and boring, and we were not in the mood to play. In normal times, with all the tall grass and trees around, it would have been an ideal place for hide-and-seek or just running around to release our pent-up energy. Now, however, this energy was supplanted by fear, uncertainty, and despair. I knew that there was something significant happening, but neither the children nor the adults could fathom the seriousness of our situation. The unknown handicapped us all, both physically and emotionally.

When we went to the forest to hide, we left everything in our house except the most valuable possessions that we could carry: our best clothes, jewellery, and money. These items had been packed in a hurry, amidst the confusion, apprehension, and stress. Physically, we all coped as well as we could under the circumstances. We were in good health and had enough food. Emotionally, the situation was different – I could sense the mental anguish of the adults and see their uneasiness. It was difficult for them to accept the unthinkable and realize what had actually happened to them in a few short days.

It was unimaginable for them to face the transition from a normal life to the life of a fugitive – in the very country where they had been born and lived all their lives as law-abiding citizens. Some older Jewish men, who had served in the Austrian army in World War I, were somewhat more optimistic. (Bukovina belonged to Austria until the end of World War I, when it was ceded to Romania.) Their belief was that civilians living next to the border were more prone to panic at the outbreak of war. They felt the situation would improve as the front moved farther away and the local civilian authority, with its more humane approach, once again took charge. They failed to understand that they were in the midst of an explicit Nazi policy to eliminate the Jewish people. The details of the policy were well-planned, thorough and brutal: The Nazis intended to utilize any method to execute their plans in the shortest time possible.

A week or so after going into hiding, word spread that everything had quieted down in our town.

"Maybe we should go home tomorrow," Uncle Schlomcu said.

"Yes, we probably should," Dad replied. "We'll wait until late at night."

On the way back, we were ambushed by a group of people, probably the local militia, who had hidden in a grain field. A voice called out in Romanian, "Stop, or you'll be shot!" We stopped. "Identify yourselves!" someone else shouted. Nobody in our group would speak; we were all too frightened. Then another voice said that if we didn't answer, we would all be shot. Without thinking I blurted out our family name, "Alpern."

Someone asked, "Which Alpern?"

I said, "Isaac." We were told to keep on going and never did find out who spared our lives. The ambush intensified our fears and left us wondering if we'd made the right decision returning home.

We arrived home to find an empty house with broken windows. Nothing remained inside except for some winter clothes that my parents had hidden under the stairs. I stared at the bare walls. Even some of the floors had been broken open, leaving gaping holes. Our hopes quickly faded. The skies appeared greyer that day than on the previous day, even though the sun was still shining.

It was very frightening for us children. As a child, I had always felt secure and safe – I knew my father would protect us from any danger. But I realized now that things were going to change. All rights, even those of protecting our own families, were taken away from the Jewish people. I was too young to anticipate the consequences that lay ahead, but I could sense the foreboding of my parents and the other adults. They were subdued and demoralized as they saw the wanton destruction of their property, for which they had worked so hard and had been so proud. Even those who had been leaders of the Jewish community were as frightened and helpless as everyone else. No heroes stepped forth to lead us.

In the morning, a Christian neighbour brought us food, along with some bad news: People had come from other towns with horse-drawn wagons and trucks, loading them with everything they could find in

Jewish homes. Some local people came with their whole families, also participating in the looting. Jewish property was seen as freely available to anyone.

Activity on the streets seemed almost normal, except that the Jews remained indoors. Only a few ventured out to visit their Jewish neighbours. Our family members gathered together in our house, and we all slept on the floor, cushioned by blankets. Everyone wanted to be with their family – togetherness gave our only sense of security. The adult discussions went on until late into the night. Fortunately, some Christian neighbours and acquaintances continued to bring us food.

For the few days we remained in our home, we were not harassed or abused. But we heard very disturbing news that pogroms and killings of Jews were taking place in some of the surrounding villages. As we sat defenceless in empty rooms protected only by walls and broken windows, not knowing what was going to happen to us, our fear intensified. The few family members who had some idea of what lay ahead kept it to themselves to avoid increasing our fear. The waiting was emotionally draining; we knew that any news would not be good. The first news that finally came was indeed disturbing: The military authority announced that all Jews were ordered to assemble in an area around the synagogue. We were to take only those belongings we could carry. This was rather ironic, considering that we had few things left. We were told that if we did not obey the orders, anybody found in his home or in a hiding place would be shot on the spot.

People, young and old, came from all directions and assembled in the designated area. The expressions on their faces told it all – they were confused and panic-stricken. I can vividly recall the scene: Few people spoke. It was like a silent movie unfolding on a screen, except that ordinary people, not actors, were participating in a tragic event scripted by the Nazis. We knew the beginning of the story but none of us could guess the ending. The only glimmer of hope that day came from rumours that we were going to be resettled.

Single people and young couples without children might have tried to avoid the round-up by hiding in the dense forest surrounding Berhomet. Without children, they could have moved from place to place, making a quick getaway when circumstances warranted. But bonds between families were unbreakable and kept almost everybody together.

Two or three hours after assembling, we were marched away by Romanian soldiers to Vijnita, a city about twenty kilometres away. As we left Berhomet behind, many tears were shed as people passed their ransacked homes and wondered if they would ever return to their place of birth. It was like a funeral procession: people with grim faces lost in their own thoughts, following each other. The only signs of life on Jewish properties were the beautiful flowers growing and, in some places, a dog awaiting the return of his master. Neighbours and townspeople stared at us through the open windows of their homes and from their front yards, with no outward expression or exchange of words. I saw one woman handing out some loaves of bread. A few others wore smiles on their faces and seemed happy to see us leaving. No foul language was used nor were any objects thrown at us, as had happened in other towns where pogroms had occurred and many Jews were beaten and shot to death. I heard later that, of the approximately 1,000 Jews who lived in Berhomet, only a few were shot during the initial days of the war.

We learned that we had miraculously escaped the first onslaught of brutal murderers who had come from the surrounding area to pillage and kill. Fortunately, we had been in the forest, out of their sight. When we arrived in Vijnita, we were put in a school, guarded by soldiers. The local Jews were still in their homes and were surprised to see us. This led us to believe that Vijnita was where we were going to be resettled. But our hopes were dashed a week later when we were ordered to assemble and were marched off again.

On the way, we were herded through small villages where we saw familiar scenes. It was easy to recognize Jewish properties by their outward appearance – broken windows and doors torn off their hinges or swaying in the breeze, banging against walls. Unrolled Torah scrolls were lying on the streets and local people were trampling on them. Anyone who tried to pick up the pieces of the Torahs was beaten by the soldiers and forced to put the scrolls back on the streets. From these scenes, we could not tell whether the Jews had been driven out or murdered.

Although our fate was unfolding before our very eyes, many were not yet prepared to accept the obvious. After a week on the road, we arrived in Storojinet, my birthplace, the second largest city in northern Bukovina. We were again interned in a school where tragic news awaited us. We heard that Romanian soldiers had entered a nearby town called Ciudeiu and rounded up the whole Jewish population of about 600 people, a number of whom were our relatives. All of them were taken to the courtyard of the jail and shot. Only a few young men managed to evade the round-up and escape to bear witness.

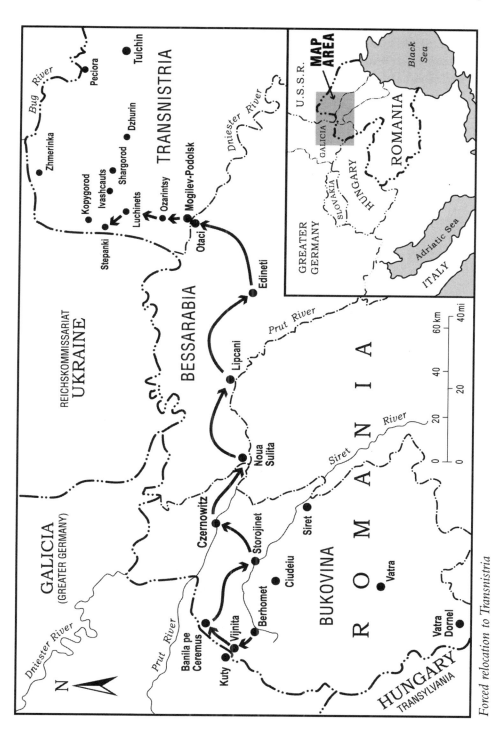

Forced relocation to Transnistria

We remained in Storojinet for about a week before continuing the march east toward Czernowitz, the capital of Bukovina. As we reached Czernowitz, we still clutched our naïveté and kept hoping that the Romanian government would stop the persecution of the Jewish people. This, however, did not happen, and we were ordered to keep marching eastward. The convoy became larger and larger as groups of Jews from other communities joined us. The Romanian soldiers who had herded us up to Czernowitz were replaced by many more soldiers who were more aggressive and cruel. They treated us worse than animals; we were driven like a herd of cattle with no mercy for pregnant women, the children, or the elderly. My father had a particularly difficult time because my sister Molly's condition had not improved. The incision to remove her appendix had not completely healed, and she was in pain. She could not walk, and Dad had to carry her as well as his own belongings in the sweltering heat.

Armed soldiers guarded the head of the convoy, both sides, and the rear. It was not an orderly march where people followed in each others' footsteps. We were scattered all over the road, walking as fast as we could to avoid ending up at the rear of the column. Those who did – chiefly the older and sicker people – were constantly beaten and abused by the soldiers. Quite often we heard gunshots from the back of the convoy, but we could not see what was happening because the column was very long. Later, we heard that marchers who could not keep up had been shot and left lying on the road. Their bodies were then robbed of valuables by the local people.

When we left home, we took all the belongings we could salvage – some carried them in a backpack, others in a suitcase. Some who had very little wore most of their clothing, even though it was extremely hot. These clothes were the only possessions they had to show for a lifetime of hard work, and having them on their back gave them a feeling of security. The march was particularly difficult for younger children and for older people who lacked the strength and stamina to carry their belongings for long periods of time on difficult roads. The very young, with their little legs and short steps, had great difficulty keeping up. They were too heavy to be carried by parents who were already straining under the weight of their belongings. These children hung onto their parents, literally being pulled along. Nobody could afford to get rid of belongings, which they needed to trade for food.

Our backpacks got lighter and lighter as we traded away our clothing and personal effects. We were never given any food or water by the soldiers. Farmers would stand on the road with bread, cornmeal, flour, potatoes, eggs, and cheese and barter with us for our belongings. We did not have much time to negotiate a fair deal for our valuables – it was a take-it-or-leave-it affair. The soldiers were always forcing us forward and away from the farmers. We were literally chased on foot over dirt and gravel roads through the provinces of northern Bukovina and Bessarabia. When the weather was dry, the dust raised by the marchers created a thick fog, which nearly choked us. When it rained, it was much worse; we walked in mud and puddles that sometimes rose above our ankles. Many older people burdened by their backpacks slipped in the mud and could not get up unless several people lifted them. Everyone in the convoy got soaked right to their bones.

We were permitted to stop for brief rests twice a day; at sundown we stopped on the road for the night. If it did not rain, the preferred place to sleep was in the ditch, where the softer ground cushioned our bones. Sometimes these overnight rests took place next to a bush that provided us with shelter and ample wood for a fire. But since we never knew where we would camp for the night, as we walked, we always picked up anything that might burn. For cooking, people scratched out small, narrow troughs in the earth and filled them with branches. They lit the branches and balanced a pot on top of them. Families took turns using the same fires, both for cooking and for drying clothing.

Our evening meal consisted mostly of soups made from potatoes or cornmeal which had been obtained by trade with the farmers on the road during the day. Sometimes the potatoes were first used to try curing diarrhea, a common problem on the road. (Dry cottage cheese was another remedy, but few could afford it.) The potatoes were baked in an open fire until the skin burned and then we ate the burned portion. It was a desperate measure; we never knew whether it really helped. The actual potato went into the soup. As our limited ingredients had to be rationed, these soups were never enough to satisfy our hunger after a long day's march. Whatever dry food we were able to get was kept and eaten while we walked.

One night some shocks of grain caught my eye when we stopped in a wide-open space next to a field. Without asking my parents' permission, I ran a short distance into the farm fields and grabbed as many sheaves as I could carry. We used the grain in soup after picking it out of the sheaves and we used the straw as bedding. Other people had the same idea, but those who were caught were severely beaten by the soldiers. We later heard that some people had been shot for this offence, so my parents forbade me to do this anymore. I was watched very closely by my father; he would not let me out of his sight whenever we stopped for the night next to a grain-field.

Each morning, when we were awakened at sunrise, we were just as bewildered as on the first day of our forced march. We were still wrestling with the trauma inflicted on us: why were we Jews being tyrannized? We were told to assemble quickly for another day's march that took us farther and farther from our home. As sunset followed sunrise, our hopes slowly faded away. People were tired and stiff from walking and from sleeping on the hard, uneven ground. I remember one man using a primitive crutch – a thick branch wedged under his arm with little branches sticking out. It must have helped as he was able to hop along and keep up with the convoy.

After approximately six weeks on this barbaric forced march, during which many people had perished, we finally arrived in a Bessarabian town called Edineti. In Edineti, we were interned in a makeshift ghetto, occupying the homes of Jews who had previously lived there. The small house in which my family stayed was shared with about twenty-five other people. This was the first night in many weeks that we had slept on a level floor under a roof. All the belongings from this house had been removed except for a cache of sunflower seeds in one room. These seeds provided a much-needed and nutritious supplement to the meagre food we received from the farmers in exchange for our limited belongings.

In one of the Jewish homes, everything had been removed except for the dead bodies lying on the floor, riddled with bullet holes. The bodies were carried out and buried by the new tenants who occupied the house. Those from the convoy who could not find shelter slept outside until it got too cold for them. Then they had to move in with the others despite the already overcrowded quarters.

A few local Jews had hidden in town. They told us horror stories about the crimes committed by the Nazis. Hundreds of Jews were massacred in cold blood and many women, including young girls, were raped. Thousands were rounded up and force-marched to unknown destinations. Some committed suicide.

Edineti became a holding camp for many thousands of Jews from parts of northern Bukovina, as well as from Bessarabia.[8] Those from Bessarabia had been lucky to escape the massacres carried out by the Nazi armies as they rolled through cities and towns in that province in pursuit of the retreating Soviet army during the early days of the war. Rumour had it that we were going to stay in Edineti until a dispute between the German and Romanian authorities was resolved. This dispute was preventing the Romanian soldiers from driving us across the Dniester River into the Ukraine. We heard that the delay was due to the fact that the *Einsatzgruppen* (specially trained German mobile killing units which operated behind the front lines) were overburdened with killing the local Ukrainian Jews in the recently conquered territory.[9]

This was the last thing we wanted to hear – it left us thinking that, once the killing units had accomplished their task, we would be moved across the river and the horrors would start once again. This time, we would be the victims as the killing units emptied the bullets from their machine guns into our flesh. Most of us could only believe the rumours to be true based on our own recent experiences at the hands of the Nazis.

Rumours determined our mood and affected our morale and daily lives. We lived in a seesaw world. When we were down, it felt like being compressed in a huge, invisible torture chamber with nothing to grab or hope for. Grasping any excuse for a brighter outlook, some of the older people passed the time by relating their experiences during the First World War. They told us about the hardships they had to endure, dodging bullets and sitting in cold trenches for weeks on end, not knowing what the next hour would bring. Hope for the future kept them alive.

The optimists among us believed that we would be sent home before winter set in. "Some minor officials must have made a rash decision to drive us out," they argued. "We've been on the road for three months and yet tens of thousands of Jews in Czernowitz, Storojinet and Vijnita, the three largest cities, remain at home." This logic sounded reasonable to some, but most did not believe it.[10]

Living conditions and hygiene in the Edineti ghetto got worse day by day. We were crowded into small rooms, and even the small amount of garbage we had to dispose of piled up and started to smell. Our bodies did not fare any better as water became a precious commodity. Some of the wells in the ghetto were laced with poison (it was not known by whom). There was a public bathhouse in the ghetto, but few people were willing to ignore the danger of the poisoned water to bathe. People became weaker from lack of food; some contracted diarrhea from the water of polluted wells, and some died from the water of poisoned wells. Their deaths alerted others, saving them from suffering the same fate, but nonetheless a large number of people continued to die daily from sickness and malnutrition.

The makeshift Edineti ghetto, the first where we were interned for a long period, turned into a death camp.[11] It became routine to see dead bodies being carried to the burial site. People ran out of clothing or valuables that they previously had hidden from the soldiers, so they had little left to barter for food. For water, we had to line up at the few remaining safe wells. Because we drew water out of the wells faster than the underground reserves could replenish them, the wells ran dry for hours at a time. There was no good time to go and fetch water – people were lined up around the clock.

We had no choice but to risk our lives to leave the camp to find fresh water. On several occasions, a Romanian military truck with a water tank pulled up next to the camp. We rushed to the truck, but not having any closed containers, we lost a good portion of the rationed water amidst the pushing and shoving of the crowd. I saw a young boy so anxious to get some water he jumped onto the truck. A Romanian soldier shot and killed him.

Throughout our whole ordeal, the delivery of the water was the only assistance we received from the soldiers. Based on the way we had been treated until then, there seems to be no logical explanation for their supplying us with water; perhaps a high-ranking official felt sorry for us and sent the trucks out of the goodness of his heart.

The only glimmers of hope were occasional rumbling noises from tanks and trucks. Rumours spread that the German and Romanian armies were in retreat and that the Soviets would soon arrive and liberate us. This turned out to be wishful thinking by desperate people who wanted to believe and hang onto any shred of good news. People even related "good" dreams they had had, and we discussed these dreams among ourselves and interpreted them as good omens.

Contrary to such dreams and our hopes, the German army had already advanced deep into Soviet territory. The *Einsatzgruppen* were busy behind the front lines fulfilling the Nazi dream of making Europe *"Judenrein"* (cleansed of Jews). This was the Nazi's "Final Solution" that targeted the Jewish people for annihilation. We all struggled to hang on to life in Edineti, not realizing that later we would envy the dead. We supported each other emotionally and tried to ignore reality, but hunger pangs would not allow us to do that for long.

We were interned in the Edineti ghetto until some time in October 1941. Decades later, when Adolf Eichmann was on trial in Jerusalem for atrocities committed against Jews, we were finally able to see the reasons behind our treatment at the hands of the Nazis. Eichmann told the court that as early as September 1941 he had received the news personally from Reinhard Heydrich, the assistant to Heinrich Himmler, who was in charge of the German SS. Hitler had ordered the destruction of European Jews, and Himmler himself had begun to implement that order.

FORCED MARCH TO OTACI

In October 1941, the Romanian government issued a decree that all remaining Jews in Bukovina (including both the northern and southern portions) be expelled from their homes. They were allowed to take only the belongings they could carry and were transported in crowded boxcars. Upon arrival at the Dniester River, they were chased out and force-marched to their final destinations in Transnistria.

By then, we had lived through almost four months of hardship and suffering, witnessed the loss of many lives and seen the horrors and tragedy of war. I had seen many people wailing over the bodies of their loved ones, something parents would not have allowed their young children to witness before the war. To shield me from grief, my parents did not even allow me to go to my grandmother's funeral in 1940. Now, a year later, I was still young and frightened, but I had come face to face with brutality. It was not like hearing or reading about it; the images stayed with me.

Molly's condition had deteriorated; she was in agony lying on the floor. She did not say much – the natural smile on her face was gone, replaced by sadness. My brothers and I tried to make her laugh, but she did not respond. My parents were heartbroken and helpless; the only remedy they had left were prayers and hope that we would not be chased for a while. Given time, they thought, nature might heal her. But their hopes were dashed when soldiers received orders to evacuate all the Jews from the Edineti concentration camp. The sick and disabled were told not to assemble, but that their transportation would be taken care of later.

As we left Edineti, our situation became desperate. Thousands of people assembled on the road amid great confusion. They pushed and shoved one another as they tried to locate family members. Children were terrified and crying. Lightning and thunder, along with periodic gunfire engulfed us with terror. The sick and elderly who could not walk cried and pleaded with their sons and daughters not to leave them behind; some would rather be killed than be left in the hands of the Nazis. But there was no choice for those who were too sick or immobile to come with us. These people were never seen again.

The sick and elderly who were able to walk joined our convoy and marched off with us. Their sons and daughters grabbed them under their arms, dragging them along with all their strength. But the weak were no match for the rainy season and the muddy roads of Bessarabia. A few hours into the march, some were completely exhausted and had to give up. Their families left them by the sides of the road, knowing in their hearts that they would never see them again. Many bitter tears were shed.

The march to Otaci started in the fall, which was a cold and rainy season. The Romanian soldiers chased us mercilessly. They learned the art of cruelty toward Jews in a few easy lessons and became masters of it. And they received a lot of encouragement from their comrades-in-arms. It was like a contest to see who could inflict the most punishment in a humiliating fashion against us helpless people. To them, it was a joke to grab an old man by his beard and pull him along the road. They would amuse themselves by kicking us with their boots or battering us with their clubs and rifle butts.

Most of us were already malnourished, weak, and poorly dressed. I was luckier because I was relatively warmly dressed in tricot underwear, heavy pants and jacket, a good leather pilot-style cap with earflaps and *bergsteiger* boots (similar to ski boots). These boots, however, turned out to be a burden: they were bulky, and they got heavier and heavier as the deep mud clung to them. The wet clay of the roads felt like chewing gum pulling us back with every step. Parents had a hard time keeping their children together and an even harder time supporting their own parents. If anyone trailed too far behind the convoy, they were shot and left for dead.

We always marched in daylight. The days became shorter late in the fall as darkness set in earlier; this gave us a longer period to recuperate. On the rare sunny day, we were warmed by the sun until it slowly set in the west, leaving us in the dark to wonder what the dawn would bring.

After we left Edineti, the soldiers usually camped us next to a forest and allowed us to make a campfire where families huddled together. The mood was sombre; I had not seen a happy face or heard people laugh for a long time, as if fun had become unfashionable or illegal. Even children no longer behaved like children – we no longer stuck together or marched side by side on the road. Our childhood common interests had been overtaken by fear, and we stayed close to our parents. Whenever possible, we sat on branches around the fire to avoid contact with the cold, wet ground. While cooking our soup, we felt the radiating heat from the flames warming our bones and drying our wet clothes. This was the only comfort we had until we fell asleep under the watchful eyes of our parents, who took turns fueling the fire all night long. This kept us warm and enabled us to get a good night's rest for a fresh start the next morning.

The emotions of parents were stretched to the limit as they watched their children struggling to keep up with the convoy, but they were powerless to help. My dad must have been exhausted because he had carried Molly on his shoulders most of the time since the day we left Edineti. He probably knew what the tragic end would be but tried to hide it from us with encouraging and hopeful words.

There was unbelievable horror one morning when we were awakened before dawn by the soldiers in a more hasty manner than usual. They were all over us with clubs and rifle butts. Shots were fired as they shouted, "Get up, you filthy Jews. Hurry up! Assemble on the road quickly or you'll be shot!"

The sick and any others who could not get up fast enough to suit the soldiers were shot on the spot. Father grabbed Molly and placed her on his shoulders. Mother embraced us and tried to calm us. The sound of rapid gunfire echoed throughout the forest, amplifying our fears. Our hopes became just as hollow as the echoes.

During the night, some individuals in our convoy must have been ordered to dig a big hole in a ravine next to where we rested. Before we marched off, the dead bodies were collected and thrown into the hole. Family members who approached the mass grave to say *Kaddish* (a mourners' prayer) were pushed in by the soldiers and shot.

That day turned out to be the most gruesome and barbaric I had encountered. Right in front of my eyes I saw what so-called human beings were capable of doing to others in the most brutal manner – without any hesitation, regret, or reason. Until then, I had seen individual Jews beaten, tortured and killed just for the fun of it. But this was the first time I had witnessed a planned mass killing and seen corpses thrown on top of each other in a big open pit. I was petrified by the scene.

This was the first of many terrifying days to come. It ended the hopes of some of the people who still had some illusion that things might improve. Their illusions vanished just as fast as the bullets that took so many lives that day. The soldiers chased us faster and faster, with malice and pleasure. Some people who could not walk anymore gave up and sat down on the banks of the road. When their loved ones tried to console them, the soldiers used their whips and clubs to chase them away. Some were willing to absorb the blows just to grab a few last, precious moments with their loved ones whom they knew they would never see again.

Molly must have felt sorry for Dad. She told him that he should put her down since she had no more pain and could walk. Dad and my older brother Shimon supported her under her arms to help her along. Poor Mother had twisted her ankle and also had problems walking, but she would not admit it to avoid making us feel bad. She hung on to me and my younger brother Avrum.

Since the beginning of our forced march, both Mother and Father had tried to keep our hope alive with frequent, reassuring words. They continued to do this even though they realized, as time went on, that there was no hope of ever returning home to a civilized and normal life. We agreed with their reassurances, if only to make them feel better. But one had to be blind not to realize our likely fate at the hands of the Nazis. Their inhumanity had already taken eight members of our family. My Aunt Esther and two of her children died during our stay in Edineti. My paternal grandmother Hughe was sick and could not walk; we had to leave her behind when we left Edineti. Uncle Moishe and three cousins died on the road to Otaci.

As we approached Otaci, rumours (which later proved to be true) spread quickly in our convoy that Jews from other convoys had been forced into the Dniester River where they were shot or drowned. Most of these rumours came from farmers on the road with whom we bartered our belongings. Our convoy did not stop in Otaci, and as we proceeded toward the river we heard shooting. Then the convoy came to a sudden stop. After a lengthy wait, we were turned back and camped next to a forest near Otaci.[12]

The shooting that we had heard earlier had been directed at a convoy of Jews coming from a different direction to the Dniester River at a crossing point leading to the city of Mogilev-Podolsk in the Ukraine. A German officer, we heard later, had given orders to force the Jews into the Dniester River and shoot them. It would have been more appropriate to call it the Red River as it flowed across the land toward the Black Sea, leaving some of its burden of Jewish blood along its banks and spilling the remainder into the sea. While the shooting was going on, a high-ranking Romanian officer arrived at the scene of the massacre and ordered the soldiers to stop. He must have ordered the Romanian soldiers who were heading our convoy to turn back toward Otaci, thus sparing our lives for a while.

After a number of disastrous days where some of us were robbed, beaten, or shot by the local people and soldiers, the convoy was ordered to assemble again to cross the Dniester River into Mogilev-Podolsk. As we approached the river, we were horrified to see German and Romanian soldiers huddled in groups at the foot of the bridge. Knowing the fate of others and fearing the worst, the tension among us reached the breaking point. Parents hung onto their children like glue. Even though they knew that they had no control over the situation, the parental instinct to protect their children did not waver.

Young soldiers with guns stood on both sides of the road, leaving a narrow path for us to walk through. This alone was terrifying. Some of us felt the jolt of a rifle butt or a kick from a boot and many were showered with spit and abusive language. The soldiers looked us over and laughed. I remember how frightened I was as I walked onto the pontoon bridge, which was supported by canoes and lay just above the surface of the water. The rushing river surged under the bridge with a deafening noise, and the bridge undulated from the weight of all the people walking across. I was afraid that the bridge would break up or sink and we would all drown, but fortunately our convoy crossed the river with very few losses. People assumed that the high-ranking Romanian officer who had halted the shooting a few days before had something to do with our relatively safe crossing.

As soon as we crossed the river, we set foot in a strange land about which we knew little, except that the *Einsatzgruppen* were there. We were in Transnistria, an area not found on any map. The name was coined by the Romanians after the war started in 1941 to identify approximately 40,000 square kilometres of territory between the Dniester and Bug Rivers in the Ukraine given to them by the Germans as a reward for their participation as an ally. They used this area as a dumping ground for Jews from Bessarabia and Bukovina to accomplish their goal of cleansing these two provinces of Jews. This goal would be accomplished by allowing them to perish from cold, starvation, and disease, rather than be murdered outright, the method used by the Germans. It was just as cruel and, in the end, just as effective. It prolonged the suffering of tens of thousands of people for another few months, as they helplessly watched the tragic deaths of their loved ones.

We had hoped that our convoy would remain in Mogilev-Podolsk where we would be allowed to occupy the remnants of buildings that had been destroyed in the recent fighting between the German and

Soviet armies. Even if the buildings were uninhabitable, they would have provided us with an opportunity for some respite. Instead, the soldiers kept us marching eastward, nobody knew where. We were always kept in the dark about our final destination. It was as if we were walking in a tunnel with our eyes open, blinded by the darkness, guessing where we were and where we were going. The physical condition of the people had deteriorated to such an extent that death was always waiting nearby; for some, it was only days away.

As we kept marching, nature would not let us forget how long we had been on the road. When we left home, the fields were colourful with vegetation; the trees were dressed in green, standing tall and swaying in the breeze. Then fall overtook summer, and farmers were busy in their fields, bringing in the harvest. The leaves slowly changed colour, fell off the trees and left them naked. Seasons slowly passed us by, recognized only by the changes in scenery and weather – summer turning into fall and slowly starting to change into winter. And still our weathered and battered bodies were chased by the soldiers.

The dirt roads in the Ukraine were just as bad as the ones in Bessarabia, and they became worse when it started to drizzle again. It was so cold it felt as though the rain might turn to sleet or snow. We hoped that in the Ukraine the soldiers would ease up on us a little, now that their goal to be rid of Jews from the two provinces of Bukovina and Bessarabia was almost fulfilled. But this was not the case – the beasts were still at our back. They were all over us like leeches, with sticks and clubs.

People were spiritless and despondent. "What's the point in living?" some asked. "We know what's going to happen to us. Even if we survive for a while, it'll just prolong the suffering." Another said, "I remember hearing about the pogroms against Jews in this country under the Czarist regime. Anti-Semitism, which has lain dormant for more than twenty years under the Communist regime, will probably sprout again under the Nazi banner. Given total freedom and encouragement, some people will take the opportunity to exploit it to the fullest extent."

We knew that the winters in the Ukraine were worse than in our former home in Bukovina – heavier snowfalls, colder temperatures and winds blowing through the wide-open plains. Our situation looked extremely bleak, and we saw no hope on the horizon. To make things worse, rumour had it that we might be chased across the Bug River to the east where the Germans were in full control. The west side of the Bug, our present location, included input from the Germans but was under the jurisdiction of the Romanian army. Under Romanian control, we might have had half a chance to survive a bit longer if the cold and hunger did not get us first. But few people had sufficient clothing left to trade; they would need it to prevent them from freezing to death once winter set in. As we kept marching, we could feel the cold wind blowing from the east. It had a mean Siberian bite to it – a prelude of things to come.

My sister's condition took a sudden turn for the worse. She had a high temperature and was in a great deal of pain. Dad had to carry her on his back again, but he no longer had his earlier strength. He struggled to keep going, especially on the slippery, hilly roads. He knew that wherever we were going, no help awaited Molly. What hurt most was that he could do nothing to help her except to keep carrying her and pray for a miracle.

After a long, exhausting day, we arrived in a town called Ozarintsy for an overnight rest. We could see that Dad was totally spent and overcome with sadness. My parents tried desperately to find medicine that would relieve Molly's pain and fever. But nobody who had any would part with such a precious possession that was irreplaceable and might one day save their own lives. We had already used what little aspirin we had brought. My parents were up all night with Molly, trying to lessen her suffering, putting cold compresses on her forehead to relieve her fever and cuddling her in their arms. Shimon, Avrum, and I sat around in a quiet, sombre mood late into the night until we fell asleep from exhaustion. We awoke, unsure of what we'd find. As soon as we saw our parents, we knew. "We lost Molly," said Dad.

My parents had done everything in their power under those nightmarish circumstances, but it was all to no avail. My sister failed to survive until dawn. Even though we knew her death was coming, it shocked us all and left us with broken hearts and bitter memories, never to be forgotten. My parents, who could not hide their sadness from us any longer, broke down and cried. Seeing our parents crying was very traumatic for us, as we had never seen them crying before. We always knew them as strong and self-assured.

Molly was the second-oldest child and the only girl in our family. We were all proud of her, always treating her with respect and love. We looked up to her. She always had a smile on her face and was kind and polite – not only to us, but also to her friends and neighbours. I remember the happy times we had together, playing or just sitting around talking. When Mother was out and I was hungry, Molly would always make my favourite open-faced sandwich for me – bread with butter topped by halvah, or honey. She was not yet fourteen when she left the world, a time when dreams are just starting to sprout in teenagers' minds and they visualize happy futures, sharing the joys of discussing them with friends. Occasionally, Molly and her friends would meet in our house and play games, pretending to be grown-ups without a care in the world. Their playing was interrupted only when they caught me spying on them.

Unlike her Christian friends, all of Molly's dreams were shattered before she had a chance to grow up and realize them. Losing a beloved sister was extremely difficult for us to bear; my brothers and I burst into anguished sobs.

That morning we were again ordered to assemble for another day's march. Soldiers used their clubs and rifle butts to persuade my parents, who were wailing over Molly's body, to join the others. "Get up! Move!" yelled a soldier. "She's not the only dead Jew here. You'll all be dead before long."

"Please, let me bury her," Dad begged, "she's my child."

"Who in the hell cares? What's another dead Jew? Get going or I'll shoot you."

My parents' begging and sobbing was drowned out by the soldiers' loud curses. It was a hopeless clash between two powerful forces: parents' love for a child and the Nazis' passionate hatred of Jews. The departure was very emotional; we had no choice but to leave Molly behind. Shimon, Avrum, and I looked on with fear, sadness and anger as we saw the helplessness of our parents as they were abused and degraded to a sub-human level. It had a devastating effect on all of us. Every day we were forced to cope with new and unexpected problems – each degrading and destructive. It seems that human beings are stronger inside than is revealed by their outward appearances.

The soldiers forced the convoy eastward by firing bullets into the air and sometimes, without hesitation, into the head of another victim, leaving another family in grief. We were being randomly picked off one by one. Our fate depended on which soldier we stood next to at a certain moment and what mood he was in. We meant nothing to them; they no longer considered us human beings.

As the weather got colder, parents had greater difficulties with their young children. They acted up, crying more than before because of their hunger and cold. They were too young to understand that their discomfort was not their parents' fault. The parents were in just as much pain seeing their children suffer but could do nothing except try to soothe them and hope they would stop crying. How could they explain to little kids that they were Jews and for that they had to pay a heavy price.

We struggled to make it to another town called Luchinets. There we were marched into a big, open space that served as a marketplace where farmers sold their produce. This turned out to be the last of many exhausting, tragic days for this convoy. The skies were as grey as the colour of our faces and squeezed every last drop of moisture from their clouds. The rain dampened our spirits even more as we stood in deep mud on ground that had turned into a big marsh while we waited for the officers to give new orders that would decide our fate. People tried to find lost relatives who had become separated in the confusion of the marketplace, but their movements were restricted by conditions on the ground and the huge number of people tightly packed together.

After a while, the soldiers split the mass of people into groups, separating more families in the confusion. Each group headed in a different direction. Our progress continued to be difficult. Our shattered bodies were pulled along by our failing legs. Some sick and older people fell to the ground without a whisper, like leaves in the fall that can no longer hang on. Because our numbers were reduced, everyone in our column was more closely observed by the soldiers, and nobody was allowed to help those who fell. It must have been agony to watch their loved ones receding in the distance. The marchers looked back with eyes full of tears, watching helplessly until the loud bang of the Nazi guns silenced their loved ones forever. Motionless bodies full of bullet holes were left scattered on the road.

I do not think we would have been able to keep going for many more days. As it turned out, our fate was determined in Luchinets when the convoy was split and our group was marched toward Stepanki.

ARRIVAL AT STEPANKI

Following the brutal death march from Edineti, which lasted about three weeks in rain, sleet, and snow, our convoy finally arrived before nightfall in Stepanki, a small isolated village in the western Ukraine. We were herded into an empty pig barn. The barn reflected our emotional and physical state – everything inside was stripped and the walls were decaying. We were welcomed by filth and foul air. Some people grabbed space next to the walls and some sat down right in the middle, not caring if they were trampled.

Many of the people who had started with us in Edineti had not made it; dead bodies had become part of the landscape through which we had walked. One did not need a map to find us – the corpses would have led to the barns. As things turned out, maybe the dead were the lucky ones. Rumours, which by now we had learned to trust, spread that we had reached our final destination.

The pig barns had belonged to the Soviet government and were part of a *kolkhoz*, a collective state farm. This *kolkhoz* consisted of thousands of acres where a variety of crops were grown. Most residents of Stepanki were employed on this farm. Prior to our arrival, all the livestock had been removed; only a few horses remained, wandering around.

By the end of our forced march, sometime in November 1941, our backpacks were empty. In contrast, our souls were filled with sorrow and bitterness, our bodies battered, and our brains weary with fear of the unknown. Looking at each other, we saw reflections of living hell – desperate, exhausted, expressionless people with not a glimmer of hope in our eyes. Most of us were strangers to one another; the only things we had in common were the losses of family members and our shared misery. Many parents were kept alive only by concern for their children.

Father picked a space away from the walls and tried to get us settled as comfortably as possible before darkness set in. Nobody was allowed to go outside to make a fire. The only thing we had to eat was the small amount of dry food we had saved. The soldiers closed the barn doors behind us and stood guard. The noise that night was unbearable. Names were shouted across the barn as family members tried to locate each other in the dark. Some people were crying, others were moaning, and others were praying for the loved ones that they had lost; in the same breath, they would ask, "God, why did you let me live to suffer?" It seems that many no longer had any desire to live – they felt as though they had been cast into oblivion as the world passed them by. People looked at them, but nobody helped or even bothered to ask why this was happening.

Dawn arrived, but we were not awakened by the soldiers. The lucky ones managed to get up. We did not know if we were going to be moved again until later that day when the soldiers told us that this was going to be our home. There were no emotional outbursts or tears shed. Like the pigs in the barn before us, we accepted it as our new home. In some ways, this was a relief; at least we would be sheltered from the wind and rain and the constant abuse of the soldiers. After five months of guessing, we had reached our final destination. We could no longer deceive ourselves by thinking that things were going to improve – the facts on the ground were no illusion. The reality of our day-to-day struggle to stay alive quickly became apparent.

We were allowed to walk outside as long as we stayed within the wire fence. We were told that anybody caught outside the fence would be shot. We went outside, bewildered as we looked over our new surroundings. From our vantage point, I could see the nearby village of Stepanki. It looked peaceful. It had small homes with smoke billowing from the chimneys. My imagination took me into those warm homes – how I envied the people living there. They lived normal lives and had not been threatened or uprooted. They had a future, along with hopes and dreams. They were real people. Our future had been shattered beyond repair and time was quickly running out for many of us. In the last five months, we had been driven close to insanity in a cruel, deliberate way. Our situation had become desperate and our perception of life had changed. Nothing mattered anymore; all we yearned for was tranquillity.

While we stood outside, our eyes were drawn to big stacks of straw just outside the barbed-wire fence. The Romanian soldiers allowed us to take the straw into our barn for bedding. It helped to keep us a little warmer, but it was not enough to prevent those without warm clothing from freezing to death. People who had warm clothes were in a dilemma – whether to trade them for food or keep them for warmth; either decision was life-threatening.

One day at sunrise, the soldiers picked my father, along with some other men, and marched them off. Mother was in panic. She had seen men in Edineti who were taken away, supposedly to work, but who were never seen again. The distress we had felt since he left turned to joy at sundown when he returned with his ration of bread and a few frozen sugar beets. "The soldiers told us to assemble each morning," Dad said optimistically. "We're going to be taken to work for the next few weeks. I'll be able to bring some food back every day." The only other food available to us came from trading the odd piece of jewellery we had left or the clothes off our backs. We bartered with farmers who came to the fences of our *lager*. (A *lager* is a camp or ghetto where Jews were held captive. *Lagers* ranged in size from a few hundred people to many thousands.)

The barn was a place of death. Some people died daily from starvation; others died as their resistance weakened, leaving them susceptible to disease. The number of deaths continued to increase, putting more families in mourning. They cried and prayed for loved ones who lost their lives in front of their eyes, just as suddenly as a flickering candle stops burning. Each morning, the bodies were taken outside and stacked like cordwood until the weather warmed up enough to bury them in the forest.

Parents were desperately trying to save their children who were crying from hunger and cold. Those who had nothing left to trade for food took unorthodox action. When people died during the night, they removed some of the deceased person's belongings and even tried to pull out gold crowns from their teeth to have something to trade for food in the morning. Nobody condemned them; they reasoned that these actions were justifiable when a life could be saved without taking someone else's. Dignity was a luxury we could no longer afford. In our desperate situation, the human personality changed quickly. Maybe this was the only way we could survive in those abnormal times.

It remained difficult for me, even after experiencing all the horrors, to cope with the daily scene of immobile people, young and old, lying in filth. Some stared at me with out-stretched arms as I made my way in and out of the barn. I considered myself lucky; I was mobile and still had parents. They practised what they had taught me about helping people in need, sharing our pot of soup with some of these people. Others who were able also shared. Despite the Nazi efforts to dehumanize us, we defied them by keeping humanity alive even in the face of death.

Within several weeks of our arrival at Stepanki, another misfortune suddenly struck our family. My older brother Shimon took sick. He tried to hide the seriousness of his condition from us, but my parents could detect that something was bothering him. He kept trying to camouflage his illness until he could no longer hide it. He started to lie down for a nap more often during the day and got up later each morning. He spoke very little, not even to his favourite little brother Avrum, whom he had always tried to cheer up. We realized the seriousness of his condition when he refused to eat and was no longer able to get up. Now he just lay on his back, keeping his hands on his stomach as if his pain was radiating from within.

The cold in the barn was unbearable. Dad used every possible method to help keep us warm. While cooking our soup, he heated stones in the fire, then wrapped them in rags and told us to keep them close to our bodies. As they cooled, they kept us warm for part of the night.

My parents tried everything they could think of to relieve Shimon's pain and avoid the loss of another child. They took turns staying awake at night to make him as comfortable as possible in those dreadful surroundings, but it was all in vain. After a brief illness, Shimon left us when he was barely seventeen years old. Like Molly, he was not given a chance to grow up and enjoy the fruits of life, nor to realize the dreams and aspirations of a normal child. We never found out the cause of Shimon's death. He had been a happy teenager and liked school; he always did his homework before he went out to socialize with his friends. He had an optimistic outlook; he had dreamed of becoming an electrical engineer. Early on, he had shown interest in this field and was encouraged by Sammy Schauber, a distant relative of ours who was an engineer. Shimon had been very helpful to us throughout our forced march. He relieved Dad by occasionally carrying Molly for short stretches and helped Avrum with his rucksack as he watched him struggling to keep up with the convoy. He was our big brother, and we would sorely miss him.

Shimon's death compounded our sadness at a time when we could see only gloom and doom. As long as he had been with us, we still had a little hope. This hope stemmed from desperation, rather than from what we could foresee in the future. Our future was bleak, like a black hole in the universe drawing us closer and closer until the day when it would draw us in for the final journey. Our only possession of any value left to trade was the three-quarter-length leather coat that Dad wore. He was able to hang onto it by keeping it dirty and scratching some of the leather, thereby avoiding a soldier's eye.

One day when Dad was at work, I spotted a small hole at the back of the barn that was plugged with straw. My curiosity attracted me, and it gave me the idea to leave the barn. Without telling my mother, I succeeded in crawling out, and since there was no fence or soldiers at the back of the barn, I started out toward Stepanki. I was frightened, as this was my first venture alone. I continued toward the village, not knowing exactly what I was going to do once I got there – whether I would turn right back, go begging or try to steal some food. After several unsuccessful attempts at begging, I finally succeeded at an older couple's house. They gave me some bread and potatoes. I returned to the *lager* by a different route. As I approached a building that looked like a hall, I was shocked to see a pile of corpses outside the building. Dead bodies were nothing new to me, but whose bodies were they? I returned in haste to the barn and told my mother what I had seen. She told me that that building housed the overflow of people from the pig barns. She also told me not to tell Dad that I had ventured out of the barn and not to do it again.

Shortly thereafter, when Dad was no longer needed for work, he happened to be outside and heard that another barn was opening up. "Hurry, follow me," he said. "Let's go to a smaller barn before it gets filled up." There were a few mangers, straw and hay against the wall, and a huge stove; it looked as if part of the barn had been used to shoe horses. We all found a spot on the ground. A few lucky people who entered first had grabbed the space in the mangers. One of these was a mother who slept with two children in a manger next to where I slept on the ground. She was so protective of them that she would not let them leave the barn, making them stay in the manger most of the time. When she no longer had anything left to trade for food, she sneaked out of the barn to go begging or stealing. One day, she got sick and soon passed away. The two children could not cope alone and they too passed away. This was the last chapter for their family; their father had died on the road to Stepanki.

Chances for survival kept on shrinking; the line between life and death grew thinner. Our own situation improved one day, however, when my father was selected again, along with other men who had a little remaining strength, to work for the *kolkhoz* in Stepanki. They gave the men soup, bread, and sometimes raw potatoes or sugar beets to take back to the barns. Dad always brought the bread back for us. Mother said that she was not hungry and gave the bread to Avrum and me. We survived with very little food – what my father brought home and whatever remained from the food he had recently received in exchange for his coat. Most of our diet in Stepanki consisted of potato or sugar beet soup, occasionally spiked with a few dried peas or beans. The potato soup was made differently from the soup Mother used to make at home. We could not afford the luxury of a real potato soup. To try to give the soup a thicker consistency, Mother took one or two potatoes, sometimes along with sugar beets, and grated them rather than dicing them. They were then thrown into a pot of unsalted boiling water. It looked like muddy water, but our brains must have been fooled into thinking we were getting a hearty, tasty meal; we could hardly wait to eat it. We barely had enough to suppress our hunger for a short time – never enough to satisfy our stomachs.

One day, the men failed to return from work before dark as they had always done. Family members who were affected gathered together in distress. There was nothing we could do except wait and hope. Later when the men did return, my dad and a co-worker were not in the group. Mother was in panic and approached one of the workers she knew. "What happened today? Where is Isaac?" she asked.

"Nothing unusual, except we had to work later today," he answered. "I'm sure he returned with us. Maybe he's outside."

I went outside with Mother but no one was there. Much to our relief, Dad and the co-worker returned later with food they had stolen. They had managed to hide before the group was marched back to the barn.

After a few weeks, the *kolkhoz* no longer needed any workers. Shortly thereafter, my father became ill. Mother became very concerned. He was our guardian and head of the family, as well as our provider. We all looked up to him; he gave us a sense of security, always trying to keep our hope and spirits up. Mother now assumed the responsibility of feeding the family. Even though it was painful for her to walk, due to an injury to her leg suffered during the brutal march, she would go into the village in search of food and I would accompany her. I felt sorry for Mother and finally convinced her to let me go alone. Any time I went into the village, Mother tried to make sure that I was bundled up. Or rather she went through the motions – there was really nothing to pull together – if she pulled some clothing to one side, the other side came uncovered. She always begged me to return empty-handed if I found it too cold or encountered peril. The look of despair in her eyes made me forget my fear and fuelled me with the courage to venture forth.

When I was caught by the local police or by young hoodlums as I was prowling around, I cried and begged them for mercy. Fortunately, I could speak Ukrainian. "Please don't beat me. Let me go," I begged.

"You're stealing. Why should we let you go?" they snarled.

"You know I live in the barn. My family is starving."

"Who cares? Better not leave the barn again or you'll be shot," they warned me.

Sometimes my pleas helped and I was able to get away from the encounter with little beating; seldom did I get away without any punishment. However, as my family was starving and my father was sick, I was not deterred from trying again and again. I was more concerned with figuring out how to survive than with the threat of being shot. I was desperate, and the only thing I had in mind was how and where to get enough food to make it through another day.

At one of the small run-down houses where I went begging, the old people told me that the house had belonged to a Jewish family. This family, along with the only other Jewish family who lived in Stepanki, had left for America in the 1920s. The local residents never heard from them again. The couple gave me some food, but I seldom returned because they told me their neighbour was a policeman.

After many mistakes and beatings, I learned the art of how to prowl around in search of food. I tried not to go into the village, but rather to go around the outskirts. I looked out for the police and soldiers instead of letting them spot me first. I would pick a small house that was not well kept as there was a good chance that older people lived there. If they caught me stealing, they would not be able to chase me, or would not even try to pursue me as the younger people would. I learned from experience that older people more often than not were good, but many of them were too poor to help me. Nevertheless, they would let me stay to warm up, and their kindness was psychologically beneficial to me – they pitied me as if I was still a human being.

The method of how to secure food was not important to me – survival was the only goal. I never gave up trying, and I learned from other people's mistakes. Negative thoughts led to negative outcomes.

Many times, I came back empty-handed, either because it was too cold or I foresaw danger and had to return quickly to the barn. When I was successful at begging, I received a few potatoes, beets, a piece of bread, or beans. At other times, I stole frozen sugar beets or "chop" out of the trough in a barn. The chop consisted of cooked potatoes and sugar beets and sometimes chaff. I picked out the potatoes and beets, and Mother made a thick soup – to us it was a gourmet meal. Chop saved our lives many times, especially in winter when my movement was restricted by the cold.

One day while prowling around, I saw a funeral procession leaving a cemetery with a priest walking in the front. It occurred to me that the mourners would proceed to the deceased family member's home and that, if I walked in during their time of grief, they might give me something to eat as a good deed in memory of the deceased. I followed from a distance and then walked into the house. To my surprise, I saw the dreaded chief of police sitting next to the priest around a table where everybody was eating. There was an icon of Mary hanging on the wall. I started talking to her as though I were saying some prayers in Jewish. I thought that this would induce them to have pity on me while I kept one eye on the chief of police. To my relief, he ignored me, and one of the women gave me a plate of cooked, dried mushrooms with chunks of meat and a big piece of bread. No magician could have made it disappear faster. She gave me another plateful, and I asked, "Can I take this back to my starving family?"

"Eat it," she said. "I'll make up a package of food for you to take back."

Unfortunately, my father was too sick to enjoy even this meal. After this incident, I watched the cemetery very closely; funerals offered my only chance for a good, nourishing meal – I was always given mushrooms, meat, and bread, which must have been a traditional post-funeral meal. I decided that it would be helpful to learn the appropriate Ukrainian prayer so I could say it aloud when I crossed myself in front of an icon. This might elicit more compassion toward me from the inhabitants of a house where I went begging. I was able to quickly learn this prayer from an old couple who had previously helped me.

My father's condition deteriorated as the days progressed. Mother tried to comfort him as he lay on the ground in the cold barn, where I could plainly see every breath he exhaled. He was dressed in his clothes, covered with the few rags we had to try to keep him warm, and cushioned only by straw. Dad never complained and spoke little due to weakness and fever. He would look at us and repeat: "Don't be frightened, I am going to get better and take care of you, as I always have." It must have been the only thing on his mind.

Avrum and I agreed with him and believed what he said, but Mother probably knew his condition was worsening and kept it from us. She knew that we would have sufficient time to grieve when it was no longer possible to hide the outcome. It was painful for us to see Dad deteriorating before our eyes. We could do nothing to relieve his suffering except sit next to him and feed him encouraging words. His eyes kept closing as he struggled and fought not to give in. He could not get up any more and slept most of the time, but Avrum and I still believed that he would fight back and recover and that we would not be left vulnerable, without a father. Even though it was no longer in his power to protect us, somehow our brains must have been tricked into believing otherwise. It was not long before the sickness and fever that Dad fought against so hard won the battle.

It was not a sudden death, but it hit us as if it had been. We broke down and cried. Mother tried to comfort us with tears in her eyes. She put her arms around us and held tight as we sat on the ground next to dear Dad's body. We were the only possessions she had left. Poor Mother, there was no one to comfort her – all our relatives who were with us in Stepanki had already died. I visualized my father as he was before this terrible tragedy – a tall, strong man who was always so good to us children. He showed his love for us and would do almost anything we asked for that was within his means. He was proud of us and enjoyed having us around him. He looked forward to our future with high hopes. I don't remember Dad ever hollering at us. We were all happy to do whatever he asked us to, without any hesitation. Whenever Mother bought apples or pears, we competed with each other to pick the biggest one to hide for him – it gave us joy to present it to Dad when he came home.

By nature, Dad was a humble man who never hesitated to go out of his way to help people in need. In the wintertime, poor people used to come to the sawmill to buy plank trimmings to heat their homes. Regardless of their religion, Dad never turned anyone away even if they could not pay. He let them take a wagonload of trimmings and told them they could pay later. The sawmill did not belong to Dad, and, if they didn't pay, he assumed responsibility for the payments.

It was a tragic moment for us – even now after almost sixty years it is a very painful scene for me to relive. The biggest regret I have was that I told Dad to keep up the fight, that we loved him too much to let him slip away from us. Many times I said: "Dad, don't leave us, we love you and need you." He said: "Don't worry, don't worry, I won't." He must have passed away with that in mind, as he murmured those words over and over again to assure us he was still with us.

Seeing our depressed state, Mother suppressed her own sorrows and tried to raise our spirits with encouraging words, but now she herself was deteriorating quickly. We could see that in her appearance, as she continued to neglect her own well-being and tried to take care of us. Even on those rare occasions when we had enough food for everyone, she pretended that she was not hungry, giving us more than she took. Her love for us was as strong as ever. Mother had a positive attitude and continually tried to instill it in us. She lived a day at a time and let each tomorrow be another day of hope. Before we lay down for the night's rest, Mother would fluff up the straw to make it as comfortable as possible for us.

Life without Dad became even more depressing and meaningless. We could no longer huddle around him, eagerly listening to what he had to say. Regardless of the topic, just hearing Dad's voice had a positive impact on our daily life and morale. The sense of security he had given us was gone. The place he once occupied was empty, a constant reminder of what had happened to our family. Mother's eyes became more teary, and she became weaker and weaker until one day she could no longer get up. But she continued to try to take care of us, talking to us very slowly and telling us what to do. She strived to give us the impression that her illness was only temporary and that we should not be concerned. Mother kept on fighting to her last breath, fully aware of her surroundings and knowing she could not avoid her last imminent journey, but still worrying about us.

Before Mother died, she said to me in a low, whispering voice: "I feel that I am going to die. Joil, take care of Avrumale and yourself." She could barely utter these words to me as our eyes focused on each other with unbearable thoughts in our minds; these were her last spoken words. Other unspoken words reached me by telepathy; it seemed she wanted to say goodbye to us but was too weak to even murmur those few precious words. I tried to encourage her – "Everything is going to be OK, Mother, and you are going to get better" – but I knew in my heart that the end was near. I had to comfort Avrum as tears slowly made their way down his face, as they did on mine. We were in despair and broken-hearted as this was the last link to the happy family we had been blessed with before the war. The happiness we had shared had been too brief, but the sorrows would last a lifetime.

One sunny morning, I could see that Mother was passing away. I was panic-stricken as I comforted her with my trembling and shivering skinny little arms. Avrum and I watched helplessly as she quickly deteri-orated, struggling to keep her eyes open for one last look at us. Our tears for Mother came from the bottom of our hearts; we were devastated. As we sat next to her, looking at her peaceful face for the last time, we felt that the sun had set below the horizon forever and darkened our lives. I still have those big, deep, raw scars in my heart; they will not heal, nor can I rub them away.

Like Dad, Mother was a good-hearted person who was always will-ing to help anyone who needed assistance. It did not matter what race or religion a person was – to her, we were all human and everybody was equal. She taught us that as human beings, it was our obligation never to refuse people who were in need of help. Whenever someone came to the house to beg, Mother always made a point of giving some money to us children to give to the person at the door. She wanted to instill in us the habit of giving and the feeling one gets from knowing they have done a good deed. She was a caring, loving mother of whom we were proud. Yes, I give a lot of *kovid* (honour and respect) to the old-fashioned moth-ers and fathers who gave their last piece of bread to their children. The only wish my parents had was that some of their children would survive to lead normal lives one day.

It is hard to put a price tag on a mother or a father. They are price-less, and they proved that in the most noble way. Rich or poor, their feel-ings for their children were the same. Who else would willingly sacrifice their lives to save their children? I know, I was there and saw a lot of fathers and mothers who could have survived if they had been selfish and had not thought of their children first.

STEPANKI, SPRING 1942

The barn served the Nazis as a death chamber during that first winter. It swallowed up hundreds of people, both young and old; only a small number were spared. By the spring of 1942, the survivors' physical appearance could be read like a book, the story of a people condemned to die. With only a few torn rags on our backs, we were starved, cold, beaten, sick, and shot at will by anybody with a gun. Some survivors, who could not walk due to weakness and stiffness, dragged themselves on their hands and knees out of the filthy barn and, shielded from the wind by the barn wall, warmed themselves in the sun. There was no visible flesh on them, and their eyes seemed to peer out of deep tunnels. They stared aimlessly at the sky; not a word was spoken among them. It was a miracle that they had survived with the little food they were given by family members or by others in the barn.

Among the people who were able to walk, there were those whose limb movements were so uncoordinated that they had difficulty manoeuvring without a stick for support. One of these starved people was a courageous young girl of about twelve. As spring progressed, she gradually managed to get up on her feet and, with determination and persistence, she straightened herself from her fetal position by supporting herself on the barn walls. She slowly started to walk upright, but pain limited her efforts to brief periods. Her stubborness in persisting despite the pain paid off. While going around begging during the summer, she found a place to live with a Jewish family who had come to Stepanki in the spring and who had managed to get shelter in exchange for some of their belongings.

For Avrum and me, the battle for survival took on a new dimension. While my parents were still alive and feared for tomorrow, I, as a twelve-year-old, felt a sense of security in their presence. The loss of our parents threw us into a state of vulnerability. How would we cope alone? Scared, confused, disheartened, and in mourning, our morale sagged to its lowest point. There was no substitute for parents whose assurance that we belonged to someone sustained us. Without them, survival seemed far beyond reach; only our youthful imaginations and the power of hope, even if it was an illusion, kept us going. We had to face the harsh reality of being orphaned and to take charge of our own welfare. There was nobody to advise or guide us. We could not draw on the experiences of other orphans; many had had disastrous outcomes. By the spring of 1942, fewer than seventy-five people remained alive out of approximately 1,000 who were force-marched to Stepanki.

The only thing that brightened our lives and warmed our souls was the sun. The spring weather gave us an opportunity to stay outside longer and survey our surroundings. Everything in sight was depressing. The clear white snow had melted, exposing the human waste that had collected around the barn but was masked during the winter. It was almost impossible to avoid stepping into excrement when we ventured out. Even after clearing the area, we had to be careful where we stepped when nature called during the night, a frequent occurrence due to the unorthodox food we consumed. A normal bowel movement was for me a reason for joy. The one sign of life that gave us hope was nature rejuvenating itself – grass, a future source of food, sprouting all over, and trees putting out buds to cover their naked limbs.

The only place with some clean snow to use for water was in the nearby forest. The earth covering the bodies that had been buried there had sagged following the thaw, revealing the graves that had been dug during warm winter days. Debris filled the empty spaces above the graves. For some reason unknown to me, most of the burials had taken place in secret without the knowledge of the local authorities. No markers were put up to identify the deceased persons' graves. By spring, few survivors could identify where their family members had been buried. Some of them had been too sick or too distressed to go to the burial sites – their crying and wailing would have carried through the forest. Others, like myself, were able to identify burial sites in relation to specific trees. Mother had picked a spot for Dad's grave that could be easily identified. It was next to the biggest tree at the edge of the forest. I did not know where Shimon was buried; my parents wouldn't tell me.

When Father died, Mother made arrangements with some men in the barn to dig a burial spot. Mother's burial was more difficult for us. There were fewer people left in the barn, and the few healthy ones were out searching for food. I took a spade, and Avrum and I went by ourselves to dig a grave next to Father's. After a while, we had to give up – the ground was still too hard for us to dig. When we returned to the barn, some of the men who were out had come back, and I asked them for help. They took the spade from me, plus a pickaxe they had hidden, and followed Avrum and me to the grave. They dug the hole where Mother lies buried.

Avrum and I must have turned into steel to be able to withstand all these terrible tragedies within such a short time. When we looked at the surroundings in the barn, we had to have been sufficiently blind, numb, or stubborn not to see the same fate looming for us, as we had already witnessed the deaths of so many people. We still firmly believed that, with some luck, two young children without their parents could cheat death, whereas thousands of adults and stronger people had failed. By sheer force of will, we were determined to live and bear witness to what had happened to the Jewish people under German and Romanian tyranny. Even then, I felt it was my duty, if I survived, to make people aware of what had happened to me and to those who perished. I was only twelve years old and my brother ten and one-half, but we were forced to shed our childhood and act like adults. Circumstances can change even a child's thinking into an adult's instinct for survival.

This was also demonstrated by my six-year-old cousin, the only child of my father's sister Bertha, whose husband had been drafted into the Red Army shortly before it retreated in June 1941. Before the war, Bertha was an extremely protective mother and her son grew up being very dependent on her. He was not allowed out of her sight. On rare occasions when he was allowed to play with other children, she felt that she had to be near him. He was so attached to her that he would not even play with his cousins unless his mother was there. Being brought up in this manner, he could not function by himself. He acted the same way in the barn at Stepanki. He slept between his mother and me and would always hang onto her when he woke up. He completely ignored me until one morning when I awoke and he was all over me, acting very friendly. I immediately became suspicious and prodded his mother, who was dead. Overnight, this six-year-old boy's thinking had changed. He knew that to survive he had to depend on his extended family. Unfortunately, he became ill and died shortly thereafter.

To stay alive, Avrum and I would have to act according to our instincts since we had only ourselves to rely on. For us, there was no right way or wrong way to survive. There were two things that could help us, and the more important was luck. The second was determination, which we did not lack. We knew that we were in a strange country where Jewish lives were not looked upon as worth saving, and mercy was not something we could count on. The only things in our favour were the approaching warm weather and the experience I had gained in prowling for food during the bitterly cold winter. We had a conviction that somehow we would survive, as well as hope, a precious commodity for persecuted people. It inspired us to think that life is worth fighting for, in spite of what the future might hold. To survive, we would have to face the unforeseen dangers head-on.

Having almost attained their goal of exterminating us, the Romanian soldiers left the local police to oversee us; a few soldiers returned periodically to Stepanki. For some reason, the police now registered all the survivors. It is ironic that they asked for our religion and where we were born. They warned us again not to leave the *lager*, saying that, if we were caught, we would be beaten or shot on the spot.

I learned later that there were more than 130 *lagers* in Transnistria, in cities, towns and villages. It was chance, not design, that determined the *lager* in which we would end up. Chances for survival, particularly during the first winter, depended to a large extent on our particular *lager*. Jews who were interned in cities and towns lived mostly in run-down, crowded houses in ghettos. They organized committees, sanctioned by the Romanian military authorities, to take charge of their ghetto. This gave people a sense of community. It might not have helped much, but it was a way of coping. We ended up in the worst kind of *lager*, a pig barn in a village. Having barely survived the Edineti death camp and the final march to Stepanki, everyone was at their breaking point – physically and mentally exhausted. No one was in any condition to take charge amidst the chaotic environment of the barn. There was absolutely no privacy or hygiene, with everybody crowded together – literally like pigs. But no matter where we were confined, an enormous number of human lives had been lost in all *lagers* by the time we were liberated by the Soviet army.

A few Jewish families came to Stepanki later and did not have to live through the terrible winter months. They had some good clothes with them, and, once they arrived, they were able to bribe the local police and make deals to avoid the pig barns. They were allowed to live in Stepanki, where they gave some of their clothing or jewellery to local farmers in exchange for a shack or a little room in a house.

Avrum and I were the poorest of the poor and had to stay behind in the barn. There were several other orphans who had family members left and a few luckier children who still had one parent alive. Some of these families left during the night, presumably for other ghettos. Those of us who remained, when not scavenging for food, sat outside the barn on a low pile of straw, warming ourselves in the sun and avoiding the stench and gases that burned our eyes. Many reminisced about the loved ones they had lost and the circumstances of their deaths. Some started to cry. These daily discussions centred on the horrors of yesterday and left us with new images for tomorrow. Some were loners, sitting by themselves, staring into space. Nobody had any encouraging words or even bothered to talk about the future, nor did they discuss the past and what they did before the war. They had their own reasons for blocking out happier times. Some older people became like empty shells; the little hope they had previously held now slowly evaporated, turning into despair. They lacked incentive to get up in the morning to fight another day's battle. Maybe they were right to think like that. Life to them had no meaning any more; they had lost their homes and families, and some felt that, even if they were to survive, they had nothing to live for. Avrum and I were young and lacked their knowledge and experience of life – maybe this allowed us to have a more optimistic outlook even in a hopeless situation.

When we looked at each other on the straw pile, we saw skinny, sick, depressed people. Some had terribly swollen legs, and others had faces covered with boils. We were dirty and wore torn rags infested with lice. The warm sun brought them out; they were so plentiful we could have brushed them off, but we did not bother. They came back as soon as they were removed; it was as if we were their property. The straw on which we sat and slept was saturated with them. What choice did we have? We had not had a bath since we left home, had nothing to change into, and slept on the ground like animals.

People's perceptions of the value of life differed greatly. Some did not want to go through the terrible suffering they had to endure under the Nazis and gave up in the early stages of their oppression. They thought it was not worth living a few extra weeks or a month under these brutal conditions and did not care if they died sooner rather than later. They did not foresee a good ending either way. Other people were willing to fight for every breath of air, even though the odds were stacked against them. Despite the suffering they had to endure, they thought that, as long as they could keep their eyes open, maybe in the near future they would see a faint glimmer of hope on the horizon. Such was the will to live of some people; Avrum and I were two of these.

Some optimists survived while others did not. My chances for survival were, at best, miniscule, but something must have fuelled my soul to keep on fighting.

Before the war, when our ordeal started, I was physically fit and quite strong for my age. I was an active, athletically inclined youngster who participated in a variety of sports. I was not particularly competitive but always tried my best at anything I did. I took part in games for my own satisfaction and for the fun of it. Now I was malnourished but still able to function.

I remember one morning when I was not able to get up. I was so weak that when I tried to rise, my knees buckled under me, just like a new-born calf. My condition could have been due to the grass I stuffed myself with to suppress my hunger or possibly to the mushrooms I had eaten the previous night. Some people had died from eating poisonous mushrooms. Avrum was very worried about my condition and ran from person to person to find out what he could do to help me. The only thing I wanted was water. I drank so much I'm surprised I didn't drown.

Our *lager* was on a hill close to a little creek that was almost dry. The day after I couldn't stand I saw a farmer planting something on the other side of the creek. At nightfall, my determination made up for my lack of strength, and I crawled all the way down the hill. Once I reached the plot of land, I used my hands to move the earth around to find what had been planted. I discovered potatoes. I always carried a home-made pouch attached to a shoulder strap. I collected the potatoes and put them into the pouch. Avrum was asleep at the time and had no idea what I was up to. I woke him up, and he made some soup.

That was the only time I remember being sick during those three unbearable years of suffering. During my illness, Avrum took care of me. I somehow recuperated and was able to get up on my feet. We had little to eat except grass and the few potatoes I had stolen out of the ground. We ate the grass, sometimes raw but mostly boiled or, for variety, we would bake grass pancakes on a piece of rusty tin. If we cooked these grass-and-water pancakes too long, they would start to smoulder like wet straw. Sometimes we found little patches of grass in the forest that looked like green onions and tasted good, especially in soup. If we were lucky enough to find a few snails as well, they were thrown in, improving the taste and appearance of the soup. I stopped picking mushrooms even though I thought I knew which ones were safe to eat. Our outdoor cooking facilities were as modern as the stone age; we made a fire between two stones and balanced a pot on top. When there were no matches available, one of the men had his own method of starting a fire. He held a special white stone with a wick-like material pressed against it in one hand. With a special piece of iron in his other hand, he struck this stone a few times until sparks were released, igniting the wick. He blew on the wick to keep the fire going until a paper or straw placed next to it started burning.

Hunger remained a constant enemy. Seldom did we talk about our future after liberation without making food our priority. Each day, we spent more time thinking and fantasizing about food than we actually did eating. There were times when Avrum and I had nothing to eat, but we pretended we were eating by chewing air and swallowing it until our jaws were sore. It did not help; the hunger pains remained. We were just fooling ourselves to pass the time. "You know," I'd say to Avrum, "if we survive the war, I'll never leave home without first stuffing my pockets full of bread."

"Yes," Avrum agreed. "Wouldn't that be wonderful – pockets full of bread! We could eat some anytime we felt like it, whether or not we were hungry."

For us, just to have it would be a status symbol.

One day, all of us got an unexpected treat. One of the men returned to the barn carrying chunks of meat. He told us that he had found a dead horse in the bush, close to the barn. Everyone who could walk rushed out and stripped the flesh off the skinny horse. Later, the bones were hacked to pieces and used for soup. For the next few days, nobody ventured out for food. Everybody was happily preparing and cooking the meat. Eating any meat was something we had dreamed about; its taste we had almost forgotten.

Sometimes Avrum and I would reminisce about the good old days and all the fun we had before our freedom was taken away. We remembered when we were like other kids; our only thoughts centred on playing with friends, and we only planned one day at a time. We would walk down the street at a leisurely pace or run, depending on our mood. We kicked a few stones around, soccer style, or went to the Maccabee Sports Club, where we jumped on the padded horse, took a few swings on the parallel bars and competed with friends in different sports activities. Whether we won or lost, it was a lot of fun. Another favourite pastime on a hot summer day was going down to the Siret River. Mother used to pack a picnic lunch, and we would all meet friends there. We would swim and play in the sand or between the willow trees. I remember Mother having a hard time breaking up our play to get us all together for lunch. Then it was more fun playing than eating. We had the mentality of children and the freedom to pursue it.

We used to walk home from school to a friendly environment where Mother would greet us with a smile. She asked us what we had learned that day and if we were hungry or thirsty, ready with a snack to tide us over until dinner was ready. Every morning she would ask us what we would like for dinner. Mother made sure that we were clean and neatly dressed. We waited for Dad to come home in the evening, and then all of us ran to greet him in an expression of joy. Yes, those were pleasant times filled with love and caring. Avrum and I talked about episodes like that to pass the time, to remember happy memories, and to forget for a while the suffering and sorrow the Nazis inflicted on us.

Still, almost a year after we were forced out of our home in Berhomet and several months after our parents had perished, we remained captive in this barn in a small, isolated village in the Ukraine. We lived in a vacuum, not knowing where we were in relation to any place or what to expect if we were to venture beyond the village. We found ourselves in an environment where common sense did not apply. Danger had to be ignored – maybe ignorance was our passport to survival.

We had found out what brutality and barbarism really are. We did not learn this from a history book or a tragic novel – reality was our teacher. My bruised body was testimony to every blow and my heart felt the sorrow through a helpless and innocent child's eyes.

SUMMER 1942

By the beginning of summer 1942, life for Avrum and me had become more bearable. We no longer had to suffer from the cold: to walk hunched up or lie curled up on the ground, listening to our chattering teeth until we fell asleep. Getting up in the morning was less of an effort; we no longer had the stiffness of sleeping in one position. We had had to avoid turning over as this would have dislodged the skimpy little blankets that we had tucked under us and allowed the little heat given off by the hot stones to escape.

But even though physical conditions had improved, emotionally Avrum and I continued to have great difficulty. It was very hard for us to accept the fact that we had lost our dear family. The worst part was waking up each morning and realizing that this was not a bad dream but that it had actually happened to us. We may have been young, but we were not carved out of stone or poured out of a mould; the pain was real. We still had human hearts filled with feeling and love for our deceased parents, and for our brother and sister who had lost their lives so tragically. Avrum and I were drawn together more closely than ever, not out of fear but out of love for each other. We always got along well before the war, but, now that we were alone, the bond between us grew stronger. It acted as a motivating force to keep on fighting and to look out for each other.

My brother Avrum is easy to describe. Gentle and polite by nature, he was well liked by his friends and neighbours. He kept out of fights at school and was always neat and tidy. He would always do what my parents asked, even doing chores that had been assigned to me whenever I asked him. He would not do anything without first asking for Mother's or Father's permission.

I was different from Avrum; I was not as gentle and polite. I occasionally did things without asking for permission from my parents when I knew they would not have allowed me to do them. I remember going with friends down to the Siret River right after school. We took our shoes off and walked in the shallow part of the river looking for fish. I was full of energy and would challenge my friends to run up the steep

bank and make it to the top without sliding down. I climbed trees that my friends wouldn't even attempt. Sometimes I would leave afternoon Hebrew classes early to play soccer or to watch soccer players practising. I had to make up excuses for coming home late, but they were not good enough to convince Mother; I was always reprimanded. But I could not resist doing it the odd time.

My behaviour did not match my upbringing. I was a spunky kid, doing foolish and mischievous things on impulse. But I never did them in our neighbourhood because I was afraid the neighbours would tell Mother. In the classroom, I stood up for my rights when confronted with anti-Semitism. I was not always a winner, but I never complained to the teacher or discussed these episodes with my parents.

Maybe my past behaviour that I had tried to hide from my parents turned out to be an asset in our fight for survival. I was proud of myself when I succeeded in stealing food without being caught or beaten. I was certainly never taught to steal at home. It is not ordinarily something to be proud of or to brag about. But now it gave me a sense of security, boosted my morale, and encouraged me to do it again. It had more of a valuable psychological effect on me than anything else. In such abnormal times, we could not think or behave as we had been accustomed to. We might have lost our gut feeling that we could survive and given up hope, a cheap source of strength necessary for survival.

Summer was progressing, and we were still in the barn. Some people had recently left us and found peace forever; for others, life dragged on. We felt no urgency; we adapted to conditions and lived from day to day. It was less exhausting for Avrum and me to find food – the farmers' gardens now held vegetables, and the fruit trees were ripening. Instead of picking grass to eat, we picked berries. One day, I came across a soft object in the bush that looked like a piece of meat and brought it back to the barn. I decided to make a meal out of it, but after boiling it for hours, it was still too tough to chew. I kept it for a couple of days and cooked it again. I finally realized that it was a piece of hide and threw it away. Avrum was right: he had told me not to boil it in the first place. Hunger was so great that we never threw anything away as long as it could be chewed and swallowed. Smell or colour was never a deterrent.

As fruit ripened on the trees, I watched it very closely. The first to ripen were the cherries and, for as long as they lasted, they filled our stomachs. While searching for them, we came across duck eggs next to a slough. From then on, whenever we saw a body of water surrounded by vegetation, we searched for eggs and more often than not were success-ful. Peas in the *kolkhoz* fields were another source of food. We went many times at night into the big pea fields where we filled our stomachs and our pouches. We literally stuffed ourselves, but our stomachs tolerated the peas much better than the grass we had eaten in the spring.

In a way, stealing was good therapy for us – it left no time for our thoughts to wander. Our minds were occupied in focusing on the object we were after and staying alert to make sure we were not caught. Avrum sometimes acted as a lookout, warning me of impending danger. Stealing provided us with the food we needed to keep up our strength to try again tomorrow. Tomorrow was a sacred word – people dreamed about living to see it, as though we lived on borrowed time.

There were days when I wished I had not ventured out at all – I was caught and severely beaten. The captors were unlike human beings, more like predators. It seems the evolution of man never progressed in some people, the bestial instinct remaining in them. Their bites were extreme-ly painful as they acted their parts to the letter. I had no choice but to forget and ignore all the threats and beatings I got. I had to try again the next day or sometimes skip one or two days to recuperate from the beat-ings I felt vibrating through my body.

One sunny day when I was casually walking next to a forest and grazing on berries, I was spotted by soldiers. I ran into the forest and hid in the thick underbrush of a big tree. I had a hard time slowing down my breathing and making it as quiet as possible. A short while later, I heard the soldiers talking as they searched for me. Shots were fired. My body suddenly trembled with fear; the pores in my skin opened up just like a shower and my whole body was soaking with sweat within sec-onds. I could hear their voices and their feet trampling on the grass. I was not able to see them, but my whole body turned into a listening ear to follow their movements. As they came closer, I was in tears, but by the grace of God their voices became fainter and fainter and my life was spared once again to live another day.

Stepanki was poor compared to other villages where I prowled for food. My chances of finding food in those villages were better, but the risks of being caught were also greater, so I tried to discourage Avrum from coming with me. Hunger overcame my fear and drove me to take chances in spite of the consequences. It was difficult to move from one village to another, some six or more kilometres apart, without being spot-ted; there was lots of open space between them. Unlike the landscape in

Romania, there were no houses between villages. In the early 1930s, the Soviet government had nationalized all the land and created collective state farms *(kolkhozes)*. Farmers lived in villages and were each allowed to own a small plot of land, roughly an acre, where they grew crops of their choice. They had a small barn to house a cow, a few pigs, and chickens for their own or commercial use. These barns were constructed of thick blocks of clay and straw that provided good insulation. They had very low ceilings, some with lofts, and often served as a shelter for me when I was out in the bitter cold and could not return to Stepanki. People living in the village were employed by the *kolkhoz* and were paid mostly in commodities that were grown on the land. They were able to sell this produce at markets in the surrounding towns and cities.

The only hiding places between villages were forests, grain fields, and patches of tall grass. This made it very difficult for me, especially in spring when people were working on the land. They could spot me right away. Some farmers ignored me, while others gave chase with hostile intentions. When caught, I paid a price for leaving the barn. My beatings provided joy for some men three or four times my age, even though my trespassing did not threaten their livelihood or freedom. It is hard to understand people with that kind of mentality. Some of them had experienced unpleasant encounters with the Nazis, and their brothers and sisters were being killed on the Russian fronts trying to stop the Nazi advance.

After seeding had been completed, few farmers remained in the fields. This made it a little bit easier for us to move around. But we did not feel reasonably safe until the grain crops were high enough and the foliage in the forest thick enough for us to hide from soldiers, police, and Nazi sympathizers.

Whenever possible, Avrum and I would go through the forest, but we did not wander in too deep to avoid getting lost. We could relax, walk at a leisurely pace, and conserve valuable energy not lost to fear. We enjoyed the peaceful and beautiful green surroundings without the need to continually look over our shoulders. It gave us the feeling of being free men, even though it was only an illusion. But then our whole existence depended on imaginary vision. It is hard to explain the joy of freedom to non-persecuted persons. Its value is obscure to them since it is free and they take it for granted, just like the air they breathe. To us, freedom had a different meaning, and the absence of freedom meant fear, hunger, despair, and probable death. Our goal of surviving until we were freed propelled us to keep on going, regardless of the hurdles in front of us.

On one occasion as we walked in the forest, we came upon an open space, startling a few deer drinking at the edge of a slough. "Oh, if we could just catch one of those deer," Avrum said. "What a feast we would have."

"Yes," I replied. "Let's look around, maybe we'll find a dead one."

While searching, we spotted a cherry tree loaded with ripe cherries. We camped under the tree until all the cherries were eaten. We always returned to the barn since it served as our home, and being among our own people helped to relieve our loneliness. Regardless of the misery there, we were still human and in need of companionship. Going in and out of the barn had become relatively easy as there were few survivors and the police no longer paid much attention to us. But we still had to be on guard – if caught outside the barn, they treated us just as harshly as ever.

When I walked from one village to another, I saw children in the distance herding cows on a big tract of government land that had no fence to contain the animals. Every farmer sent one of his children to watch his cow. There were usually groups of about ten children guarding these cattle. The lunch bags they took with them were always piled in one spot. While they were looking after the cattle, the children would play together. I would hide in the grain fields or in the bush. If the children were far away from their lunch bags and their view of me was obstructed by a hill or bush, I would sneak up and take some food from each pouch. I took only part of their lunches so that they would not notice that anything was missing and I would be able to return another day. My success the next time depended again on how far from their lunch bags they played. If they were too close, which they often were, I had to leave with an empty stomach, as I had not forgotten previous encounters with them. They had attacked me like a swarm of bees. After they finished with me, they walked away laughing happily, and I was left lying on the ground. I did not get up until they were some distance from me since I feared they might return and continue the beating. I then retreated to my hide-out nearby to recuperate. Even though I feared these children, some of whom were older than I was, I did not give up. I continued to approach them, albeit with caution, because I considered their lunch bags a good source of food.

My targets in summer also included elderly people driving a horse and wagon to sell their produce in the markets in Kopygorod, Shargorod, or Luchinets. They always took along a package of food to eat, keeping it at arm's length at the back of the wagon. I used to hide in the grain fields or forest near the top of a hill where the horse would walk at a slow pace. If the farmers were young or middle-aged, I ignored them. If they were elderly, I would sneak up quietly behind the wagon once it passed by. I was barefoot and made no noise. I looked for the package of food, and if I was lucky enough to spot it, I grabbed it and ran back to my hiding place. Sometimes the farmers happened to look back before I could reach the food and tried to hit me with the horse whip, making me leave empty-handed. When I was successful in snatching a bundle, I did not try to duplicate my good fortune the same day. I headed straight home with joy to share the food with Avrum. Both of us had smiles on our faces as we ate full mouthfuls without interruption. It was real food and plentiful. It helped us bridge a few more days in our struggle for survival. After a good meal, our morale was high; our conversation centred around food and the future, as though we had just won a lottery.

We daydreamed that our fight to be free would be realized and that the day would come when we would be able to walk the muddy roads back to freedom and regain our right to live as human beings. In sorrow, we would pick up the broken pieces of our lives which had been shattered and try to put them back together again. But in our hearts we knew that this would be impossible as there were too many irreplaceable pieces missing. The memories of Transnistria could never be forgotten.

Leaving our dreams aside, our daily struggle for survival continued. We were like deer, whose natural instinct for survival is to watch the hunters' moves very carefully, trying to out-guess them. We had to take the same precaution to elude the Nazis and their sympathizers. We were too young and helpless to protect ourselves; we were subject to the bestial behaviour of total strangers. Somehow we got used to being abused and accepted it as normal – that was the only way we could cope. What other choice did we have? Our goal was survival, a difficult task since the Nazis left us with the impression that we could only live until our turn came to die. This did not leave us with much room to breathe. Realistically, the only peace we could foresee was the peace of the grave into which we would be thrown.

I have often been asked how I survived such terrible conditions without my parents and at such a young age. My answer is simple. I was young and daring and not naïve – and very, very lucky. A rational person would not attempt to do something without first weighing the

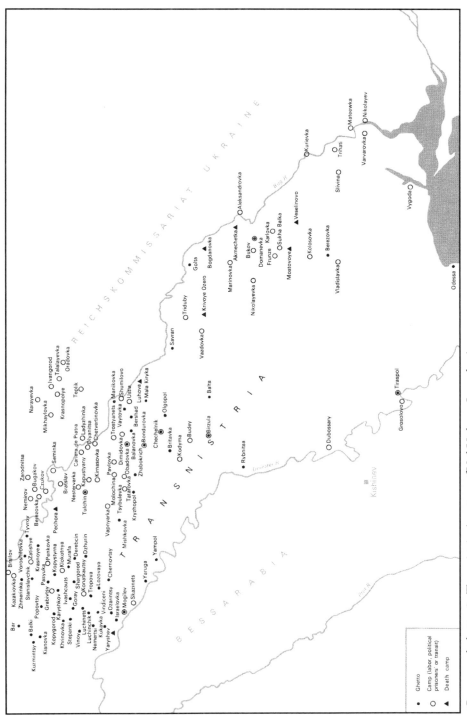

Camps and ghettos in Transnistria (courtesy of Yad Vashem, Jerusalem).

chances of success. Most of the time, the actions I took to survive were taken on impulse; I saw through tunnel vision, like a dog chasing a cat across the street, never thinking of the consequences. Maybe the disregard for danger was the reason for my survival. I also trusted nobody, having learned from hard experience. The black and blue marks on my body were a constant reminder that we had no friends – just a lot of enemies who were always looking for us and trying to take our freedom and lives away.

One day, when Avrum and I were roaming the outskirts of Stepanki in search of food, we came upon a house where an old man was picking apples from his tree. As he walked into the house, I realized that he was an amputee with a wooden leg. We thought this man might not only share some food with us, but would let us stay with him in exchange for doing his chores. Avrum stayed behind in the weeds outside the yard while I slowly walked into the house. The old man was sitting alone at the kitchen table and eating. "Hello," I said, "I'm hungry. Can you please give me some food?"

He looked up at me and, within seconds, lunged toward me with his cane. His sudden angry reaction caught me by surprise and I headed for the door. As he came after me, he started to swear and rant. "You Jews, you're all a rotten bunch of communists," he yelled. "You deserve to die. I'm going to report you to the police."

Avrum was surprised to see me running out of the house empty-handed. He got up and we both ran through a field and hid in the bush to recuperate from the unexpected scare. It bothered me a lot that an old man like that, without any provocation, would act like a Nazi against a defenceless child. Knowing that he could not run after me and I would be safe, I said to Avrum, "I'm going to come back alone tomorrow and steal as many apples as I can put into my pouch."

The next day, as I climbed up the tree, he happened to come out and spotted me.

"Come down, you dirty Jew," he hollered.

"Come up," I said sarcastically. "I'm Stalin's grandson. He's going to come to liberate us soon. I'll get even with you fascists then." I shook a branch, causing a bunch of apples to fall on his head. He walked back into the house, and I ran away without a single apple. I did not realize the stupidity of my actions at that time. He could have had a gun in the house and shot me. But a kid is still a kid, even in such a terrible situation. I never returned to that house again.

On the rare occasions when we were lucky enough to beg or steal enough bread to last us for a couple of days, we could not fall asleep until it was safe in our stomachs. Every so often, we would sit up, break off another little piece of bread and eat it. "We should leave the rest for tomorrow," I'd say, and lie down again. But we kept on breaking off pieces until it was all gone. Some people saved the little food they had for tomorrow and went to bed hungry. For us, tomorrow was today.

Whenever we returned to the barn with food, we proceeded with extra caution. We were more concerned with having our precious food taken away than with being caught and beaten. Being beaten did not hurt me as much as seeing Avrumale beaten. Any time he was caught before I was, I stood my ground and interfered by throwing stones at the captor. He would let Avrum go and come after me. When caught, I absorbed the beatings. In the meantime, Avrum ran away. I was very protective of him; he put a lot of trust in me and felt secure when we were together. There was a lot of similarity between us, not in character but in the will to live; we both had the same drive and conviction. We hoped this momentum and our determination would carry on until the Nazis lost the war. We had no idea who was winning or where the war was being fought in the summer of 1942, but we strongly believed that eventually we would be liberated by the Soviet army.

The only close human contact we had was with the few survivors in the barn. Even rumours, good or bad, that had so often been discussed and repeated before were no longer heard. The barn took on a life of its own. Nights followed days and days followed nights without a horizon to look forward to. There was not much left for the imagination unless one turned a blind eye to the present and focused on the future. The barn was not the place for us to look for encouragement.

In the meantime, Avrum and I continued prowling the countryside. There were lots of places to hide when we saw danger, but one day a group of kids must have seen us coming as we walked on a path in the bush next to the road. As soon as we approached their hiding place, they jumped on us, wrestled us down to the ground, and beat us. We had no chance to defend ourselves. Fortunately, a man driving by in a wagon heard the commotion and saved us. After this episode, I suggested to Avrum that it would be better if I went alone to avoid putting us both in danger. He was not too keen about the idea, still insisting on coming along occasionally. He was just as concerned for me as I was for him.

I made many solo forays for food. On one occasion, I ran into a house that had an aroma of fresh bread and found nobody home. There was a clay oven in which the bread was baking. The opening to the oven was covered with a piece of tin to keep the heat in. I removed the tin, saw bread which appeared to be baked, and reached in with my hand to grab the loaf. The bread was only partly baked, and my hand went into the hot dough, which stuck to my fingers. I ran out of the house in agony. There was only slight relief once I put my hand into a puddle of water. Before long, my fingers were full of blisters, and I continued to be in a great deal of pain. I took a rag and tied it around my hand; it was the only remedy I could think of.

The pain and blisters did not subside, so I went to see Marusia, a Ukrainian woman whom I trusted, hoping she knew of a remedy that would heal my hand. She had recently been helpful to me when I limped into her house. I had developed a lump on my heel which was full of pus and extremely painful, hindering my movements. She had told me to put fresh cow manure on the heel every day, tie it up with a rag and avoid putting pressure on it; this would pull out the pus. I took her advice, and, after limping along for four or five days, the pus was gone and I was cured. Now she advised me to put unsalted butter on my fingers. This, she said, would soften the skin, prevent it from drying, relieve the pain, and help the healing. Unfortunately, she was so poor she could not afford butter. Luckily, I managed to get some butter from a woman who took pity on me when she saw my blistered hand. I kept putting it on until my hand healed.

I also learned some survival techniques from my own experience. They did not always work, but they helped more often than not. In summer, I was always barefoot, frequently cutting and bruising my feet on glass or stones as I walked through the weeds in the back of barns or homes while searching for food. I improvised my own remedy of applying clay to stop the bleeding.

I first met Marusia, a woman in her late twenties, in early spring. I had walked into a small, sparsely furnished, one-room house on the outskirts of Stepanki. Inside were two young children, about three and six years of age. The older child told me that her mother was at work. I stayed there for a while to warm up before leaving. A few days later when I came back again to warm up, Marusia was home, having dinner with her children. I started talking to her and was invited to join them for dinner. She was the first person in Stepanki with whom I sat at a table and discussed my problems. She took a keen interest in listening to me, asking many questions. Knowing I was Jewish and that I lived in the pig barn, she was curious to know where I was from and why we had been sent to Stepanki. She told me that she periodically worked in the *kolkhoz* but had experienced difficulty feeding herself and her children since her husband was drafted into the Red Army. She had no idea where he was or even if he was still alive.

Marusia's house was one of the poorest that I had entered in Stepanki while searching for food. The room was so small that even the sparse furniture filled it. Against one wall was a clothes chest elevated on legs. A narrow picnic-style table took up a good part of the room. Against another wall was a bed made out of planks covered with straw, which served as a mattress. A blanket enclosed the straw. A narrow, long, clay stove that was used for cooking as well as heating the room was next to the clay oven. There was one small window with four panes of glass that was permanently closed. A couple of boards used for shelving were attached to a wall. The room had a dirt floor. A shack attached to the house was used to store straw and wood and held a pail that served as a toilet.

The constant search for food took me to unfamiliar territory. One day, I got lost in the forest and couldn't find my way out. I must have walked in circles. It was summer and I wasn't worried; eventually I'd find my way out. I picked berries to eat and drank water from sloughs. Avrum knew that I wouldn't always return the same day when I went to different villages looking for food. While walking in the forest, I spotted a big house that looked like a mansion. I cautiously approached it to make sure there were no soldiers. When the absence of military vehicles convinced me that there were none, I decided to walk in and beg for food and directions. The people in the house were well dressed and polite. They knew by my bedraggled appearance that I was Jewish and looking for something to eat. I was given food without even asking.

"Where are you from?" the owner asked me.

"I live in a pig barn in Stepanki," I told him.

"There's a village called Ivashcauts, not far away, where Jews also lived in a barn. But I think they're not there anymore," he said. "Farther on is a town called Shargorod. The Jews there live in a ghetto, but I heard that many have perished. For your own good, you can't stay here too long. I'm a forest manager, and officers often come here. Some stay overnight. But any time you have a chance, when there are no soldiers around, you can come in and I'll gladly give you food."

"I'm lost," I said. "Can you tell me how to get back to Stepanki?"

He gave me directions and I left.

I made a number of return trips to the forest manager's house but would frequently have to leave empty-handed when soldiers were present. On one of the return trips, I got lost again. As I was walking in the forest, I saw two soldiers in the distance carrying rifles in their hands as though they were going hunting. I turned around and walked in the opposite direction to distance myself from them and hid behind a big tree. I lay down in the grass until late afternoon. When I got up, I was disoriented. After walking for a while, I heard a bell ringing. I headed toward this sound, and, as I came closer, I saw a cow with a bell around its neck. I decided not to go farther but to wait until someone came to look for the cow. Shortly after, a young boy appeared. I followed them from a distance; before long I could see a village. I remained on the outskirts of the forest.

Once darkness set in, I proceeded toward the village and came upon a shack. I looked in the window and, to my surprise, saw Jewish people sitting at a table eating. It was easy to recognize them by their appearance. I walked in like an unexpected guest.

"Where are you from?" one of them asked.

"Stepanki," I said.

"Come sit down; have supper with us. How did you find us?"

I told them how I got there. They were surprised to hear that there were any survivors still living in Stepanki. They heard that almost everybody there had either starved or frozen to death, and that the few survivors had left. Three families lived in that shack – one man was a shoemaker, and one was a tinsmith. In return for their work, they received food and were thus able to survive. They told me there were a few more Jews in that village who had come in the early spring of 1942. I stayed overnight, sleeping on the floor. The next day, I returned to Stepanki with potatoes they gave me.

Whenever I returned after being gone for a day or more was like a happy reunion with Avrum. The first thing he wanted to know was whether I had encountered any danger. I did not always tell him the truth because I did not want to upset him. I pulled the loot from my pouch, showing it to him with great satisfaction. I told him how and where I got it and whether I was planning to return to that place again. Unlike in winter, I usually brought back something in my pouch.

One night while prowling around Stepanki, I was attracted to a well-lit house. As I came closer, I could hear singing. I was curious and ran into the nearby barn to hide. When I looked out of the barn I could see through the house windows that there were a lot of people eating, drinking, singing, and having a good time. I did not know the reason for the celebration, and I did not care. I was only interested in finding food.

The hallway door was open, and, under cover of darkness, I sneaked in. I spotted a large pot. I grabbed it by its two handles, but it was so heavy I could hardly carry it. I took it behind the barn. When I examined it, I found that it was a pot of borscht. As it was too heavy to carry back to the barn and too precious to spill any of its contents, I decided to eat as much as I could. It would get lighter, and I could take the remainder back for Avrum. I ate so much so fast that, when I got up, I felt sick – as if I was going to bring it all up or even die. Although I was afraid that I might be caught if I did not leave right away, I had to lean back and support myself against the barn wall. I was unable to move. After a while, I felt a bit better, but I was still too sick to take the pot with me and too scared to wait until I felt well enough to carry it. Regrettably, I had to leave the borscht behind, barely making it back to the barn.

I led a hazardous life; my daily struggle for existence placed me in constant peril. I never knew what awaited me as there were many hidden trip wires along my path. I had to be on guard for police, soldiers, and those local people who were faithful to the Nazi cause and had a passionate hatred for us. Many people were willing to kill us, but few were ready to stop them. The sad thing was that these people did not even know who we were and why we had been sent there. They only knew that we were Jews, and this was sufficient reason for them to hate us. I did not know whom to trust; unfortunately, there were not too many that I could.

Chances had to be taken out of need rather than through the application of logic. Logic made no sense in this environment where we were forced to live at gunpoint, not knowing if there was going to be a tomorrow. Hunger directed my moves; most of the time I was desperate to avoid starvation. Weather permitting, I ignored the dangers as well as the blisters and sores on my feet. I was always on the go in search of food. Until I became familiar with the surrounding area, I had no planned destination; I just wandered around aimlessly in whichever direction my eyes were attracted. No matter which direction I chose, all roads led to enemy territory. The days were long, tiring and, without Avrum, lonely. I had nobody with whom I could talk or exchange views to interrupt the tortuous silent fears that whirled in my mind.

The hostile environment sometimes turned into a joyful setting. Once when Avrum came along with me, we gathered enough food without encountering any hostility. We stopped to eat at the edge of the forest. While absorbing the sunshine, we looked around, awed by the beautiful and peaceful surroundings. The endless grain fields were swaying in the breeze under the clear blue sky as far as the eye could see. Colourful butterflies floated around, skimming over the heads of grain. (The grain at this stage was not ripe – I had tried eating it, but I became bloated, and it caused me a great deal of pain.) Behind us were tall green trees that were home to many birds of different species and colours. They flew freely from one tree to another, chirping songs with not a care in the world. I spotted a deer grazing in leisurely fashion, raising its head and chewing its cud while looking around, as if admiring the view.

Scenes like that, which I frequently saw while walking in the forest, were beautiful to observe. They had a calming effect, temporarily relieving my misery. It was as though I had ascended into an illusory world of peace, stepping into a dream beyond my reach. Unfortunately, this state of tranquillity did not last long because I had to interrupt my reverie to continue the search for food. How I envied those carefree inhabitants of the forest. It is human nature to hope and dream that your wishes to be free will come true one day. Without imagination and hope, a person's will to fight for survival can be destroyed. I kept on fighting – I was frequently disappointed, but I never gave up.

Avrum and I often spoke about the two *lagers* that the forest manager had made me aware of.

"What do you think, Avrum?" I asked. "Should we go explore these *lagers?*"

"Well, we can't remain here," he answered. "The weather's nice, and if we have to hide, there's lots of places in the greenery and bushes. We probably should go now – there's food available in farmers' gardens."

After some hesitation, I decided to go alone. Avrum wanted to come along, but I discouraged him. I felt he would be safer in the barn than wandering with me in unfamiliar territory with its unknown perils. Reluctantly, he agreed to stay behind. We stole enough vegetables and fruit to last him for several days. Even if I were to stay away longer, by now, Avrum had sufficient experience and was daring enough to take care of himself.

He surprised me – I always thought of him as being passive. After we were left without our parents, his inner emotional strength surfaced and his behaviour became more aggressive. He disregarded danger, always wanting to come with me. Regardless of his courageous attitude, I still felt he should stay out of harm's way as much as possible, and the barn was the safest place to be to avoid being physically threatened.

Heading out, I planned to stop in Ivashcauts because it was on the way to Shargorod. After hours of walking, I could see a village, presumably Ivashcauts, and spotted a big barn on the outskirts where Jews were supposedly interned. I headed straight toward the barn. When I got closer, I watched it for a while but did not observe anyone entering or leaving. I had a strange feeling that maybe it was the wrong village. I slowly approached the barn and finally walked in. Foul-smelling air greeted me. There was silence and no sign of life. I was apprehensive as I stood motionless, my eyes slowly wandering around the deserted barn. There was evidence that people had lived there.

I bypassed the village and walked toward a house on the outskirts to ask for directions to Shargorod. While in the process of stealing food from a garden, I cut my foot, and it started to bleed. My first reaction was to secure my safety. Ignoring the bleeding, I ran for cover. It must have been a deep cut as it bled profusely. I applied clay to the cut and wrapped a rag around my foot. I rested for a while, but when I started walking, it began to bleed again. I decided to sleep overnight in a grain field.

When I got up at sunrise, the bleeding had stopped, and I continued on my way to Shargorod. As I limped along to avoid putting pressure on my wound, I saw a horse and buggy approaching in the distance but did not take evasive action because of my foot. As soon as the buggy reached me, it stopped. I saw a Romanian officer with a young woman. The officer jumped off the buggy in haste and lunged at me. My first reaction in situations where I was caught and could not run away was to put my hands in front of my face, bracing myself for the expected blows. He started to curse and hit me. At the same time, the woman stepped off the buggy, pleading with the officer in Romanian to stop beating me. Surprisingly, she seemed to be concerned about my well-being and succeeded in stopping him from hitting me further. After climbing back onto the buggy they drove away, leaving me standing on the dusty road with a bloody nose, an aching foot, and a sense of bewilderment. His hatred toward Jews must have been so strong that abuse against a child took priority over a pleasure ride with a woman. A bloody nose was not uncommon for me, but the fear of what might happen if I were caught in Shargorod remained.

When I left Stepanki just a day before, my spirits were buoyant, anticipating that some good would come out of this venture. I had set out to scout the area to see if we could improve our situation. Maybe I would come across some of our relatives, or, if not, I might learn some lessons from a larger pool of people who might have different ideas and more optimistic outlooks than the survivors in Stepanki. I limped along at a slower pace than before with less enthusiasm, my thoughts conflicting on whether or not to proceed. Until now, I had only ventured into villages; going to Shargorod would be a new experience for me. As time went on, I started to see some houses in the distance. As I drew closer to Shargorod, I could see people working on their small plots of land next to their homes. I was apprehensive as I passed their houses. My greatest fear was that I would encounter soldiers with the same attitude as the Romanian officer who had just beaten me.

As I continued walking, I reached a bridge spanning a small river. I went down the bank and took shelter under the bridge. While I tended to my wound, I could see several Jews across the river searching for something around a flour mill. I crossed the bridge and asked them where the ghetto was. I told them what I had seen in the Ivashcauts barn and what had happened to me on the way to Shargorod.

"You're lucky," one of the men said. "That young woman with the officer is Jewish. She's his mistress."

"Many of the people from the Ivashcauts barn made it to the Shargorod ghetto," another man said. "In fact, one of them is right here."

"Do you know if there are any people here from Berhomet?" I asked.

"No, I don't. But go into the ghetto, you'll meet more people. Maybe you'll recognize someone."

Most of the homes I saw were old and run-down, but to me they looked like palaces compared to the pig barns in Stepanki. I walked around in the ghetto, feeling perplexed – I had not seen so many Jews in one place since our convoy was split up the previous year in Luchinets. It gave me a feeling of security to be among my own people where I could let my guard down; I became more relaxed and felt relatively safe. But the fact was that the people living there had also suffered many losses. They, too, felt threatened, never knowing what tomorrow would bring.

I watched people as they walked back and forth. I looked for relatives or a face I could recognize, but they were all strangers to me. The lucky among them still carried some items of clothing on their arms, probably for sale. Small groups huddled and talked among themselves; nobody paid any attention to me. I walked alone for a while until I ran into a group of bedraggled and malnourished children, some younger and some older than me. They wore rags and went barefoot – mirror images of myself. I started talking to them, telling them where I was from and about the loss of my family. They, too, were orphans – some of them told me their own sad stories and talked about the difficulties they had encountered while struggling to survive on their own. They seldom wandered away from their area of confinement, doing most of their begging and stealing in the ghetto.

They were a friendly bunch so I hung around with them the remainder of the day. We had a lot of unpleasant experiences to talk about, and we understood each other's sorrows. We realized how difficult the road ahead would be without our parents. We had no one to give us moral support or the reassuring feeling that we belonged to someone who loved us and whom we could love in return. We were all lonely souls drifting around in an environment where everybody had too many problems, enduring hardship and losing family members to hunger and disease.

For us orphans, it was difficult to survive the struggle on our own long enough to learn to cope. Time was not on our side, and for some it was already too late. There were orphans I saw that day who did not say much but just straggled along. They did not have enough life or strength to grapple with their hunger and loneliness much longer. The chubby cheeks that adults always liked to grab and pinch were long gone. In their place were only bones and dried-out skin as tight as a drum. The only positive thing they had going for them, along with warm summer weather, were their few friends who encouraged them to get up every morning and join them in roaming the streets in search of food. The momentum generated by the group carried the weaker orphans along, making them forget or ignore the inevitable fate awaiting them. Only by the grace of God would they survive.

Justice was a meaningless word to us orphans. We had yearned for it, but we had never experienced it. Injustice and cruelty were the way of life we knew. The few of us still surviving stubbornly clung to that life with our bare hands on the edge of the cliff, trying not to be swept away by the raging current created by the Nazis to destroy us.

This venture to Shargorod was an eye-opener; it filled me with enthusiasm and determined my next move. I liked what I saw; after being

down about as low as I could be in the barn, the ghetto seemed to be an improvement. It is amazing how the mind leaps ahead, viewing anything different than the state one is in as an improvement.

It was late in the afternoon when I decided to return to Stepanki, planning to sleep and rest my foot on the way. Before I departed, I told my new friends that my brother and I would join them soon because I thought my chances for survival would be better among my own people in Shargorod. I planned to talk it over with Avrum before we made our move. The main concern behind this decision was the need to find shelter for the coming winter.

As I left Shargorod, a horse pulling a wagon trotted along the road. The old couple on the wagon stopped to ask me where I was going. When I told them to Stepanki, they told me they were going to a town nearby and offered me a ride. I quickly jumped onto the back of the wagon. They asked if I was hungry, and after my response they gave me all the food they had in their bundle. I ate some, leaving the rest for Avrum. They asked me a lot of questions, and we continued talking until I fell asleep.

It was late at night when they woke me and directed me to the road to Stepanki. I got off the wagon and started to limp along the lonely road. I could hardly wait to reach the barn to bring the good news about the ghetto to Avrum.

It was dawn when I reached the barn, where everybody was asleep. I lay down next to Avrum to continue my own interrupted sleep. When we got up, he was surprised and happy to see me; he hadn't expected me to return so soon.

"What did you see?" he asked. "Did you find any relatives?"

"No," I replied. "But I saw lots of Jewish people. You know, Avrum, Jews are living in houses in Shargorod and walking the streets! Some even wore good clothing like we used to wear at home. It's a different world there. I should have gone to Shargorod as soon as the forest manager told me about it; we could have been living there by now."

"Well, it's not too late," Avrum said. "But did you find a place for us to stay during the winter?"

"No, I didn't. I was too anxious to come back to tell you about it. I'll have to go again."

We were so upbeat that we told an elderly woman who had taken a liking to us and always engaged us in conversation. "Go," she said. "You're young and have a lifetime ahead. If you stay here, you'll die. It's too late for me. My husband and all my children are gone." She could barely walk and did not care to live any longer. Her legs were so swollen and the skin so tight that they looked like they would burst at any moment. Even though it was summer, people continued to die, leaving a few more orphans in the barn.

I remember two of them; they were boys a little older than me. One told me his aunt had spoken to a man who had just returned from Mogilev where he had gone to search for relatives. The man had found a brother and came back to get his wife. He told the aunt that the Jews of Bucharest, the capital of Romania, had bribed the officials to allow the opening of orphanages in Mogilev, where thousands of Jews were interned in a ghetto. (Romanian Jews, other than those living in the provinces of Bukovina and Bessarabia, had been allowed to remain at home during the war. Having lived under Soviet occupation for a year, the Jews of Bukovina and Bessarabia were looked upon as harbouring communist ideals; it was a pretext for ridding these provinces of Jews. Ironically, even though southern Bukovina had not been occupied, the Jews from there were also deported.) The orphanages were to try to save as many orphans as possible from disease, starvation, and death. Hundreds had already perished on the streets, the only home they knew after their parents died.

Both boys tried to convince us to go with them to the orphanage as they were concerned about going alone and felt that our experience in roaming the countryside would help. It was hard for us to believe stories about orphanages after we had witnessed the merciless killing by the Nazis of both young and old alike. They argued that, if the rumours were not true, we could always return. The possibility of an orphanage appealed to us, diverting us from our plans to return to Shargorod. Avrum and I leaned toward Mogilev, but we were both skeptical and decided that we should wait before making a decision. The two boys left for the orphanage.

The days slowly ticked away as Avrum and I impatiently waited for word, but we had no way of finding out what had happened to them. We hoped there really was an orphanage and they would not return. It was early fall, and we would soon have to make our move. Winter, the enemy we feared most, was not too far away, and we were both barefoot and had little clothing on our backs.

In the meantime, we followed our usual routine. The harvest was in full swing and farmers were in the fields. The grain fields in which I had previously hidden were being cut down, making it more difficult to get from one village to another without being spotted. There were, however, fruits and vegetables that I could steal from farmers in Stepanki.

I remember one little episode involving a tall pear tree that grew on a piece of land belonging to an older couple. Avrum and I feasted on that tree until most of the sweet and juicy pears, our favourites, had been picked by either the farmer or us. I spotted three remaining pears bunched together at the top of the tree. Having heard in the barn that it was Rosh Hashanah and that Yom Kippur was a week away, I decided to climb the tree to camouflage those three pears by tangling up the leaves around them. I wanted to save them for breaking the fast on Yom Kippur night. It sounds silly now, but it was even sillier then, when we were forced to fast unwillingly most of the time. My Jewish religious background was still imbedded in me, and I tried to carry on its traditions.

More than a month had passed since the boys left for the orphanage, and they had not returned. We assumed that things had worked out for them; this helped us decide to go to Mogilev. We hoped we would be relieved of a great burden; we would be housed, fed and taken care of, and that would ensure our survival. Avrum and I decided that we would leave Stepanki as soon as the harvest was completed and the farmers were out of the fields. Farmers were already harvesting the grain, leaving behind the odd heads that fell to the ground. They never bothered picking these up, letting them rot in the fields. Only the people from the *lager* tried to gather these precious kernels. We were not allowed to do this, and we were beaten when we were caught. To avoid being caught, we went early in the morning before the farmers started work on the land. One day, a man with a horse and buggy closed in on us very quickly. Avrum and I ran into the bush, barely escaping a whipping. The older people were too slow and were not as fortunate. They later told me that this man was the mayor of the village. Beating the Jews was a sport to him.

When we returned to the barn, we rubbed the heads of grain between our hands, blew away the chaff and ate some of the kernels right away to satisfy our immediate hunger. We placed the remaining kernels on a piece of tin over an open fire, browned them, and put them into soup to add some substance and flavour. These luxuries only lasted for the few weeks of harvest, and only for those people who had the courage and strength to go into the fields.

THE ORPHANAGE IN MOGILEV

The cooler nights and the falling leaves were a daily reminder that winter was fast approaching; we could not delay our departure any longer. We were encouraged by the fact that the two boys had not returned, because that indicated to us that there was an orphanage in Mogilev. Most of the crops had been harvested, allowing unlimited visibility in the open fields. We decided it was time to go, and that it was best to walk at night to avoid being detected.

Our luggage consisted of two small torn blankets. We wrapped them around our shoulders during the day and draped them over our bodies at night. We had a hard time deciding which parts to keep warm because the blankets were not big enough to cover our whole bodies when we lay down to sleep. We had no shoes and tried to keep our feet warm at night by putting them into our caps. We wore pants that had been torn by dogs and fences and branches while searching for food. Falling apart from wear and tear for over a year, the pants were tied around our bodies with pieces of string to prevent them from disintegrating. We each wore warm tricot underwear (tops and bottoms), a shirt, and a torn jacket. Layers of rags were attached to our clothes to help keep us warm. We had enough food to last us for a couple of days.

Before we ventured out of Stepanki, I had gone to see Marusia to ask for directions. She could only direct us part of the way because she was not familiar with the territory closer to Mogilev. We left with high hopes of lessening our suffering and improving our chances for survival. We hid and slept during the day, and whenever we got tired at night we slept in huge straw piles that were formed when farmers threshed grain. We had no problem getting food; sugar beets were still in the ground.

It must have taken us four or five days to reach Mogilev. We kept our bearings by stopping at farmhouses on the outskirts of villages to ask for directions. We approached Mogilev sometime during the night and hid in a straw pile until nightfall the next day. We chose not to proceed in the daytime for fear of soldiers. Although shielded by darkness, we were both frightened as we entered the city. We didn't know which direction to take to find our way into the ghetto. As we hurried along,

I saw somebody in front of us with a blanket draped over his shoulder. I knew he must be a person from the ghetto. We caught up with him and realized that it was an old woman. I asked her for directions to the orphanage; she told us to follow her. She appeared just as frightened as we were and told us not to talk. After walking for a while, she stopped and directed us to the orphanage.

As we approached the structure it reminded me of a school I had attended. It was dark, and there was nobody outside the building. After a little hesitation, we walked in and saw a doorman. "We are orphans," I told him.

"Who sent you here?" he asked.

"No one. We were desperate. We came by ourselves."

"Which ghetto did you come from?"

"The pig barn in Stepanki," I answered.

He looked us over, shaking his head, "I've never heard of Stepanki. It must be far away. The staff has gone home, but I'll put you up for the night. You'll be processed in the morning."

As we were led up the stairs, I breathed a sigh of relief – "We made it!" I said to Avrum. We had finally come to a place where we would be taken care of and find warmth and peace. The doorman opened the door to the room. As we entered, an unbelievably strong stench hit us. He told us that we would have to sleep on the floor. Children were lying in crowded beds; a few others in nightgowns were sitting and talking in a small adjoining room. All the ones I saw looked malnourished; a few lying in bed looked lifeless. Avrum and I looked at each other; we could not believe what we saw. As soon as the doorman left, one of the children called me to his bed as if he knew me, but I did not recognize him. He was one of the two boys who had tried to convince us to go with him to the orphanage. He was extremely happy to see a familiar face. He slowly got out of bed, and we joined the others in the small room.

"You're lucky to have arrived at night," he said in a weak voice. "You still have your clothes on. You've got to run away. Look around, see for yourself; most of us are malnourished and sick, and some have already died."

My friend was filled with frustration and anger, bitter about the injustice done to him by some of the officials in charge of the orphanage. He had been told by workers who felt sorry for the orphans that there was a better orphanage in Mogilev. Justice, however, did not prevail – they told him that some parents who still had valuables bribed officials and put their children, some as old as twenty, into the better orphanage, knowing that they would be better off there than where they lived. These children were fed, clothed, and taken care of – and took up some of the valuable space intended for real orphans. This was the original intention of the Romanian Jews who supplied the necessary provisions to save as many orphans' lives as possible.

My friend told us that, when he arrived, he had been processed and his clothes immediately taken away. Maybe this was done as a preventive measure to get rid of lice. He was given only a nightgown and a little food to eat. The orphans' movements were so restricted that they could not even go to a bathroom; chamber pots were placed under their beds. The doors to the rooms were kept locked and only opened when food was brought in or when the chamber pots were emptied during the night. We learned that tonight would be our only opportunity to run away before we were processed in the morning and had our clothing taken away.[13]

We did not know what to do; we were in a panic. Our minds pondered every angle, trying to figure out how to escape. Time was closing in on us, and we were already tired and sleepy. As I took my friend back to his bed, he whispered: "You can see our fate. You must get out – tonight is your only chance." We sat next to him until he fell asleep. It would probably make his day if he did not see us in the morning.

Our eyes surveyed the room, stopping at the window, but we realized that it was too high above the ground for us to make it without breaking our bones or getting killed. We returned to the only possibility – the door. We were afraid that we might fall asleep and miss our one opportunity, so we decided to take turns sleeping. Still we remained afraid that both of us might fall asleep, until Avrum noticed that the door opened into the room. This relieved our anxiety, and we both lay down with our heads against the door.

Sometime during the night, we were awakened as the door was opened. Without paying any attention to us, the workers came into the room to empty the pots. Avrum and I got up quickly, left through the open door, and made our way down the stairs. We ran into the dark, mysterious night filled with terror and uncertainty. Our short-lived happiness at making our way out was overtaken by fear. We panicked and ran from one street corner to another, not knowing whether to turn left or right, nor even knowing what we were looking for. My heart was pounding. Bewildered and breathless, our greatest fear was being spotted by soldiers or police and shot. We were two young children who were easily recognizable as being Jewish and felt trapped in the city where the Romanian military headquarters of the region was located. German officers and soldiers were also stationed there. They were all in their glory days, their trigger-happy fingers looking for any easy target.

After a hair-raising time, which seemed like an eternity, we finally succeeded in finding our way out of Mogilev without being caught. It was a miracle. Powered by fear, we kept on going, running and walking up a hill with whatever strength we had left until we came to a big straw pile. We bored our way in and lay there for the remainder of the night, shivering, dozing on and off, totally exhausted. When we awoke in the morning and peered from our hideout, we were completely disoriented – we did not know where we were or what direction to take. Being anxious to get away as fast and as far as possible from Mogilev, we decided to proceed in the daytime. We had no choice but to return to the Stepanki *lager,* although we knew it would be impossible for us to survive the winter in the clothing we had.

We had lived with hope until now and would somehow manage again – hope was our life force. It generated a vision of a brighter future and prevented us from succumbing to despair. Our lives depended on visions of tomorrow occupying the spaces of yesterday's sorrows.

I thought of two people in Stepanki who had previously shown pity on us. They might let us stay in their homes for a while. Marusia was one; the other was an old woman whose name I did not know. She was very poor. She lived in a one-room *zamlianka* – this was more or less a cellar, two-thirds below ground and one-third above, with a few windows to let light in. During the previous winter, she had let me come in to warm up. She thought of me not as a Jew but as a person who was being unjustly persecuted simply because I was born into a different religion, one which did not suit the Nazis. Our other option would be to go to Shargorod and take our chances there.

While walking in the rain, we saw a soldier on a horse approaching us. When he confronted us, he said in Romanian, "Stop! Where are you going?"

"Home," I said.

"You are Jews, you have no home here. I'm going to shoot you," he said.

Avrum started to cry, and I tried to comfort him as the soldier dismounted. The soldier looked very young and his manner of speaking was not nearly as harsh as that of other soldiers we had encountered. We were kids, wet, cold, barefoot, and pitiful to look at.

"Please let us go," I begged him, "We're the only ones left in our family."

He took his rifle off his shoulder. Motioning toward me, he said to Avrum, "Stand in front of him. I don't want to waste two bullets on you Jews."

As Avrum continued to cry, I pressed him to my chest to calm him down. My own body started to tremble from head to toe as I looked helplessly at the barrel of the gun that the soldier pointed at us from a few metres away. Our only defence was Avrum's tears and my trembling body. He fired. We heard the sound of death. We were so focused on dying, we didn't realize that he had deliberately missed us. As he mounted the horse, he warned us not to leave the ghetto and wander around as we might not be as lucky the next time. It turned out that he was only trying to show his authority and scare the hell out of us.

This was the closest we had ever come to death, and it was terrifying. Avrum's tears kept flowing just as easily and fast as the rainfall that day. He was sobbing so hard he could not even speak. The dirt road in the area was rich in clay, making it very slippery. We had to hang onto each other. While I tried to comfort Avrum, the aftershock of our close call hit me. My own tears started flowing, blending with the rain. Even the weather that day was against us. The skies were grey with dark patches encircling us as far as one could see. It was a very traumatic day; we were so confused and scared it did not even occur to us that we might be on the wrong road.

We kept going in the rain, our spirits dampened by our close encounter. But hope was still alive; the sun would shine on us again – if not tomorrow, then the day after. We came across a field of sugar beets and stopped to pull some to eat. While looking for a straw pile in which to sleep, we ran into another Romanian soldier on a horse. This one was quite a bit older. He did not ask us where we were going or who we were. By our bedraggled appearance, it was obvious. Still sitting on his horse, he started spewing venom. He appeared to be drunk, and all I could make out was "You dirty little Jewish bastards! How far do you think you're going to get?" Without warning, he whipped his lash toward Avrum since he was the closest. Being positioned in front of the horse, I stuck out my arm to prevent the lash from hitting Avrum. As I raised my arm, the horse got scared and stood up on his hind legs. While this was happening, the leather from the lash twisted around my arm and the soldier tried to pull it back. Somehow his saddle must have shifted, and he fell partly off the horse, getting himself entangled. While he was trying to extricate himself, we ran away toward a clay hill nearby. Luckily, this hill had a lot of small tunnels dug by farmers who used the clay to smear the dirt floors in their homes to create a fresh look. We crawled in and hid in one of the tunnels.

We were petrified and remained motionless. Our eyes were wide open and our ears listening hard for any sounds of the soldier. The silence surrounding us kept us unsettled and in a state of fear. We were trapped, having no choice but to await our fate. We huddled together to keep as warm as possible until finally we fell asleep.

In the morning, we slowly crawled out of the tunnel. The rain had stopped and the sun was shining. We decided it was too risky to walk in the daytime, but the tunnel was too wet and cold to be our hiding place. We had to look for a straw pile to keep us dry and warm until nightfall. After a short walk, we spotted one and crawled in to hide. We ate sugar beets and rested. After sundown, we started walking into the cold night, desperately trying to survive in this hostile environment. We were lost, disoriented, and too frightened to approach a farm house to ask for directions. We decided on one direction, hoping it was the right one. Unfortunately, it wasn't. I didn't find this out until the next evening when I stopped a farmer riding on a wagon and he directed us toward Stepanki. We had encountered nothing but bad luck ever since running away from the orphanage. We survived only on sugar beets that had not yet been harvested from some patches.

After many long, scary, and exhausting days, we finally arrived in Stepanki at night. We had gone to Mogilev with high hopes and returned disillusioned. Our determination to persevere had dwindled but still had not vanished. Avrum and I kept thinking and talking about our experience at the orphanage – I believe it was Orphanage Number Three. This incident occurred sometime in October or November 1942. We concluded that it was not a time to look for mercy, and we were lucky to have survived; the Nazis had forced us all to live in the shadow of death.

The weather now took a sudden turn for the worse, and I hoped that Marusia would let us stay with her for a while. As we walked into her house, she looked surprised to see us. "What are you doing here? Didn't you go to Mogilev?" she asked.

"We couldn't stay and had to return," I replied. "Please," I begged, with desperation in my voice, "Can we stay with you for the winter or at least until we find another place?" I had in mind the old woman who lived in the *zamlianka;* the only other option left to us was to go to the Shargorod ghetto.

Marusia had only one bed where she and her children slept. She agreed to let us stay for a while. We felt as though we had been granted a reprieve, especially now that ugly winter was staring into our eyes with a predatory look. I could not forget the previous winter that had taken the lives of hundreds of people in the pig barn, turning living human flesh into blocks of ice overnight. Marusia told us to go into the shack to gather straw for bedding. This was our happiest moment since leaving home. A dirt floor to sleep on may not sound like much, but for us it meant the difference between life and death.

I feared the cold more than hunger. I had witnessed people dying from both circumstances. A hungry person can linger for weeks with a lot of unbearable pain, but as long as he can keep his eyes open, his hope remains that one day he may be saved by a miracle. Cold is not as painful, but it is a silent, treacherous killer. People would lie down on the ground for a night's rest; the cold then appeared to act as an anaesthetic. One would not hear a sound from them all night; in the morning a family member or friend next to them would give them a push to wake them up and realize that tragedy had struck.

We got up the next morning with tired, aching feet; our soles bruised and sore. Our spirits reflected the condition of our feet. We collected and bundled up the straw and put it back in the shack. We were hungry, and I pulled the few remaining sugar beets from my pouch. Marusia told us to save the beets and join her for a hot meal. Seeing the condition we were in, she offered us food until we were able to go out. It took several days for Avrum and me to regain our composure and recuperate from the trauma.

After being restricted to the house by rain and sleet, I was anxious to get out and search for food. I did not want to give Marusia the impression that she would have to feed two more mouths, something she could ill afford. I told her that I would help with chores and assured her that we would not need her food. After we had been in the house for a while, Marusia told us that we could remain with her for the winter. My joy was so great that I started to cry. Avrum and I had just been given a new lease on life.

We couldn't understand why Marusia was so different from others that we had encountered. We intruded on her privacy, carried straw in and out every day, and must have been underfoot at times. But she never criticized or complained about us and tried to cheer us up whenever we were down. How can one describe the inner feelings of a person like Marusia? It's as difficult as describing a specific shade of any given colour. To say she was a good-natured person is to do her an injustice. She was much more than that. A heavy-set, good-looking woman with a pleasant disposition, she treated us with respect. Despite her poverty and meagre existence, she displayed optimism. Dressed in traditional Ukrainian garb, she always wore a kerchief covering her hair.

We kept as quiet as possible and helped by doing chores around the house, breaking up branches and keeping the fire going. We also played with her children. They were cute-looking, well-behaved kids who were always happy and liked to play. It didn't take much to keep them occupied; any little thing they found in the house became a toy. Avrum had more patience to play with them than I did. He'd take a round potato, roll it toward the kids and they'd roll it back. To make it a little more of a challenge, he invented a new game. He stood up a small piece of board on the floor, and the kids rolled the potato to try and knock it over. They always got excited and jumped for joy whenever they succeeded. When their mother was away and I tried to help the younger child, the six-year-old sometimes got annoyed and said to me, "You don't have to help me. I can take care of her, I'm not a baby anymore."

As the weather was now too cold for me to go outside barefoot, I asked Marusia for a pair of scissors to detach some of the rags that I had sewn to my blanket and wrap them around my feet. She gave us other rags and told me to leave the blankets alone. I wrapped the rags around my feet and they felt good and warm. I decided to go into the stubble fields to collect heads of wheat. As soon as I had taken a few steps outside, slush seeped right through the rags, but I was determined to keep going. Who could predict the weather in November? Tomorrow, the going might be even more difficult.

As I reached the stubble fields, the heads of wheat were covered with a thin layer of wet snow. Luckily there was a field of sugar beets nearby, and I pulled out enough to fill my pouch. I had to return quickly as my feet were becoming numb from the cold, wet rags. After this episode, I tried another method to keep my feet warm. I wrapped the dry rags around my feet and covered them with a lot of straw. I then took string that I had made out of rags and tied the straw over the rags to keep them from falling apart. This helped a little, but after a while, mud collected on the straw and my feet became heavier and heavier, with a snowball effect. When I returned home, I removed the strings, leaving the muddy straw outside. I dried the wet rags in front of the stove and put them back on my feet to keep warm. While the slushy weather lasted, it was difficult for me to wander out in search of food.

WINTER 1942-43

Avrum and I ate meagrely until it got colder and the snow stopped melting. I then modified my improvised shoes. I used two rags, sandwiched a thick layer of straw between them, and tied it all up with string. This allowed me to walk around in the powdery snow and keep my feet dry and warm for longer periods. I even slept in my "new shoes." I kept adding any rags I could find until I no longer needed the straw.

I would walk into a run-down house and beg the people for anything they could spare. If they had nothing, I begged them to let me look through the garbage. If I was lucky, I found potato peels. Sometimes I found chicken bones and pieces of *makuch* (the residue left over after unshelled sunflower seeds had been pressed to make oil).

Most of the time, I was fortunate enough to bring back food to sustain our lives for another day. Only severe cold or strong winds prevented me from going out. One day when I was foraging for food, I saw a piece of leather sticking out of the snow. I pulled it out; it appeared to be a sleeve from a leather coat. I took it back, cut the sleeve in half, and sewed the ends together to make a pair of shoes. Unfortunately the leather had deteriorated to such an extent that my shoes quickly fell apart. I kept the pieces, adding them to the other rags that I had managed to attach to my blanket. The little grey blanket I started out with became three times as heavy and took on the look of a patchwork quilt.

The weather got colder, and Marusia had to burn more wood to keep the house warm. One day, she asked me to come along with her at sundown to gather wood from the forest. She gave me a thick sweater to help keep me warm. I had to tie it around my body as it was too big for me – she was a hefty woman. Since this was the beginning of winter, the snow wasn't too deep, and we found many dry branches that had fallen to the ground during summer. We collected the branches, tying them together in two bundles with rope that Marusia had brought with her. She had a creative method of carrying the bundles. We put them on our left shoulders, shifting more weight to the centre back where it was supported by a long, strong stick slung at an angle over our right shoulders. This stick underneath the bottom of the bundle distributed the weight

more evenly to both shoulders. Even though my bundle was smaller, returning home was difficult as the load on my shoulder was heavy and it was hard to keep pace with Marusia. I fell behind quite often, but fortunately made it home without incident and was proud of my accomplishment.

As winter progressed, there was more snow on the ground, and we could no longer find enough fallen branches. We tried to break off the underbrush around big trees, but the branches snapped in the cold weather, creating a loud noise that carried throughout the silent forest. The forest was patrolled, and Marusia was afraid of being heard. She decided to take a small saw on future trips to reduce the level of noise. We made many trips and were caught only once as we walked into the forest. Marusia threw the saw into the snow, and, when asked by the patrol why she had come to the forest at night, she talked herself out of her predicament.

Even though I felt the cold, I was always happy when Marusia asked me to go with her to the forest. I felt useful, and it made me feel good to give something in return, although it was very little in comparison to what she did for us. Had it not been for her, who knows what our destiny would have been.

Winter had now set in for good, and Marusia made sure the wood-pile never got too low. She always had enough wood to keep the house warm for a couple of weeks. If it was too cold for me to go with her, she went alone or with a neighbour. Like Marusia, the neighbour did not have trees on her small piece of land and could not afford to buy wood.

Avrum remained house-bound during the winter. I would not allow him to go out alone, nor could he. Neither of us had adequate clothing, and I always took his blanket when I went out. There wasn't much for him to do except play with the children, tend the fire, and await my return. Avrum's presence gave Marusia more freedom to get out of the house, whether to go to work or visit a neighbour. She did not have to worry about the children playing with fire or getting into other trouble.

Avrum and I spent evenings sitting in front of the clay stove where we kept warm and cooked our meal before or after Marusia cooked hers. The majority of our meals consisted of watery potato or beet soup, occasionally supplemented with peas, beans, or browned kernels of grain. Sometimes, if we had flour, we thickened the soup. When we had a few extra beets, we splurged and baked them in the ashes of the fire, but we were rarely able to wait until they were fully baked. Beets were more accessible than potatoes. I found them frozen in barns or in the hallways of farmers' homes. Once frozen beets were thawed, they turned soft, sweet, and juicy, and we ate them raw or cooked. The hardest part was getting enough of them to fill our stomachs and let us fall asleep at night. In the morning, as soon as we opened our eyes, our stomachs reminded us of our priorities for the day.

Occasionally, I was lucky enough to get some bread, flour, cheese, or the odd piece of pork by stealing or begging. Unfortunately, the times I was able to obtain such foods were too few to give us a healthy diet. We lacked nutritious food during most of our growing years. But then we did not look for healthy food – anything that would keep us alive was good enough. Surprisingly, even with so little nourishment, we were able to survive three long, bitter years.

One relatively warm winter day, I ventured out of Stepanki, helped along part way by a sleigh ride. As I approached a nearby village, it started to storm. I made it to the village and walked into a barn, hoping to weather the storm. The barn was empty of livestock, holding only hay. I crawled into the hay to keep warm, but after a while it got very cold and I was afraid I might freeze. I decided to go into the house and beg the people to let me stay overnight. I looked through the window and saw an old man sitting on a stool next to the stove, feeding the fire. There was a large kettle with a coiled pipe attached to it sitting on the stove. Something was dripping out of the pipe into a bottle. I walked into the house and saw that the man was alone.

"Can I please stay with you overnight?" I begged.

"Yes, you can," he said. "How did you make it in this storm?"

"I've been hiding in your barn, but I was afraid I'd freeze to death. I'm an orphan. I live in Stepanki and ventured out to look for food. Can I help you with whatever you're doing?"

"I'm making home-brew," he said. "I'm tired and I want to go to sleep. You can help by keeping the fire going and changing the bottles once they're filled. Here, I'll show you how to test the strength. Every so often, take a spoonful and hold a flame to it. If the liquid catches fire, the brew is still strong enough. As soon as it doesn't, wake me and I'll replace the mash."

He gave me some food, poured himself a drink and went to sleep. Out of curiosity, I tried the home-brew; to me, it tasted awful. Even though my job was not difficult, I was afraid that I might mess things up. After a while, the brew no longer caught fire, and I woke the man up.

I helped him replace the mash, and he told me to go to sleep. When I awoke, it was daylight and everything was cleaned up. The kettle of mash on the stove had been replaced by a pot full of borscht and meat. We sat down to eat, and he was amazed at my capacity. The following day, the weather improved and after another hearty meal I left for Stepanki with a pouch full of food and a *valienka* (tall felt boot) I had seen in the barn.

By now, Avrum was used to my absences. The only disagreements I ever had with him came when I had to convince him not to come along with me. Even though he helped Marusia in the house, he felt guilty that he was not doing his share and that I was taking all the risks for his survival. I always regarded him as my little brother, and, even though we were only eighteen months apart, I did not want him to take any unnecessary risks. Going together would have placed us in double jeopardy, especially in winter when the danger of both of us freezing to death was a distinct possibility.

I took the *valienka* and cut the top half off to sew together a second one. I continued to wrap rags over these new boots. They were a lifesaver, they kept my feet warm and were not as bulky, allowing me to get around more easily.

Very few Jews remained in Stepanki by the beginning of winter 1942. Those that did were fortunate to have found shelter in shacks or in the homes of farmers. Nobody in our condition could have survived another winter in the pig barn.

I came to know several of those who found ways to survive outside the barn. These included three sisters in their twenties who lived in a shack and made their living by knitting sweaters, scarves, and mitts for farmers out of home-made yarn that the farmers spun on spinning wheels. In return, they were given food. To keep their shack warm, they also went to the forest for wood. I used to talk to them after the harvest in the fall when they picked grain off the same stubble fields that I did. In winter, I had conversations with them when I walked into their shack to warm up.

One of the Jews was a shoemaker who was able to support the few surviving members of his family by offering his services in exchange for food and a roof over their heads. He was always searching around the pig barns for old torn shoes with crepe soles. He melted the crepe down, turning it into glue. He was then able to fix rubber boots or anything else made of rubber for the farmers. His skill was in demand because everything was in short supply during the war.

Another family living in a shack had been uprooted in the late fall of 1941 from a city in northern Bukovina called Vashkovits. Their name was Steinhauer; they had one son and four daughters. Their survival was due mainly to their father's trade – he was a tinsmith who repaired leaky pots and pans for farmers in exchange for food. The Steinhauers were helpful to me and showed their kindness by inviting me into their crowded shack to warm up and have a bowl of hot soup. The whole family was friendly to me, which meant a great deal to a lonely child. Unfortunately, I did not meet them until the beginning of the winter of 1943-44.

One man whom I recall very well had known my family before the war. He had a heart of gold. I met him one day in late 1942 when I went begging for food. As I opened the door to a farmer's house, I saw a Jewish man visiting with the farmer. We recognized each other.

"Where is your family?" he asked. "Where are you living?"

I told him what had happened to my family – that only my brother and I survived and that we had found a place to stay with Marusia.

"Where does she live?" he asked.

"The last house in the outskirts of Stepanki," I said, pointing in the direction.

He told me that he and his wife and daughter were living in a room across the hallway from the farmer he was visiting.

One stormy day shortly after we met, this man came to visit and brought us food. This surprised us and boosted our morale. It was the first time since we had lost our parents that somebody had actually thought of us and went out of their way to help us. Avrum and I did not know his name so we decided to call him Messiah – we thought it an appropriate name for the good deed he had done. He told us that any time he could spare some food, he would bring it to us. After he had brought food several times and visited with us, I got to know him better and asked him how he was able to get food and live in the village. He told me the story of how his wife became a fortune teller.

When the war started in 1941, the Soviet Union mobilized young and able-bodied individuals into the army. The families left behind were anxious to find out what had happened to their husbands and sons and daughters, as many of them had never been heard from. It was an ideal situation for somebody with imagination to become a successful fortune teller by telling people what they wanted to hear. To gain people's confidence, the fortune teller had to become knowledgeable about each family, its members, and circumstances. My father's acquaintance and his wife somehow eluded the pig barn and were fortunate enough to get a room in a farmer's house. The wife started to gather information about families in Stepanki as soon as she arrived. She believed that fortune-telling was their route to survival, knowing it was in demand during wartime. As soon as she had sufficient information about a few families, she went to them, offering to tell their fortunes in exchange for food. After telling a fortune, she managed to get the family talking about their neighbours so she could accumulate more information. Once she established credibility by correctly giving the number of children in each family and their gender, her listeners were inclined to believe whatever else she told them. They were interested in hearing where their loved ones were and, since nothing could be verified, she always told them that their family members were alive, either as prisoners sent to Germany or still fighting with the Red Army against the Germans. This fortune-telling gimmick was the couple's passport to survival, enabling them to avoid the hardships that most of us endured.

There were a few others who came to Stepanki in late 1942 and never went through the terrible hardship in the pig barn. They were fortunate enough to be deported to the Dniester River by train and were allowed to take all the belongings they could carry. After walking for several days, they reached Stepanki. They had enough clothes or jewellery to arrange for rooms with farmers and to obtain enough food to feed their families.

I met one of these families one cold day when I was desperate for food and went into Stepanki to beg. I entered a house and saw a family with two young children. It was morning and, to my surprise, the father was in his *tefillen* praying. For a moment, I felt good as I was sure I would get something to eat, or at least a place to warm up. But because of the way I was dressed, the man's reaction was to call me a parasite and chase me out of the house. I was stunned. Abandoned and demoralized, the only visible reaction at that moment came from my eyes, which were releasing instant bitter tears, but my inner feelings of loneliness and sorrow were more painful. Beatings were easier for me to absorb than this because I just did not think about them; being abused by a man wearing *tefillen* was devastating.

What an example for a father to set for his children! My parents had taught me to refrain from asking questions and always to help a person who puts his hand out to you. If you have no means to help, a few kind words will do. By now, I had learned from my own bitter experience how right my parents were. I was just like a tree during a dry spell, extending its roots farther and farther to capture some moisture and avoid drying up and dying. My soul needed to hear some comforting and encouraging words to be rejuvenated; it was hollow and withered from the sadness I had experienced.

How I envied those two nicely dressed young children sitting at the table, eating in a warm house. This scene brought back memories of happier times that I, too, had once enjoyed. These children did not have to worry where their next meal was coming from, or in what dirty barn they might have to sleep; they had parents to take care of them. Since it was too cold to go elsewhere in search of food, I returned to Marusia's house, the place I called home, hungry, cold, and broken-hearted. Avrum and I had very little to eat. This was not the first or the last time that we went to sleep hungry. With only straw between us and the hard, cold ground, we curled up like little balls, cuddling a few hot stones that we had heated in the ashes. We must have had an incredible tolerance for hardship because we were capable of surviving when given the slightest chance.

One winter night in early 1943, we were awakened by loud banging on the door. A Romanian soldier entered, accompanied by a civilian. The civilian shouted in Ukrainian, "All of you, take shovels and get out on the road." We were all chased out even though Marusia had only one shovel. It was an extremely cold, clear night, and as we approached the road I could see many people shovelling snow. We learned that a Romanian general was coming through Stepanki the next morning and for him the road had to be cleared. Avrum and I had no shovels so we just stood there shivering.

Standing with nothing to do, we were easily spotted by a Romanian soldier. He came up quickly, cursing us. As soon as he was close enough to see that we were huddled in blankets and without shovels, his tone of voice changed. He motioned with his hands for us to go back home. He probably didn't realize we were Jews and could speak Romanian. As soon as we came into the house, we added more wood to the fire and huddled around the stove. Marusia returned later, and, even though she was warmly dressed, she was extremely cold. She joined us around the stove and told us that we were lucky the soldier had sent us back home; otherwise we could have frozen to death. Marusia felt sorry for us and told me not to go out looking for food until it warmed up. Even though she did not have much, she shared it with us for the next few days. The man we called Messiah also brought us some food. It was like manna from heaven.

The calm and inactivity in Stepanki during the severely cold winter days was broken by movement and activity during the night a few weeks later when we were awakened once again by loud knocks on the door. Avrum and I became frightened: Not again! We all got up and Marusia opened the door. Three or four men dressed in sheepskin coats, with automatic weapons, walked in, telling us not to be alarmed. They were Russian partisans. They told Marusia that they were going to occupy the village for several days; their comrades would be coming into her house periodically to warm up and eat. Since her house was the last on the outskirts of the village, they had put up a tent beside it. It was to serve as an observation post to protect themselves from a surprise attack by Nazi soldiers.

Marusia lit her kerosene lamp, something she seldom did, and heated a pot of water on the stove for *kipitok* (hot water), a beverage used when tea was not available. One of the partisans left and returned with a sack of meat and bread. We all feasted, and the atmosphere in the room turned joyful. After they left, another group came in to warm up and eat. It was late when Avrum and I happily went back to sleep with full stomachs. When we got up in the morning, there were no partisans in the house. "Where are they? Have they left already?" I asked Marusia.

"No," she said. "In fact, the whole village has been occupied by partisans, and nobody is allowed to leave. There's meat and bread on the table; go ahead and eat, they gave us permission to use as much food as we want."

Once Avrum and I had our fill, we hid some food under the straw in the shack and stepped outside to see what was going on. There were partisans mingling on the road and others in the tent who engaged us in conversation. We soon got too cold and went back into the house to huddle around the stove.

The partisans were warmly dressed and cheerful. They knew who we were and about our suffering. "Kids, it's too bad you're not older," one of them said. "You could join us and help in our struggle to defeat the Nazis. Be brave and don't give in to despair. Before long you'll be liberated by the Soviet army and be able to go home as free men."

They told Marusia that their job was to disrupt the Nazi military supply line wherever possible. This would make it more difficult for the Nazis to re-supply their forces on the Russian front.

I asked Marusia where the partisans got all the food. She told me that they had ordered the more prosperous farmers in the village to bake bread and slaughter pigs to supply them with food. Several days later, the partisans left the same way they came, during the night. Before they left, they brought us more meat and bread. Avrum and I were sorry that they were gone; their presence had given us hope and a feeling of security that we hadn't experienced before. And to us the food had been like a dream – a long feast beyond our wildest imagination. We hoped they would return soon.

After being confined to the house by the partisans, I went with Marusia to the forest to replenish the woodpile. It was getting low from the continuous burning required day and night to keep the house warm while the door was continually opened and closed. Marusia gave me her thick sweater, as she always did when we went to the forest. I had an unusual method of keeping my face warm: I put my pouch on my head and pulled it down over my face. I could see out through little holes that had opened through wear and tear. I always carried my pouch to store anything I was able to collect or steal, including frozen dead birds. I usually carried this pouch like a shoulder bag, allowing me to use my hands freely.

After we had walked for a while on a snowy trail, we noticed somebody hacking away at a snow-covered pile. "There are probably potatoes in that pile," Marusia said. "They belong to the *kolkhoz*. Let's go and see." As we walked toward it, the man ran away, leaving a small opening and a sack. Marusia had no idea who he was. She grabbed the sack, quickly filling it with potatoes. I removed my pouch from my head and she filled it, too. Before we left, Marusia tried to cover the hole as best she could so that no one would notice that it had been tampered with. We walked home in fright as fast as we could.

As soon as we got home, my fright subsided, and I was ready to go back. "Can we go get more potatoes?" I asked Marusia.

"No," she replied. "I'm afraid to go."

"Well, I'll go back myself," I said.

"No, you can't. The police or someone from the *kolkhoz* may see you. They'll follow you back home and find this batch of potatoes. They'll accuse me of opening the hole."

The thought of all those potatoes nearby bothered me all night. They were a rare, precious find for Avrum and me. They could keep us alive for a long time without the need for me to risk my life so often in search of food. Even though it was very cold the next day, I was curious to see what had happened to that pile of potatoes. Without telling Marusia, I went out and walked toward the pile. From the distance, I could see two sleighs with horses and people taking the potatoes out of the hole and putting them into the sleighs. They must have been workers from the *kolkhoz*. Unfortunately for me, somebody must have noticed and reported to the authorities that the pile had been tampered with.

The *kolkhoz* had no storage facilities for potatoes over the winter. They had a unique system – they dug a big deep hole in the ground, lined it with a lot of straw and put the potatoes in. They then covered the potatoes with more straw and a thick layer of earth to prevent them from freezing. In spring, they opened the hole and took out the potatoes. Once a hole was opened during the winter, all the potatoes would freeze as it was impossible to reseal it. The earth was frozen and too lumpy for a tight seal. Marusia knew that taking branches off trees and occasionally cutting down a small tree was not nearly as damaging as ruining a large pile of potatoes. They were probably destined for use as seed for planting in the spring.

Some time later when I was out prowling for food, I noticed a similar snow-covered pile not far from the road. I removed the snow and was faced with a pile of earth that was frozen solid. When I got home, I asked Marusia if she would come with me at night to make a hole. She said that it was too dangerous as the potatoes were government property. If we were caught, she would probably be put in jail and I, being Jewish, would suffer severe consequences.

The cold and deep snow lasted until some time in late February or March 1943. During this harsh winter weather I survived by stealing from barns and from the hallways of homes in Stepanki; begging alone would not have kept us alive. I had to bypass many homes where I had experienced previous hostility; some of them had chained dogs who got excited when they saw me in the yard and were anxious to break loose to taste a piece of me.

Chronic hunger is a potent force that can drive a person to unorthodox actions. Sometimes my hunger pains were unbearable – the first thing I did when I opened the door to a farmer's house was to look for the cat's dish. I would run to it, immediately devouring whatever food was there. I was always afraid that I would be chased out of the house and would have lost an opportunity to get at that dish. It does not sound too hygienic or human-like, but for me, it was a small price to pay for survival.

At other times, I looked for an icon as soon as I entered a house. I kneeled, I crossed myself, and spoke aloud the prayer I had learned in Ukrainian. I knew the words well – I had had a lot of practice. I hoped the farmer would have mercy on me. It was disturbing for me to kneel and cross myself in front of the icon, but my life depended on it. I never told Avrum what I did as it was inappropriate for a Jew to kneel in front of an icon.

Luckily, the man we called Messiah came to our rescue by supplementing our meagre rations when we were most desperately in need. He usually brought us bread, potatoes, or beans hidden in his pockets or under his coat. The reason he was so surreptitious never occurred to me until one day when I walked into his place to beg for food and he wasn't home. Even though his wife knew who I was, she chased me out with a fiery burst of curses. The loud echoes that followed me rang in my ears long after she slammed the door behind me. Hurt and angry, I snapped back at her and sadly walked away. The next time Messiah brought us food, he told me not to come to his place, but that he would bring us food whenever he had a chance to sneak some out without his wife's knowledge. He was so upset he could barely hold back his tears.

As the weather got warmer, I ran into other problems. The snow started to melt and the rags that had kept my feet warm during winter now had the opposite effect. They absorbed moisture, making my feet cold. My solution was to stick to the neighbourhood, only venturing out at night after the ground froze. The pickings were slim. One day, I came upon a barn where the chop contained a lot of potatoes. For the next few weeks, I would sneak into the barn before dawn and hide in the straw pile. I waited until morning when the farmer brought the chop to fatten up the pigs for market. I could hear the pigs running to the food and could hardly wait for the farmer to leave the barn. As soon as she left, I came out of hiding, competing with the pigs at the trough. They were tough competitors, and I had a difficult time squeezing myself in. I scooped out the potatoes and waited for the right moment to escape unseen. The smell never bothered me – I must have lost my sense of smell during the first winter in the pig barn.

Food and warmth were more important for my survival than hygiene. Keeping clean was the least of my concerns. I had not taken a bath or changed clothes for more than a year and a half. I had nothing to change into. Even in the summer of 1942, I was afraid to take off my clothes, which were held together by rags and strings, for a bath in a creek or slough; I feared I would not be able to put them back on, especially if I had to make a fast getaway. The upper part of my pants was tied in such a way that I could pull it down partially when nature called. The rags felt like part of my skin – I felt quite comfortable, as though I had been born in them. Misery had become part of my life. Living under sub-human conditions had taught me that one can adapt to life without many of the "necessities" to which I had been accustomed, but only if one's will to survive was stronger than the Nazis' determination to kill. It seemed my mind would ignore the darkness and always see the light at the end of the tunnel. I would sleep anywhere to keep warm and eat anything that my stomach could digest.

SPRING 1943

As the cold of winter abated, the ground thawed and the sun turned the roads into mud. Marusia waited until night when the ground froze before setting out for the forest. The white snow that had cushioned my soles and brightened the trail turned into a dark, cut-up road with deep ruts made by wagon wheels. Walking became a challenge. It was difficult to keep my balance and avoid falling when I took a wrong step, especially with a bundle of wood on my shoulder. Although wrapped with rags, I felt the sharp edges of the ruts cutting into my feet with every step I took. But I ignored them – warmer days were ahead, and unlike in winter, the plans I made before lying down for the night's rest could be followed through in the morning and not cancelled due to bad weather. My only forecaster in winter had been simple, primitive, and accurate – my own body. I would step outside in the morning to see if I could withstand the cold, and, if I couldn't, I turned back.

Avrum and I were elated that we had survived a second bitingly cold winter and beaten the odds that were heavily stacked against us. This gave us a sense of accomplishment. Survival was not easy in spring either, but our chances improved. We did not have to fight the bitter cold, and I was able to move around, day or night, whenever I thought my chances of securing food were best. It did not matter how long I had to stay out because freezing to death was no longer a threat.

Many times during winter, we had supplemented our nourishment with optimism. I would stand in front of the small frosted-up window, watching the branches of the trees bending to the rhythm of the wind as the snowflakes swirled around and formed snow banks. I would convince myself that the storm would soon subside and that conditions would allow me to go out – if not later that day, then certainly by the following day. Those thoughts carried me through until I was finally able to venture out. I remembered Mother's advice – to live one day at a time and let each tomorrow be another day of hope. Our minds were occupied from dawn to dusk with finding our next meal and getting away unscathed. It did not matter how – stealing or begging. We had long since lost any feelings of guilt or shame.

Time meant nothing to us. Maybe it was good that we didn't know when the Jewish holidays occurred. They had been a time of joy and laughter, but now they would have had the opposite effect of increasing our sorrow. We didn't even know when our birthdays arrived – celebrations were the last things on our minds. Our only orientation to time was the changing seasons of nature.

The smell of spring in the air lifted our spirits, filling us with inspiration that had slowly evaporated during harsh winter days. What really mattered in the spring of 1943 was that we were still alive and able to look forward to better days ahead.

Spring finally took shape – grass started to appear, trees budded, farmers were back working on the land and even the birds were chirping their songs. The vibrancy of life filled the air. The sun not only shone on us but also warmed us. I removed my improvised shoes, overjoyed to see that all my toes were still attached. I felt happy and free as a bird that had been locked up all winter and finally let out of its cage. It reminded me of the times before the war when my parents got me a new pair of shoes. I was happy and excited, hardly able to wait to try them on and get the feel of walking in them and kicking a few stones around. I had the same feeling when I removed the rags from my feet. It was good to feel the ground with my bare feet even though my soles were still tender and felt every little pebble – before long they would toughen up. Movement became much easier; I could walk normally at any pace and even run. It is difficult for me to describe the happiness I felt when I took the filthy rags off my feet and started walking barefoot. What happiness is to one person is not necessarily the same to others; to me, happiness was surviving.

There was a lot of spring work in the *kolkhoz* and Marusia was gone all day, leaving some prepared food for her children. Sometimes when I stole some sweets or made a hot meal, I fed the children, too. Most of our stealing took place in the morning when I knew the farmers were seeding in the fields. When it rained and the farmers could not seed, I usually stayed home, eating whatever we had. The seeding lasted two or three weeks. After it was finished and the trees were still naked without their leaves, I went to other villages at night and slept in farmers' barns.

In the outskirts of one of these villages, I hid in a barn for an overnight rest. When I got up the next morning, I saw an elderly couple digging up a patch of land behind their house. I decided to offer my help, hoping to receive food in return. They accepted my offer; I took the spade from the woman and started digging alongside the old man. She went into the house and brought me some food. After we had finished digging the plot, she called us in and served us a hearty lunch. Not only did I enjoy the meal – I also felt at ease talking with them. I always found that people who helped me wholeheartedly were interested in my past and listened with sympathy. Before I left, the woman gave me enough food to last us a couple of days. I put it in my pouch and was so happy with it that I decided to go back in the daytime instead of waiting until dark.

Walking back to Stepanki, I ran into a streak of bad luck. I encountered four or five boys, my age or a little older, coming toward me and singing. They did not look threatening. As soon as we came face to face, they attacked me, grabbed my pouch, spilled the food on the muddy road, trampled on it, and beat me up. They walked away with pride, singing and laughing as though they had accomplished something that day. Besides enduring pain from the beating, I lost most of the food except for the few potatoes and sugar beets I could salvage. I picked them up, put them back in my pouch, and continued my lonely way home.

Sometimes events like that dampened my spirits, and I started to feel sorry for myself. I was their age, barefoot, draped in rags, and only trying to survive in the most primitive way. I did them no harm, yet they couldn't resist attacking me.

I kept on walking until I came to a small wooden bridge leading to a short but steep hill. I went down to the creek, washed the potatoes and sugar beets, crossed the creek and climbed up the bank. When I reached the top, I looked up the hill and saw three German officers on horses, sauntering down the hill toward me on a very narrow road. Their fancy caps revealed their ranks. They had their tommy guns in their hands in front of them, as if they were expecting something to happen, or maybe they had spotted me. I was always an optimist, but this time I lost my self-assurance and was petrified.

A multitude of thoughts raced through my mind as my trembling body walked up the hill. My heart was beating hard and fast. The guns came closer and closer, staring into my face. I thought that my luck had finally run out and that the day I feared most had arrived. My body would be left lying abandoned on the road, riddled with bullet holes – a recurring scene that never left my mind. The encounter was brief, but it packed a punch that left me in a daze. When I was beaten up by the young kids, it hurt, but I did not cry. The three officers did not touch me, only looked at me, but as soon as they passed, I started to sob. Our lives had been ground down bit by bit every single day. I was barely thirteen, but felt I already had a lifetime of experience behind me with no end of suffering in sight.

When I got home, I told Marusia about the encounter with the German officers. I didn't mention the kids since they were Ukrainian, as she was. "The Germans did not let you go free out of the goodness of their hearts," she said; "they have their own problems now. Partisans have become very active in this part of the Ukraine. Those three officers must have been afraid of the partisans and were on the lookout for their own lives. They were probably loath to fire their guns unless attacked," she added. "They feared they would endanger their lives by revealing their whereabouts."

It might seem that I was involved in an inordinate number of unusual situations. Like me, there were other children who survived pig barns in isolated villages and were left alone without parents, having to fend for themselves. We had no choice; unlike the situation in most ghettos, there was no one in charge in the pig barn to help us or to offer any advice or support. We were among the remnants of those who had battled the severe winter of 1941–42 in the pig barns and suffered great losses. We were left rudderless, drifting around in the wide open spaces of the countryside. If we still had the strength to get up in the morning, we had no choice but to wander in search of food. We were chased out of homes, in some cases as soon as farmers saw us in their yards. They came roaring outside with curses and threats that they would report us to the police. We ran away in panic. We had to cover a lot of hostile territory and were exposed to great danger, consequently getting into sticky predicaments.

Winter was especially difficult for orphans. Some were found frozen in the open fields or on the roads, where the blowing winds had covered their footprints and their curled-up bodies with snow. Had they survived, they could have told unimaginable stories about their bravery and the cruelties committed against them; they all had enough experiences to fill books. It may seem strange that young children were willing to put up such vigorous battles to stay alive, regardless of their suffering. They had more fight than some adults, who became increasingly passive as time went on and more of their family members perished.

Thousands of orphans paid with their lives at the end of their heroic fight. They were attempting to overcome odds that were almost impossible. They were not cowardly or lazy, nor did they just lie down and die, going to their graves willingly – they fought to their last breaths with determination and stubbornness, trying to carry on the little flame of life that was left from their large families and not to be one of those counted in statistics or remembered in history books. Sadly, they took their hopes with them into unknown and unmarked graves, just as innocent as the day they were born.

To live, we had to be constantly on the go. Once again, I decided to head to the house of the forest manager to beg for food. I knew I would get some as long as there were no soldiers present. I left in the afternoon, planning to sleep on the edge of the forest and not venture into the bush until daybreak. Caution was necessary since I had already been lost twice before. As I walked, I saw a big house out in the open by itself, away from the village. Isolated houses were unusual, but I decided to walk in and beg for food.

I opened the door, and to my surprise, saw two Romanian soldiers having dinner. I ran away as fast as I could, but one of the soldiers pursued and quickly caught me. He brought me back to the house. "Please don't beat me," I pleaded as I started to cry. "I'm on my way to Stepanki and I got lost."

"We won't harm you," one of the soldiers said. "Calm down. Relax. Join us for dinner."

They asked the farm woman in broken Ukrainian mixed with Romanian to make me a plate of food.

"Where in Romania do you come from?" the other soldier asked. "Are your parents still alive?"

"I'm from Berhomet in Bukovina," I said. "My parents are dead. I have only one brother left."

"I'm originally from Bukovina too," he said, "not far from Berhomet." We continued our conversation until it got late.

"Stay here overnight and have breakfast with us in the morning," one of them said.

I was frightened and restless all night as I did not know what to make of their unusual friendliness. After we had eaten breakfast, one of the soldiers pointed to their rifles and asked, "Will you stay to clean our rifles and polish our boots?"

"Yes," I said, "I'll be happy to do that."

They took their rifles apart, gave me the tools, and showed me what to do. I cleaned the bores and the trigger mechanisms and polished the rifles while they sat at the table writing. After lunch, they asked me if I would like to stay another day.

"I want to go back to Stepanki," I said. "My brother is alone and hungry."

They told the farmer to make up a parcel of food for me to take back. They took their rifles, mounted their horses, and rode off. I left, still surprised and puzzled over the unusually kind treatment I had received.

After a long walk back toward Marusia's, I heard shooting in the distance just before I reached home. It was dark and I became frightened. I ran the rest of the way home. "There's been a big fight nearby," Marusia said the next morning after returning from her neighbour's. "The partisans ambushed a German convoy. Many Germans were killed and their damaged equipment was left scattered all over the road."

The following day, Avrum and I walked to the area where the skirmish had occurred, thinking we might be able to salvage some food and clothing or anything that could be traded for food. As we approached the area, it looked as though everything had already been plundered. There were no people – only birds picking away and bodies stripped of their clothing lying in the ditch. Blown-up guns and burned-out vehicles were scattered all over the road and fields next to the bush.

I poked a stick into the burned piles to see if I could find anything salvageable. There was nothing except ashes and charred pieces of metal. I looked inside a covered truck, shocked to see burned naked bodies stacked up like cordwood. I continued searching the area until bullets suddenly hit the ground near me. The sounds of the shots came from the nearby forest. We took off like bullets ourselves and headed home, empty-handed.

When Marusia came home from work, I told her that we had gone to see the area where the ambush had occurred and described what we had seen. "All the people at work are happy, talking about the skirmish," she said. "Listen, Avrum, I've got some good news for you. I persuaded a farmer to let you help his young nephew herd the farm's two cows in a pasture not far from here. In return for your work, you'll be given three meals a day."

"Oh, that's good," Avrum said happily. "When do I start?"

"I'll take you there tomorrow morning," she said.

Avrum was so excited about earning his keep and helping me that he could hardly wait until morning. When it arrived, Marusia, Avrum, and I went down to the farmer's barn where they had just started to milk the cows. Marusia left us and went back home. Once milking was finished, we went into the house where we were served breakfast and Avrum was told what his duties would be. After breakfast, Avrum and the nephew chased the cows out of the barn and into the pasture. It was more like a rough piece of land between the road and the grain fields with no fence to keep the cows in. Watching them was to be Avrum's and the nephew's job. I left shortly thereafter because I did not want to give the farmer the impression that his family would have to feed two of us.

Late in the afternoon, Avrum came home with some of the food he was given and had saved for me. He was a different Avrum – happier and acting with more confidence than I could ever remember. He even tried to boost my morale with encouraging words. "Don't worry, Joil," he said to me, "I'll bring some good food home every day."

It is amazing what a touch of freedom and the opportunity to earn one's own keep can do to a person's self-esteem and morale, regardless of their age. Avrum even encouraged me to explore the surrounding district to look for some of our relatives from whom we had been separated in Luchinets. We had frequently spoken about them, wondering where they were and how many were still alive.

Even though we were tough and outwardly acted like grown-ups, inside we were like normal children who yearned for family support. Loneliness had engulfed us and added to our misery. The long nights, when we had nothing to do, were the most difficult. Marusia and her children went to bed early. To shorten the cold nights lying on the floor, Avrum and I warmed ourselves in front of the stove, delaying going to sleep. The only sound was the crackle and sizzle of the burning wood. As we sat silently in the dark, with just the light from the stove or the moon, our losses and pain reappeared, frequently accompanied by tears. We slowly wiped them away, trying not to attract each other's attention. We had no one to talk to in our mother tongue to distract us from our sadness and lessen our anguish. We felt that being together with some of our relatives would ease our loneliness and lift our spirits.

Avrum and I decided that I should go now while the weather was good. I waited a little longer to ensure that Avrum still had his job. Each morning, he got up, looking forward to going to work. When evening came, he brought me food with a smile on his face. We discussed his work and he told me what he was given to eat, and how his day went. We debated about whether I should go to Kopygorod or Shargorod, the closest towns with large Jewish ghettos. I chose to go to Shargorod because I had been there before.

THE WORK CAMP AT TULCHIN

On my way to Shargorod, I stopped at the forest manager's house once again to beg for food. This time I was successful; there were no soldiers present, and I was able to walk in. I was given not only food but also an old pair of pants and a shirt. After I ate, I continued on my way. I was so attached to my rags that I didn't take them off – I put my "new" old clothes on top of them. Once it got dark, I stopped for an overnight rest. I got up early the next morning and, feeling confident in my "new" clothes, decided to take a chance and walk on the road hoping to pass as a Ukrainian.

I was successful until I approached Shargorod. As I walked across the small bridge into town, two Romanian soldiers on foot approached me. With a stern voice, and motioning with his hand, one of them yelled, "Come, follow me." I realized that I was in trouble. We walked a short distance before reaching a big open gathering place where many Jews were already assembled, guarded by Romanian soldiers. Nervously pacing around looking for a way to escape, I recognized one of the soldiers; I had recently cleaned his gun. I approached him and he recognized me.

"How did you get here?" he asked. "These people are being sent to Tulchin to be interned in a work camp. You're too young. Wait here. I'm going to see if I can get you out." He left and I stayed in the same spot, anxiously awaiting his return. I never saw him again.

While standing lost and confused, I was suddenly embraced. "Joil, I'm happy to see you." It was my second cousin, Marcus Sussmann. "What ghetto are you in? Where are your parents? We always talk about your family."

My silence said it all. Our happy reunion turned sombre. After I composed myself, I told him what happened to us after we were split up in Luchinets in the late fall of 1941.

"Where is your family?" I asked. "Did everyone survive? What happened to your brother Chaim?"

"My parents, my sister Clara, and I live in a crowded room here in the Shargorod ghetto. You know, Chaim retreated with the Soviet army in 1941. I hope he's alive."

"Is anyone else from our family here? Did any of them survive in other ghettos?"

"No, not that I know of."

"How come you're here? Were you also caught?"

"No, there's a Jewish committee here that administers the ghetto and has its own police force to keep order. When the Romanian authority needs workers, they inform the head of the committee. The committee then picks the workers. I was told a few days ago to report here to be sent away to work."

"What's life like here?" I asked.

"Well, like in other ghettos, we're not permitted to leave. Thank God, we're lucky; we have a roof over our heads and we've managed to survive. I hope our luck holds out. Many people I know, both young and old, have passed away, some of them in a very short time."

The people assembled for the work detail were restless, frightened of the unknown. They knew that Tulchin might not be their final destination; they might be sent across the Bug River to the German side, as close to hell as one could get. Few had ever returned.

After mingling in the open field, we were ordered to line up in a column. Some older people were told to get on the few wagons standing nearby; the rest of us marched on foot. As the convoy moved out, guarded by Romanian soldiers, there was a lot of hand waving and crying among family members who had gathered around the field during the day to see what would happen to us. This scene compounded my sorrow and loneliness – I realized there was nobody who cared or would shed a tear for me as we marched away in a cloud of dust behind the wagons.

After a long march, we came to a train station where we were taken to a track with empty boxcars. The soldiers counted a certain number of people for each car, told us to jump in, and slammed the door shut. Few found room to sit on the floor. The heat was unbearable. We pounded and shouted for them to open the door to let in some fresh air, but it was to no avail. Only when the train started to move did we feel the fresh air rushing in through the small openings in the boxcar. We literally breathed a sigh of relief. At the end of our journey, the car doors were opened, and we were greeted with loud curses that rang in our ears. Some of us felt the jolt of rifle butts. The harsh treatment upon our arrival gave us an indication of what to expect at our final destination. We were lined up in column formation and marched off. Some had a hard time keeping up with the column.

As we entered the camp and marched toward one of the barns, I saw hundreds of people mingling in the open space. They came running toward our column to look for a familiar face. Some were lucky; shouts of recognition were exchanged. Once we reached the barn, we were told that this was going to be our new home; anyone trying to escape would be shot. The barn had a dirt floor and built-in plank bunks stacked up along both sides. There were no mattresses and no partitions or designated spaces for sleeping. We all rushed to grab a place, some preferred the lower bunk and some the upper. We slept crosswise, our heads toward the alley. It was tight as a sardine can, making it almost impossible to turn around during the night. Once we moved out of our spot, we could not squeeze ourselves back in.

This was my first experience in a work camp. The camp, located outside Tulchin, must have been a *kolkhoz* before the war. It was a big open space surrounded by barns and encircled by barbed wire. There were a few huge mounds of straw inside the fence. A small house in the middle of the yard served as an office and living quarters for the *kapo* and his family. The *kapo,* who was Jewish, was the work camp foreman.

Early the next morning, we were awakened, chased out of the barn, and told to line up for our breakfast, which consisted of cornmeal cereal cooked without any salt. The worst part was that many of us did not have a container to hold our rations and we were not given any. Some people had brought cans, which they used to hold their food as well as that of their friends. The others tried to get hold of anything that would hold our mostly liquid rations. I saw one man trying to chip a hollow in a small, thick piece of rotten wood from a post.

After breakfast, soldiers marched us off to work in the peat bogs.[14] I did not know what a peat bog was, or what we were going to do there. The workplace was four to five kilometres away, and we had to pass through a small village to get there. I spotted a rusty can in a farmer's yard, ran in, grabbed it, and quickly ran back. It would serve as a dish for my rations. Other people also managed to find containers in yards or near the peat bogs where soldiers threw away the empty cans from their rations. When we arrived at the place of work, the peat bog looked like spongy, moist soil. We were told that, after it was dug out and dried, it burned like coal.

We were split into groups. Some workers in each group were given specially shaped shovels. This shovel, once pushed down into the ground, would cut out a brick-shaped piece of peat. The peat did not fall apart but held together very firmly. Workers without shovels carried the pieces out of the trenches, stacking them on level ground as high as they could reach. We dug steps in the trenches to carry out the peat. Some of us switched jobs, alternating between digging and carrying.

Years later, when I saw the movie "The Ten Commandments," in which Jews were depicted as having been forced into slavery in Egypt and had to work hard to make bricks out of clay and straw for meagre rations, it reminded me of Tulchin. History does repeat itself, regardless of how long it takes.

At noon, we stopped for lunch and had to stand in long lines, even though there must have been at least six columns of people standing two in a row. When I reached the front I saw a military-sized pot filled with soup. Two men from our workforce were serving with big ladles. Every worker was served one full ladle of soup and a piece of *mamalega* (a solidified cereal made out of cornmeal). Some workers with containers received two ladles of soup, one for themselves and one for a friend who was with him but who did not have a container. After receiving our food, we walked ahead about twenty metres before sitting down on the ground to eat. Soldiers stood guard between our eating place and the soup pots to prevent us from going back for another serving.

After a brief rest we were ordered back to work until five or six in the evening before marching back to the camp. Some of us went right into the barn and lay down on the bunks. Others mingled, hoping they would recognize people from home or find out about their family and friends from other *lager* people. For the first few days, we all went into the barns before darkness set in. We were afraid to stay outside as we were unfamiliar with the grounds that were patrolled by soldiers. We tried to squeeze ourselves onto the bunks to sleep. In the morning, we were awakened and repeated the same routine.

After observing the way food was served, I figured out a way of getting an extra ladle of soup and an extra piece of *mamalega*. I gave my pouch with my can inside to Marcus, and we stayed close together as we approached the soup pot. I told the server that I had no container and that he should give my portion to Marcus. Marcus walked past the soldiers, sat down on the ground and started eating. At the same time, I walked up empty-handed to the soldier in the next column and told him that I had no container and was going to get one from someone who had finished eating. He let me go and I went over to Marcus, pouring his soup into my clean container and taking his dirty container back to the same soldier right away so that he would remember me. He let me through to get another serving, which helped to ease our hunger a little longer. There was not much substance to the flavourless soup – it was slightly thickened coloured water, which sometimes included meat from dead horses. We were given barely enough food to survive, let alone enough to have strength for the work demanded of us.

The work was hard, and we were always under the watchful eyes of the soldiers. They put a lot of pressure on us to move faster, disregarding the fact that we were weak from hunger and exhausted from standing on our feet all day long, sometimes in unbearable heat. As we dug ourselves deeper into the peat bog, we were harassed by them but not hit, because they did not want to come down to the trenches and get dirty. Even at times when we were not watched, we could not sit down to rest because it was too wet. The only time I could hide and rest was when I carried out the pieces of peat from the trenches to stack them. Then I had a chance to hide between the big stacks, but I continually had to be on the lookout for soldiers who went searching for individuals trying to slack off work.

The work was physically difficult, but it did not bother me as much as the mental stress caused by my concern for Avrum. It had been more than two weeks since I left Stepanki, and I knew that he would have expected me back by now. At least I knew where he was and what he was doing, but he had no clue about my whereabouts. My long absence was surely causing him a great deal of anxiety. He had no idea that people were taken away to work, and all he could do was wonder if I was still alive. He must have been anxious to go home after work to see if I had returned. What a disappointment for him every day. He probably had a lot of sleepless nights. This was the longest we had ever been apart. We had been functioning as two separate components who relied on each other's support to strengthen our determination to survive. Being alone might weaken the link, cause us to drift away from our positive outlook, and slowly allow us to slip into a state of depression that might lead to a tragic outcome. We were children, not grown-ups. Just seeing each other in this hostile environment would boost our morale and keep us going. My need to escape became urgent.

I did not even know where Tulchin was in relation to Stepanki, but this would not deter me from trying to get back. Rumours started to circulate that people had been shot while trying to escape, even after they had managed to get as far as ten to fifteen kilometres from the camp.

Some workers told me that several of their friends had been shot closer to the camp. This put a damper on my plan, and I decided to put it off for a while – I did not want to stretch the luck that had been with me so far. It may sound strange to describe the previous two years as lucky, but I related to that word because I was still alive.

The first time I heard a man called a *kapo* was in Tulchin, and the *kapo* there was a ruthless man with no conscience who ruled with an iron fist for his own sadistic satisfaction. He was a power-hungry individual with no principles or respect for human beings. Being in a position of authority, he could exercise power according to his discretion; he could have been either good or evil. He chose the latter, and I feared him more than the soldiers. One morning, I somehow ended up in the shrubbery close to the kitchen. It was under a canopy supported by big poles. There was a long, wide table made out of wood. I saw the kitchen workers pour the thickened cornmeal onto the table and spread it out evenly with a flat piece of wood. I hid, waiting for an opportunity to grab some. By then, it had cooled and hardened; the workers cut it into squares and left. The Romanians called this *mamalega*.

There were soldiers around, and I watched them closely while I tried to appear occupied, to avoid arousing their suspicion. When they were looking elsewhere, I snatched a piece, but the *kapo* noticed and grabbed me.

"Please let me go," I begged, "I'm hungry."

"You little brat, you're going to get it," he yelled as he hung onto me. He told the soldiers standing nearby to beat me. They took me to a table and told me to bend over, with my hands stretched out. While one soldier held my hands down on the table, another hit me all over my back and buttocks with a whip. I started crying from the pain while the big, strong *kapo* stood by watching. Every lash felt like an electric shock as the whip bit into my body. Even though he was the father of two young children my age, he exhibited no pity toward me. By the time they let me go, I was in a daze, barely able to walk. Later, when I touched my back, the pain intensified, and I could feel huge welts all over. I was black and blue, remaining in pain for weeks until the swelling subsided.

By now, all of us were familiar with the area, mingling freely in the big open space after work. The *kapo* frequently took his two well-fed, dark-complexioned young sons for a thrill ride through the camp in a wagon hitched with two black horses. Like a maniac, he drove the horses around the yard as fast as they could run, often steering them directly toward groups of people. We had to move quickly out of his way. If we were close, he tried his best to hit us with his whip. I made a point never to forget that *kapo*'s ruthless behaviour, especially his supervision of my beating. I was determined to get even with him after the war when justice would prevail instead of the power and discretion of a *kapo*. Unfortunately, the only thing about him that I was able to learn from other survivors in Israel was that he came from Putila, a small town in northern Bukovina.

Tulchin was a back-breaking labour camp with no consideration given for our well-being. Even though we worked hard to provide the Nazis with peat, we continued to receive meagre rations. They treated us worse than slaves, not caring if we lived or died. They knew that we could easily be replaced by Jews from other *lagers*. Our bodies were already drained from the last two years and ready to give up. The added stress and lack of food showed in our faces and in our hollow cheeks. People were exhausted. Many no longer mingled after work but went directly to the barn to lie down and rest. Others stayed out longer when they found it too hot in the barn. Most sat in groups on the bare ground discussing the latest political rumours, theorizing about the safest means of escape, and describing tragic stories about their families that were common to all of us. The more we sat around and listened, the more depressing the stories became, but this was the only recreation we had after a hard day's work. The alternative was sleeping, and in summer that was often impossible. The barns were extremely hot, and the stench was so strong that our eyes burned. There was a joke going around – "I could not sleep last night. There were so many big lice that the noise of them falling off the bunk woke me up."

To avoid the barns, some of us slept outside under the stars, either on the ground or in the straw pile if there was a free spot. Some lay down early to get a spot near the bottom of the pile. Others, like me, came later and had to crawl over people to find a place higher up. We would inadvertently step on the others, and they would either pinch us or grab a leg and give it a hard twist. The only way to avoid this was to quickly run up the slightly sloped straw pile before they had a chance to get hold of you. Once you reached an empty spot, you bored yourself in so you wouldn't slip down. It was quite an art to do this on a nightly basis. Some people were not able to do it and slipped on the straw pile, ending up at the bottom where they were cursed and forced out by the people who were sleeping there.

I spent a lot of sleepless nights in the straw pile thinking about Avrum, wondering how he was coping alone. I had already postponed a few escape attempts because I heard rumours practically every day that somebody had been caught and shot.[15] I decided to wait for an opportunity when I thought I would have a better than fifty-fifty chance.

Rumours circulated in the camp that the German army was retreating with heavy losses. We thought we might soon be liberated if only we could hang onto our lives a little bit longer. But we couldn't gauge the rumours by the behaviour of the soldiers. They harassed us just like always, with no mercy shown to the young, old, or sick. Anytime they had an urge to hit someone, they did not hesitate. Their hatred was so intense that, even after they threw away a cigarette butt and ground it into the earth with their boots, they would beat anybody whom they caught picking up the tobacco residue. This tobacco was a precious commodity that could easily be exchanged with a smoker who was so addicted that he was willing to give up his ration of soup. At that point, I made up my mind that I would never smoke.

We were lucky it was summer, enabling us to survive on a minimum of calories. We did not know how long we were going to remain in this work camp. Some took desperate measures to get more food at the risk of being shot by the soldiers. As we marched to work and back, some of us ran into farmers' or *kolkhoz* fields and stole whatever was edible. Pumpkins were precious because they served a dual purpose. We ate half and used the other half as a soup bowl, which was later eaten once it started to spoil. I did not see anybody shot while stealing food, but some were caught and severely beaten.

After living in Tulchin for a couple of months, people became more subdued. Fewer mingled and the groups who socialized became smaller and smaller. We were getting weaker from the hard work and long walks to and from work. It felt as if the road was getting longer and longer every day, uphill both ways. We were digging and carrying peat all day long and felt pain and weakness from the lack of food and the sleepless nights spent worrying about our families. The soldiers continually forced us to work faster, watching us like hawks to make sure we did not slack off or hide between the stacks of peat.

One of the workers in the camp was a young man with a pleasant voice who occasionally provided entertainment that touched our hearts and kept our eyes moist. He would lie on the grass or sit, leaning against the barn wall, singing *chazzunic*, or sad Yiddish songs. Jewish history is

Under the direction of Romanian soldiers, Jews are deported from Bessarabia
and Bukovina to Transnistria. Two German soldiers are visible to the left.
National Archives. Courtesy of USHMM Photo Archives.

Romanian Jews en route to Transnistria assemble on the west bank of the
Dniester River during a deportation action.
Yad Vashem Photo Archives. Courtesy of USHMM Photo Archives.

Joil's mother.

Avrum, the small boy second from left. Probably taken in Bucharest in 1944.

Avrum, bottom right. Taken in Bucharest in 1945.

Avrum in a photo that was probably attached to a military document, August 1946.

Joil in Russia, 1946, when he was given a medal for his work as a sapper.

Working in Security in Scuola Cardorna, Milan, 1948.

Max Reger, Beno Grobstein, Joil, and Isiu Schneider. Milan, 1948.

Avrum, far right, instructing comrades in Israel.

Avrum, in the centre, herding goats on a kibbutz in Israel.

Avrum on an outing, somewhere in Israel, 1948.

Joil in Winnipeg in the early 1950s.

Joil and Ida's wedding, December 15, 1963.

Uncle Schlomcu (left) and Uncle Simon in Israel, 1980s.

Avrum's gravestone at Mount Herzl, Jerusalem.

burdened with great tragedies, resulting from struggles to preserve our heritage. Many songs had their origin in those tragedies and reflected the suffering of the people. The words and melodies are very sad. Some workers found it too difficult to listen and walked away. But others would stay and listen while the singer's own eyes filled with tears, especially when he sang his favourite song over and over again. When asked why he sang this song so often, he said that he visualized his mother, whom he dearly loved but who was now gone forever, singing it to him.

Another song of his caught my attention – it was as though the lyrics had been written for me, the words reflecting my life. I always asked him to sing "Papirossen" for me. I remember the tune and some of the words – it was about an orphan left alone, whose father had died first and his mother shortly thereafter, leaving him alone with a younger sibling. Desperate, frightened, and hungry, he walked around in rags, searching and begging for food, but nobody was willing to help, no matter how many tears he shed. He slept under trees during drizzly, cold nights, frightened whenever winds shook the branches of the trees.... I listened to this song as he sang it in a soft clear voice; the tears slowly threaded down my face.

The lowest point of my horrible time in Tulchin was a barbaric and devastating event carefully staged by the Nazis for their own amusement. It happened one morning in our camp. We were all ordered to line up in columns in the middle of the yard. Once I got there, I noticed a gallows with about eight nooses spaced closely together and benches beneath the gallows. We all stood there, dumbfounded and scared, with our eyes focused on the gallows. Our bodies trembled with fear – we knew what this meant for some of us. But we could only stand there, powerless to defend ourselves against the Nazi murderers. We did not know who would be selected – the young, old, or sick. It did not really matter, because we were all victims and none of us was prepared to die. We had fought disease, hunger, and cruelty for more than two years, and we all yearned for the day when we would regain our freedom. It was not hard to guess what was going through people's minds: they could see the nooses and visualize the victims dangling from them.

I stood motionless with my eyes fixed on the gallows, remembering Avrum as I had last seen him before I left Stepanki. The smile on his face and the self-confidence gained from his job was my only consolation. I knew I was as close to being selected for the gallows as eye contact with a soldier or a finger pointed in my direction. It had been some time since

I was this frightened. Whenever I had been caught before, I had always tried to escape, either before or after a beating. My mind was too occupied then to think of any consequences. Now I was among hundreds of people of my own faith – they were stronger and older, and they, too, were immobilized by fear. Maybe this made me realize the gravity of the situation; some of us were going to pay with our lives, and I might be one of them. Thoughts raced through my mind with lightning speed while time seemed to stand still. Every second seemed like a year as I stood petrified, awaiting my fate and that of the others.

Suddenly, our fear was compounded by another distressing scene in the distance. A group of officers, some Romanian but mostly German, were approaching us in their impressive neat uniforms with shining buttons and glittering caps as though they were going to a parade. The method of how to kill us was in place, awaiting only the selection of the helpless and frightened victims. Our eyes shifted from the gallows to the officers as they came closer and closer. When they reached the gallows, they stopped and directed some soldiers to go to the columns and pick men to fill the nooses.

The soldiers approached us. Deathly silence descended. My body turned to stone, except for my trembling knees. Everyone held his breath, waiting to see who was going to be picked by those men with murderous-looking eyes who would decide within seconds who would live and who would die. For some reason known only to the Nazis, they selected the tallest and strongest men. The soldiers did not point their fingers at the men they selected but pushed through the rows and grabbed the victims one by one, acting as if they knew they had the guilty ones who deserved to die. The grimaces on those innocent people's faces revealed their pain and innermost feelings. This was the last living image we had to remember them by as they were marched off. Some of us could not watch, and we turned our faces aside as they took their last few steps. Once they reached the gallows, they were told to step up onto the benches. Their hesitation to obey the Nazi instructions was overcome by prodding guns, and the nooses were placed around their necks. The soldiers removed the benches from under their feet, literally taking their lives away as they left them dangling in the air. All their suffering and hopes had been in vain. Within seconds, their lives vanished on that beautiful sunny day.

Despite having seen so many brutal murders in the past, it was still hard to get used to scenes like that. Our outer crust might have given the appearance of being tough and not caring, but inside we still had hidden human feelings for our fellow man. The horror of the event shaved years off our lives. Some of us broke down and cried, some said *Kaddish,* and all of us were disheartened. If one could strip away the officers' impressive uniforms and look into their hearts and minds, what would the ruthless, inhumane interior of a Nazi look like? If they were thirsty for Jewish blood that day, they could have taken eight people and shot them, but this was not good enough to quench their thirst. They used a dramatic setting to make us all feel the pain and bitterness even more deeply. Afterward, without showing any emotion, they casually walked away from the horrific scene in the same calm manner as carnivores after they have indulged in their kill.

One German officer stayed behind and made a very short, powerful, and intimidating speech. "Don't any of you think for a second that you'll get out of here alive," he said. "What you just saw, that's what's awaiting you in the future." We were dismissed, except for a few who were ordered to stay behind to remove the bodies from the gallows after they had been on display for several hours. Sad and dispirited, we slowly walked away in a silent, sombre mood. Some went straight into the barn and lay down, while others sat outside silently grieving. Not a word was spoken – the only motion came from our hands as we wiped away tears that kept flowing down our faces.

Those who had been sick that day were lucky because they had stayed behind in the barns. They did not have to go through the stress of watching with their own eyes. One of the people who was hanged could have been their father, son, or brother. It was hard for all of us to watch these tragic deaths that could have happened to any of us. The hopes and suffering of those poor people were gone forever, but not for their families who were left behind in the *lagers,* awaiting the return of their loved ones. One day, they would find out about the tragedy and have to live with it all their lives. It is impossible to hermetically seal a human mind that has lived through such a tragic time. Some of the bad memories always come seeping through, regardless of how hard one tries to block them out.

The hanging and the threatening speech were intended to rob us of any hope we still had hidden in our hearts. People in the camp became more desperate; some gave up hope of ever seeing their families again. I grew more restless and frequently pondered my chances of escaping and being reunited with Avrum. My best opportunity came when there was a big downpour and I could not sleep in the straw pile because it was soaked with water. I did not want to sleep in my assigned barn as it was too crowded and had a powerful stench. Instead, I went into a small barn at the end of the camp that nobody was assigned to and had no bunks. I walked in, surprised to see at least forty to fifty people lying on a little straw on the dirt floor. I lay down next to them for the night's rest. It was drizzling, and the men next to me were whispering to each other that this was the night to escape. I decided to follow them in the dark without being seen by them. But God must have been on my side; I fell asleep. They left the barn, barely getting outside the camp before they were all shot to death by the soldiers. This put real fear in me. After that, a lot of people who were contemplating escaping gave up the idea for the present. These deaths were not just rumours any more; they had happened right outside the camp.

When I got up the next morning, I found a yellow object that looked like a small piece of soap with a very hard exterior. I told my cousin Marcus that we might be able to trade it with a farmer for food. Since we passed a small village every day on the way to work, Marcus thought it was a good idea. I gave him the piece of soap. As we walked to work, he ran into a farmer's house and made a quick deal to exchange the soap for potatoes. Soap and salt were in short supply during the war and were very easy to trade. He told the farmer he would pick up the potatoes on the way back.

Marcus and I always walked together to and from work. He was a few years older than me, but we got along like twin brothers. No matter which one of us was lucky enough to steal some food from farmers' gardens, we always shared. That day, I decided to walk ahead of Marcus on the way back. I arrived first at the farmer's house and asked her to give me the potatoes for the soap. Without hesitating, she handed me the potatoes. I put them in my pouch and walked out. Marcus walked into the farmer's house later and also asked for the potatoes. She said that she had already given potatoes in exchange for the soap. Marcus did not know about my scheme and convinced her it wasn't him. The farmer gave in and Marcus left with another batch of potatoes. Once Marcus caught up with me in the camp, he told me that the farmer had tried to pull a fast one on him but that she could not fool him. I told him my story, and we both started to laugh. We were not laughing at the farmer; we were just so happy to get more of those precious potatoes. The good-natured farmer must have felt sorry for Marcus.

We both returned to the small barn to look for more soap but could not find any. Later on, we realized that what we had thought was soap was actually a one-hundred-gram piece of dynamite, probably left behind when the Soviet army retreated in 1941. I was relieved to learn that it could never be blown up without a detonator; I did not want to see innocent people hurt.

The people in Tulchin work camp came from many different *lagers,* different backgrounds and a wide range of ages. Each of us had different problems and aggravations to deal with. We were all thrown together without knowing each other and lived and worked in cramped quarters at all times − both in the barns and in the trenches. It is amazing that tempers did not flare more often. Anger surfaced only on rare occasions, when shouted words would echo throughout the camp.

The longer we were in the camp, the more depressed we became. That changed a bit one day when we heard rumours that some people, mostly from Mogilev, were going to be sent back to the ghettos where they had previously lived. We heard that the older people, the sick, and a few minors were the groups who would be sent back.[16] We were all happy because this seemed to be a good start − maybe we would all be sent back eventually. A few days later, the designated groups of people were told to go to the camp office to register. Those people who thought they qualified, including myself, went to the office. As I stood in line waiting my turn, my hopes of seeing Avrum lifted my spirits. But they were quickly dashed once I reached the desk. I was turned down by the *kapo,* who said I was not sick and could still work. I told him that I was young, but he ignored me and kicked me out of the office. Anybody who was accepted was given a small piece of paper identifying them as eligible to leave. I was determined to leave with this group, no matter what. This might be my best chance to escape. I picked up a scrap of paper from the floor in the office just to have something to hold in my hand so I could pretend I was accepted.

A few days later, all the workers in the camp were told to assemble in a column. As we lined up, I noticed military trucks parked behind a fence. A Romanian officer, holding a list in his hand, told the workers to leave the column and walk toward the trucks when their names were called. As names were called, the people marched out one by one from various parts of the column. I felt my adrenalin kick in as I watched the proceedings − I was excited and apprehensive at the same time.

I had to quickly make my move before they completed calling out all the names or I would be left behind. I stepped out of the column, pretending my name had been called. I held the piece of paper in my hand and confidently walked toward the trucks, thinking that I had been successful in fooling the officers. As I approached the fence, I noticed that there was a small opening that served as a checkpoint. Some people had gone through and jumped onto the trucks, but there were many people behind the checkpoint, pushing and shoving while waiting to have their slips checked. I realized my scrap of paper was worthless and in the confusion – out of desperation and without much thought – I jumped the fence and ran straight to the closest truck, not noticing that it was still empty.

I jumped onto the canvas-covered truck and hurried all the way to the back. I lay down on the floor, shaking and terrified. It seemed like an eternity until I heard people running toward the truck and saw their faces as they started to jump in. Marcus had seen me leaving the column and observed my moves. He had decided to do the same thing and also succeeded in getting onto a truck. After everybody was loaded, the trucks started to move, slowly picking up speed. So did my rhythm of joy. But some of the people whose wishes had come true were now skeptical. They had previous experience and knew how tricky the Nazis could be. We didn't really know where we were headed.

DESTINATION UNKNOWN

After riding for a while, we arrived at a train station. The soldiers ordered us off the trucks and made us line up in a column. We were then marched across a few sets of tracks toward freight cars, some open and some closed. I was happy to catch a glimpse of Marcus in the distance. The soldiers split the column into groups and ordered us into the cars. Many of the elderly and sick who could not pull themselves up into the cars had to be helped by others, causing a delay. At the same time, soldiers used whips and clubs to move us in an urgent manner, as if the train were waiting for us.

I ended up in an open car. Unlike the closed boxcars, it had no roof, only solid sides about a metre high. Once we were all loaded, we had a long wait until we left the station. In the meantime we were a source of entertainment for the German and Romanian soldiers milling around. Laughing and enjoying themselves, they observed us as though we were creatures in a zoo. Using us for target practice, they honed their throwing skills by tossing stones at us and shouted abusive language as if we were the guilty ones who had committed crimes against humanity.

Crammed for hours in the freight cars like cattle, hungry, thirsty, and tired, we tortured ourselves wondering why they had picked the less productive people. The cars were finally coupled and started to move slowly out of the station, accompanied by grinding noises from the car wheels and tracks. Rumours spread among us that the train was moving in the wrong direction. Others argued that we were moving in the right direction. Since we did not know the direction to Mogilev, it was anybody's guess. As the train picked up speed and moved along faster and faster, people next to me felt sorry that they had registered in Tulchin to leave the camp. They became suspicious because most of them were old and sick and could no longer produce enough peat for their keep. They felt that they had been picked out for extinction and were being sent to their deaths. They talked about a dreaded *lager*, thinking we were heading there.

This was the first time I had heard the name Peciora, and it meant nothing to me.[17] The word spread quickly in our car, like burning gasoline, and in no time the car was engulfed with frightening rumours. The people from Mogilev knew that death had awaited *lager* people who had previously been sent to Peciora. Some of them had been taken from that *lager* across the Bug River to the German side where, after working for a while, they were shot by German soldiers. Others who were left in that *lager* were beaten, abused, and shot more than in any of the other *lagers*. As I listened to the conversations, my hope of seeing Avrum was fading fast. I prayed that the train would slow down or stop at a station during the night, giving me one last chance to escape before arriving in Peciora where the end of my life was imminent.

As the train rolled along, my heart was beating just as hard and fast as the wheels of the cars pounding the tracks. The wind and noise in our open car, combined with the red hot sparks shooting out of the locomotive chimney in the dark, compounded our fear. The sparks looked like flying stars moving toward us, creating an illusion that we were moving faster than we actually were toward our rendezvous with death. As we travelled through the night, I could not see the expressions on people's faces, but I could hear frightened voices praying to God and asking for help.

After a long ride, I could hear the grinding noise of brakes pressing against the wheels, slowing down the train. The last turn of the wheels brought the train to a dead stop outside a small station. Conversations and prayers ceased. We did not know if this was our final destination or just a normal stop. I did not wait to find out; my prayers for a chance to escape were answered. Without hesitation, I lowered myself from the open car, jumped off, and ran into a field. Fuelled by fear and panic, I kept running until I was overcome by exhaustion and lay down in a bush to rest for the remainder of the night.

When I got up in the morning, I felt great relief at having succeeded in my escape. Searching for something to eat, I looked out of the bush and saw a field of sugar beets. I pulled some out and ran back into the bush. I hid until nightfall before resuming my walk. After dark, I kept walking in a direction that I hoped would lead to the vicinity of Stepanki. The weather was nice, I did not encounter anybody, and I walked until I got tired. I looked for a bush in which to lie down and rest.

In the morning, I was jolted awake by an old farmer. He must have come into the bush to relieve himself. I told him I was on my way to Stepanki but wasn't sure which direction to take. He didn't know where

Stepanki was, and I realized then that I was lost. He recognized me as being Jewish.

"I'm on my way home," he said. "It's not too far from a town called Dzhurin. There are a lot of Jews living in that town. If you want, you can get a ride with me."

I hopped onto the wagon, and, after a long ride, he stopped at a crossroad, pointing out the direction to Dzhurin. I got off the wagon and walked toward the town. As I came closer, I saw a woman working in her yard. I asked her how to get to the Jewish ghetto, and she gave me directions.

As I walked into the ghetto, I saw people milling around the street. Some were cooking their meagre meals on grates, some were walking, and others were talking in small groups. I approached a group, listened to their conversation for a while, and then told them my story. One man in this group called me aside. "I have a proposition for you," he said. "I'll take you home and we'll discuss it." During dinner, he told me what he had in mind. He was a Ukrainian Jew who, along with his wife, had escaped the massacre by the *Einsatzgruppen* in 1941. He and others had recently been drafted by the Jewish committee to go to work in Zhmerinka and were to report to the Romanian authorities the following morning. He wanted me to be his stand-in. "They won't accept you and they'll let you go free as you're too young," he said convincingly. "If not, you'll have no problem escaping since you're a kid and the soldiers in this ghetto aren't abusive." This is the only time I can remember being naïve and trusting, falling for the bait.

He showed me what he was going to give me for standing in for him – a pair of worn-out sandals, an old pair of pants, two shirts, and a loaf of bread. I asked him to let me stay at his place overnight; I would think about it and let him know in the morning. He agreed. The used clothing acted as a strong incentive for me. Since I thought the chances of being rejected were good and, if not, that I would be able to escape, I decided to accept his offer. I thought I would then return to Stepanki with some clothes for Avrum and me. My only desire was to see Avrum again, not only in my thoughts and dreams, but to experience the joy of hugging and kissing him. This would revive our spirits, injecting new life into both of us.

Early the next morning, the man woke me up, and I accepted his offer. He gave me a piece of paper with his name on it, telling me that when his name was called, I should respond. He escorted me close to the assembly point where soldiers awaited us. He was going to wait until I joined the group, probably to ensure that I did not run away and get him into trouble. After a short while, a Romanian officer appeared and ordered us to form a column. He had a list in his hand and told us to acknowledge our names when they were called. After all the names were called, they counted us. We remained in column formation for a short time before marching off.

I walked out of the column, approached a soldier, and told him I was too young and had not been drafted, but had just wandered into the group by mistake. Without hesitating, he hit me with his whip and ordered me back to the column. I realized then what a grave error I had made. I had come so close to realizing my dream and now blamed myself for getting into a dire situation by selling myself for a few pieces of clothing. As we walked, I thought that I might have a chance to escape during the night. The soldiers who herded us were young and mean, exhibiting their authority with rifle butts and whips. Their actions were just the contrary to what I had been told and had believed. After marching for hours, we stopped to rest. Everyone had taken some food with them; I nibbled on my loaf of bread. I looked around to see if I could escape or hide my small body in the grass or behind any obstacle, but there were none. The soldiers must have had previous experience herding Jews by foot. They knew what they were doing.

After the soldiers had eaten their lunch and rested, they got us up on our feet, making us march until sundown. They did not trust us to sleep outside under the stars. They found a barn that was too small to house us all, even standing up, and physically pushed us all in. The last of the people to be forced in took the brunt of the beatings. It was so tight that the soldiers were barely able to close the barn door. We begged them to open the door to let in some fresh air. They refused until we were able to come up with some valuable items to give them. One man volunteered to give them his watch. The soldiers wanted more valuables, but nobody had any or, if they did, would not willingly part with them. The soldiers finally agreed to open the door, allowing some of us to sleep outside near the door under their watchful eyes. I was surprised that someone had volunteered to give away his watch. I was told that he had lung problems and, if the door had not been opened, he would not have made it through the night.

In the morning, we were counted again and marched toward Zhmerinka. As we entered the city, I could see German trucks and soldiers on the street. I felt uneasy; we had entered a German environment. It was the first time I had seen soldiers wearing black uniforms with the insignia of a human skull. Tulchin and the recent hangings staged for the amusement of the German officers popped up in my mind. What was their purpose in bringing us here?

We kept on marching until we reached a large building next to an orchard. The building was surrounded by a tall barbed wire fence, the wires very tightly spaced. I well remember that fence as I immediately looked it over, thinking about the possibility of escaping. We were told to go inside and pick places to sleep. There were a lot of big, empty rooms with wooden floors. The spotlessly clean rooms must previously have housed German officers or officials. The unusually high fence would have provided security for them. After mingling for a while, we each found a place and lay down on the bare floor to sleep.

We were awakened early the next morning by a new group of soldiers, mostly German, who told us to form a marching column in the yard. After we assembled, they inspected us closely as though they wanted to make sure they had received the right merchandise and had not been cheated. "Don't any of you try to escape," one of them yelled in German. "The fences are electrified, and there's only one penalty for attempting to escape – death!" They then told us that we had been brought there to work at the railway station. After the inspection, a soldier walked along the column, picking out about ten people; I was one of them. We were to remain in the camp to work as cooks and helpers. After we all received a portion of bread, the others were marched off to the railway station.

The people left behind were given shovels and were directed how to dig holes to hold two big kettles for cooking soup. Stairs were carved out next to the holes to allow a person to walk down into the pit to put wood underneath each kettle. Once this project was completed, we were assigned to different jobs: some to chop wood and keep the fire going and others to cook. Being the smallest, I was assigned to keep the fire going. In the beginning, I thought I had an easy job, but it was not to be. I had to get up very early to start the fire as the watery potato or, sometimes, cornmeal soup had to be ready by 6 a.m. The biggest problem I encountered was the smoke in the pit, especially when the wind blew – as it often did – in my direction. I had to run out of the pit many times when my eyes teared and I could not stop coughing. I had no choice but to return to feed the fire under those huge kettles to ensure that the soup was ready in the morning and also in the evening for the workers when they returned from work.

As I tended the fire, I had time on my hands to reflect with sadness on the past. At the same time, I thought about the stupidity and poor judgment that had caused me to land up in Zhmerinka and prolong my yearning to be reunited with Avrum. But my hope was not broken – my gut feeling was that I would somehow be able to escape. My mind and eyes were always on the alert for different avenues of escape. I thought my best chance might be to dig a hole underneath the barbed wire fence. I would avoid being electrocuted, run into the orchard, and keep going from there. I would have had to dig myself out by hand, so I looked for a soft spot next to the fence. That's where I was caught by the patrolling soldiers. "What are you doing here?" one of them asked.

I had a ready excuse: "I'm gathering dry weeds to start the fire in the morning."

They believed me and kept on patrolling. The second time, I was caught by other soldiers; they gave me a stern warning not to come too close to the fence or I would be shot. I took their threats seriously – they were a mean group who acted on impulse against a people they loved to hate.

Unlike the situation in Tulchin, the people in this camp did not mingle much after work. The fence that contained us was approximately fifteen metres from the building, and the soldiers, always in pairs, constantly patrolled the grounds. This did not give us much of a comfort zone. Besides, the evenings were now cool and darkness set in early. We felt safer being inside the rooms, out of view of the German soldiers. Sitting on the bare floor, leaning against the wall for support, I passed the time thinking about Avrum and listening to conversations. Most centred on our chances for survival and what the future might hold for us. Sometimes there were disagreements between the optimists and pessimists. As evenings wore on, we grew tired, stretched out from our sitting position and lay down for the night's rest with doubts in our minds about what the next sunrise would bring.

Every morning after breakfast the workers assembled in a column and marched to the railway station. Thousands of German soldiers were travelling to the Russian front via this station, and, at the same time, it was a stop for trains carrying wounded soldiers back to Germany.

The German officer in charge wanted to ensure that the Jewish workers did not contaminate the soldiers. A few days after we arrived in camp, he ordered the soldiers to march us down to the communal bath-house to get cleaned up. We had never expected such a treat. Once we got there, we were split into groups; the bathhouse was too small to hold us all. I was in the first group, and, as I started to undress, I realized it had been more than two years since I had had a bath. The "new" old shirts and pants that I had recently acquired came off easily, but I had to strug-gle to untie the knots in the strings that kept my original clothes from falling apart. Before I'd finished, everyone in my group had already undressed and gone in for their showers. I became so frustrated, I tore my clothes off piece by piece. They had deteriorated to such an extent that the pieces came off as easily as the petals of a flower. My tricot underwear was full of holes, but it still held together. Once I had finally removed my clothes, I was shocked to see how skinny my body had become. Even the feel of my skin seemed strange; how detached from my own body I had become. I stopped feeling sorry for myself, quickly walking in to join the others in the showers.

After we'd had our showers, we were directed to another room con-taining pails of naphtha. The soldiers made sure we completely washed our bodies with it and that our clothing was sprayed with a white powder. These measures were taken to kill the lice with which we were infested — they were the only commodity we never lacked throughout the war. My skin turned red and itchy and burned; it felt like a bad sun-burn. After everybody had been through the showers, we were marched back to the camp. In a way, we were lucky because we had never heard about Auschwitz at that time. There, when poor innocent Jews went in for showers, instead of getting water from the shower heads, they were gassed and all perished.

I returned minus my pouch, which I had treasured for so long like a trophy. It must have been stolen while I was in the shower. Back at the camp, I ran around asking people if they might have taken it by mistake, trying to spot it myself. I never saw that pouch again. It had been like a security blanket to me and had served multiple purposes. It was a stor-age place for food and a cushion to sleep on, or an extra cover to warm my feet at night. It complemented my cap when it was cold in winter, keeping my head and face warm. It also had a sentimental value for me. If it had not been stolen, I might have kept it as a souvenir and would still have it today.

I always lay down early for the night's rest as I had to be up by 4 a.m. The on-going conversations in the room did not bother me. Instead of my pouch, I now used a piece of wood, cushioned by my cap, for a pillow. Each morning, as I walked outside to start the fire, my eyes automatically focused on the fence, and my heart started to beat faster as I gathered the courage to attempt an escape – until I saw the patrolling soldiers rounding the corner, coming toward me. The window of opportunity to make an escape was very brief because the soldiers' circuit was short. Disappointed, I would go down into the pit to light the fire. Maybe my lucky break would come tomorrow. I always prepared the wood the night before, putting some underneath the kettle so that I did not have to get up even earlier. One of the men in our group who was a cook slept beside me and had a pocket watch. He woke me up every morning. This man seemed to need little sleep. He was very edgy and always discouraged me from thinking about escaping by pointing out that it was futile; nobody had ever been successful.

I became more restless as I realized how remote were the chances of escaping from the camp. I felt my chances would not improve unless I switched jobs with one of the men who went to work at the railway station. These workers toiled in groups spread out all over the station, and there were no electrified wire fences to pen them in. I approached an older man to ask if he would like to switch jobs with me. He quickly agreed. He thought I was crazy since my job was relatively easy and I could scoop out the thicker portion of the soup, rather than the watery soup that he got after a hard day's work. I introduced him to my co-worker with the watch and told him that we were switching jobs. My co-worker tried to talk me out of it but, as I was determined to escape, he was not successful.

The next morning, guarded by soldiers, I marched off to work with the others. Some people on the street stopped to stare at us. Once we arrived at the railway station, we were randomly assigned different jobs. Some workers were sent away from the station to shore up gravel beds next to the tracks. Another group worked around the station doing the same work, as well as picking out the big stones from the gravel and throwing them into an open rail car. We then pushed these cars by hand to different parts of the yards to fill holes or low-lying terrain. We also moved and replaced small sections of track. Still others collected garbage that had been dropped in the station by the German soldiers travelling through Zhmerinka. The largest portion of the garbage came from wounded soldiers returning to Germany.

As I worked at the railway station, my morale rose. I could sense that the opportunities for escape had increased. I realized that there were many risks involved. Soldiers with sharp eyes guarded us. Even if I were to succeed in escaping from the work area, I might still be spotted by other soldiers who patrolled the station for security reasons. The clothing I wore would give my identity away, particularly during daylight hours. But at least we were no longer corralled within a barbed-wire fence.

The traffic through Zhmerinka was heavy – it must have been a main line in the southern part of the Ukraine leading to the Russian front. It seems priority was given to soldiers travelling to the front. I often saw whole trainloads of tanks and guns, as well as trainload after trainload of soldiers singing German songs at the tops of their lungs. Their stop at the station was very brief. By contrast, the wounded soldiers returning from the front were frequently switched to a side track for hours or even a whole day. Some heavily wounded soldiers returned in boxcars. Once the train stopped, the doors were opened. When I worked as a garbage collector and was right in front of the boxcars, I could see double-stacked bunks inside. Some wounded soldiers were lying on stretchers and others on bunks. They were attended by nurses, and I could sometimes see blood seeping through their bandages. Many of the soldiers were fed by the nurses.

If one of us was lucky enough to be standing next to a boxcar door when a nurse threw out an empty chocolate box, we could sometimes find a piece of chocolate mixed up with the papers. You had to be fast to grab it before another worker did. We all kept our eyes open to catch such a treat. Being small, I was frequently assigned to be a garbage collector. How I envied those nurses as they sat on the boxcar floors with their feet dangling outside, casually eating. I could not imagine eating like that; I would have swallowed a sandwich in two fast bites and reached for more.

I purposely worked very slowly picking up the garbage in front of the cars. I stared at them like a dog; the desperate look on my bony face should have had a more powerful impact on the nurses than spoken words, understandable in any language. I hoped they would have pity on me, ignore the fact that I was Jewish, and throw me some food, not just the garbage. But they did not respond or perceive me as a human being who was worth saving. They ignored my silent pleas and continued eating and chatting with their colleagues as I made my way from boxcar to boxcar collecting garbage off the ground, hoping to find something to chew on. I can remember only a few who felt sorry for me and gave me some food. One even engaged me in a conversation.

"Where are you from?" she asked.

"Bukovina," I said.

"Where are your parents?"

"I have no parents, they're dead."

"What happened to them?"

"They starved to death in a pig barn. I'm Jewish, you know."

She looked at me with pity. "I know," she said, "I'm surprised you speak German so well."

My eyes started to tear as memories came flooding back, and I walked away.

Yes, small details like that I remember. These acts of kindness rarely happened and meant a great deal to me. I had always been under the impression that a nurse was good-hearted and made an effort to help people. Out of the many nurses that I saw passing through Zhmerinka, only a few helped me. Most *lager* people remember very well the few times they received aid, since it happened so seldom. They also remember, regardless of their age at the time, the painful hunger, beatings, and fear they had to endure. It is not that one is remembering such tragic events out of pride; the reality is that they are impossible to forget. My memories are vivid because my life remains connected to the past. One remembers the images more than the words. I have often spoken about these experiences over the years with Holocaust survivors and others interested in knowing how I survived the war. It is painful but something I must do.

One evening, while working near the station, I heard loud German singing coming out of the open doors. As I came closer, I could see that the hall was full of soldiers eating and drinking. What caught my eye was a soldier holding a big drumstick in his hand. He took a bite and proceeded to wave the drumstick like a conductor moves his baton. My eyes were glued to the drumstick, and my mouth watered as he moved his hands up and down in an atmosphere of camaraderie, joy, and laughter. I felt sad, seeing the enjoyment those murderers were sharing while I, the innocent, was held captive, standing motionless in the shadow of the boxcars, hungry, robbed of everything, and full of fear. One had to be more than an optimist to imagine the day when I would not be afraid to walk out of the shadows and reveal my true identity.

Another incident I recollect because it was unique involved a group of Jews on a train. As I was working close to the tracks in the station that day, a train slowly pulled out. By our appearance and clothing, and maybe because the workforce had young as well as older people, these people on the train must have recognized us as Jewish. They stuck their heads out of the cars and hollered at us in Yiddish, "We are Hungarian Jews returning from a labour camp." At the same time, they threw out some small pieces of bread, probably part of their rations for the day. One man threw out a pair of pants. The train picked up speed, and we lost contact with them. Everybody working close to the tracks tried to grab some bread. I attempted to grab the pants off the ground, but an older man snatched them, practically out of my hands.

Working at the railway station was an eye-opener for me. I was always distracted from work by the activity on the street, which reminded me of what freedom really meant. For more than two years, I had been isolated from civilization, and now I had the opportunity to observe it again. It was just across the tracks from where I was working, yet beyond my reach. How I envied those people mingling freely, without fear. Walking up and down the street, some peddled their goods in the open, ignored by the soldiers. Physically, I was only a leap away from freedom, but the presence of the soldiers, with their guns and trigger-happy fingers, kept me captive behind invisible bars. I frequently saw older people begging on the streets, and this gave me an idea about how I might escape from Zhmerinka; if I could only blend in among them. Once I paid for my observation with lashes. I was picking stones that day at the station, and, as I relaxed for a few minutes, I was caught gazing at the people on the street. A soldier sneaked up behind me, hitting me with his lash. I felt intense pain from the first lash, but he did not stop there. I knew from past experience that pleading and crying would not help when soldiers were looking for any excuse to exhibit their authority and create some excitement for themselves. They were not responsible to their superiors for their acts whenever Jews were involved. We were at the total mercy of these beasts.

My first attempt to escape was a failure. I had to turn back before crossing the last few sets of tracks when I was spotted by a man in civilian clothes walking toward me in haste with a big dog. I had no idea who he was or if he was even working for the Germans, but I did not want to take unnecessary risks. The soldiers who guarded us were becoming more aggressive as time went on. They watched us like hawks, venting their frustration on us with their whips and clubs for no apparent reason other than seeing so many of their wounded comrades returning home. This put us in great danger; I was afraid that one day we would all be shot. The frequency of traffic, both to and from the front, increased dramatically, putting more pressure on us to work harder. We were in constant fear, not knowing what they were going to do to us next.

We were always surrounded by soldiers and had no access to news or even to any rumours from the local population. We had no idea how close or far away the front was from Zhmerinka. We could only guess by the increased traffic that there must be heavy fighting going on, with big losses being inflicted on the German army. I hoped and prayed the Germans would lose the war while I was still alive and able to rejoice at their defeat. But more important, I wanted to be a living witness to their horrific acts, even if it meant being carried into a courtroom on a stretcher to reveal the truth and deny them the luxury of telling the world it never happened.

More than a month had gone by, and I was still in Zhmerinka, but my thoughts were with Avrum in Stepanki. It must have been at least four months since we had last seen each other. What was he doing, and how was he coping alone? He probably did not have his job anymore because the cows would no longer be feeding on the grass due to the change in seasons.

It was getting colder, and it rained frequently. Sometimes I was able to hide under a boxcar to keep dry. Luckily, I was not spotted – my small body was shielded by the wheels of the freight cars. Some of the workers were better dressed than others and were able to keep warm. But I started to feel the cold, especially in my feet, because I wore only sandals. I was lucky to find some rags amongst the garbage. I wrapped them around my feet and tied them up with pieces of bandage. With the clothing I wore, my chances of surviving in the approaching cold weather were slim. Sympathy from the soldiers guarding us was not something I could count on. They perceived me only as a shadow and couldn't have cared less if I didn't survive. I became desperate to escape and knew I had to do something quickly, even if it meant taking bigger risks.

I had a couple of ideas in mind. Instead of going back to the camp with the rest of the workers, I would hide in an empty boxcar and make my getaway during the night. I was reminded by a co-worker that this was like committing suicide – he told me that German soldiers patrolled the grounds at night with dogs and searchlights. Some people had been caught in boxcars and shot. I returned to the idea of blending in with the local people, including beggars, walking freely on the streets. I could speak the languages that were spoken in the district. I felt I had a good chance of getting lost in the crowd by passing myself off as a beggar – if only I could cross the street and reach the buildings across from the station without being detected.

The days got shorter, and we worked into the darkness, giving me a better opportunity to succeed. Unfortunately, I had to put off several escape attempts as the nights were clear and there were too many soldiers walking around on the street that I had to cross. This dampened my courage – not out of fear, but out of logic, which I had very seldom used until now. I had a strong conviction that somehow, some day soon, I'd be able to make my escape, and I didn't want to jeopardize my chances. I had no choice but to go back with the others to the camp.

Finally, one evening, luck was on my side. I succeeded in crawling underneath several boxcars and getting across the street. It was foggy, and nobody noticed my escape. I hid in a doorway, looked for passers-by, and started begging for money to buy clothes to keep me warm, but my main concern was to hide my identity on the way to Stepanki. Some people ignored me while others gave me money. It got foggier, and I could not see the passers-by until they came close. I was startled when a German officer suddenly appeared as I held out my hand. He stopped, reached into his pocket, and handed me some money. Not a word was exchanged. I got scared, promptly leaving for the outskirts of Zhmerinka to look for a barn in which to stay overnight. I felt safer in isolated surroundings.

On the way, I came across a small house, and when I looked in the window I saw an elderly couple. I walked in and begged them, "Please, will you let me stay overnight? I'm returning to Stepanki, and I've lost my way." By my appearance, they could tell I was Jewish and a fugitive on the run.

"Are you one of the Jews who work at the station?" the old man asked.

I froze. Not knowing what his reaction would be, I hesitated, but finally said "yes."

They agreed to let me stay and gave me some food. I told them what had happened to my family and myself. They had no love for the Nazis either; they had their own tragic story to tell. One of their sons had been killed by the Germans. He was a partisan who fought the Germans behind their lines. Their daughter had left with the Soviet army when it retreated ahead of the German advance in 1941; they had not heard from her since. I sensed I was welcome in their house and felt secure enough to tell them what I had in mind.

"I want to beg on the street at night to get enough money to buy some old clothes," I said. "Can I stay with you a few days?"

"You're welcome to stay," the old man replied, "but don't venture outside in the daytime."

The next evening, I returned to the same area to start begging. I thought it would be safe as I became lost in the midst of the pedestrian traffic, but, as soon as I reached my destination, I became apprehensive. It was a clear night and soldiers were all over the place. This was not such a good idea after all! I went back to the house and asked the old man if I had enough money to buy a second-hand *kufaika* (parka). I gave up the idea of trying to buy anything else and would have to make my way back to Stepanki in my sandals. After I told him my problems, the old man had some encouraging words for me. "Don't worry kid, go to sleep," he said. "I'll see what I can do in the morning."

The next day, I gave him the little money I had received from begging and he left. He returned with some old clothes: a parka, a Russian winter cap, and a pair of leather boots that were too big. He gave me some rags to wrap around my feet – they felt warm and comfortable in the boots. This couple perceived me not only as a Jew, but as a person. They willingly spent some of their own money to save my life. Their act of kindness relieved the pent-up tension in my body and filled me with encouraging thoughts. How strangely the mind works: a deprived person needs very little to ignite the flame of hope. Things were finally turning in my favour, and it now looked as though I would be able to realize my dream of being reunited with Avrum. They told me that I could stay a few more days to rest and get back some of my strength before I began my journey back to Stepanki.

RETURN TO STEPANKI

After only one day, I became impatient and anxious to start the trek back to Stepanki. I got up in the morning and told the couple that I had decided to leave. While we sat at the table eating breakfast, I was also fed encouraging words. As I listened, I wondered how different the world would be if people would act with such kindness toward each other. After we finished eating, I put on my parka and Russian cap. My new clothes were a novelty to me. They changed my identity – I took on a civilized look. As I left, they blessed me and gave me a parcel of food for the road, along with an old pair of mitts.

It was a cold, frosty morning, but my spirits were buoyant, knowing my chances of reaching Stepanki had improved. I was dressed like a native, hiding my skeletal body from being recognized as a Jewish fugitive. The Russian cap with its big ear flaps hanging down added extra protection. Very little of my face was visible. Even my boots were standard local apparel.

The narrow dirt road that led to the main highway was peaceful and quiet, except for the sound of the partially frozen ground breaking under the weight of my boots. As I reached the highway leading out of Zhmerinka, I became apprehensive again. I spotted the group with whom I had worked. Guarded by soldiers, they were working across the highway on the railway tracks. I ignored them and increased my pace, heading in the direction the old man had told me to take. On my way, I encountered light traffic – mostly horse-drawn wagons driven by local people going to Zhmerinka.

As I continued on my way, the tranquillity was periodically interrupted by German military trucks, but they ignored me. This assured me that I was being perceived as a native and relieved me of some of my fears. I started to walk in a more relaxed manner. I felt comfortable in my clothes and had enough food for another day. It was dark when I finally came to the outskirts of a village. I walked into the first house I saw and begged the people to let me stay overnight. They agreed. In the morning, they offered me breakfast, and I asked them for directions to Kopygorod, a town not far from Stepanki. Unlike

Stepanki, Kopygorod was large enough that most people knew where it was located.

After I had walked for a while, light snow started to fall and became my companion. The road became muddy, making walking more difficult. My oversized boots started rubbing one of my feet. This slowed me down. Traffic was light, mostly Romanian and German soldiers motoring by and riding on horse-drawn wagons. I was of no interest to them.

As I limped along, two horses pulling a wagon came from behind and stopped. A young man who appeared to be in his twenties told me to hop onto the wagon. Without hesitating, I jumped on. "Where are you going?" he asked as we drove away. "Why are you limping?"

"I'm on my way to Kopygorod," I said. "My boot has been rubbing my foot."

"I'm heading to a town in the vicinity of Kopygorod. If you want, you can stay with me overnight."

"Yes, that would be good," I said.

"You're Jewish, aren't you?" he asked.

"Yes," I replied. "How did you know?"

"You speak with an accent, and I know that there are many Jews confined in ghettos in this region."

I immediately became uneasy and started to worry. He was young, well dressed for the cold and had two fast horses. Maybe he was in some position of authority, working for the Nazis. My fear increased as he questioned me about Jewish life in the ghettos.

We headed into town and drove up to a house. Upon entering, I saw seven or eight young men sitting around. There were guns on the table and scattered all over the room. The driver said to his comrades, "I picked up this young Jewish lad on the road. He's going to be staying with us." Motioning to the men, he said to me, "These men are all partisans. Don't be scared of the guns; you'll be safer here than in the ghetto. For security reasons, you'll have to stay with us three or four days until we leave town."

They were a happy amicable group of young men who quickly made me feel at ease.

"Where are you from? Where did you learn to speak Russian?" one of them asked.

"I'm from Bukovina. Our territory was occupied by the Soviet Union in 1940. I attended Russian school for a year."

They accepted me as one of their own and asked me my name.

"Joil," I said.

"I've never heard a name like that," one of them said. "Can we call you Juri? It's a nice Russian name."

The atmosphere in the room was relaxed and joyful. They were all volunteers, anxious to fight in defence of their country. I was envious of them; they showed no fear and were ready to engage the enemy against whom I stood alone, defenceless and in fear. Listening to their conversations, I gathered that there were other groups of partisans in the vicinity. The men spent their time discussing the war, their patriotism, their willingness to die for their country, the families and girlfriends they left behind, and what they planned to do after the war. There was no doubt in their minds that the Nazis were going to be defeated, and pay a heavy price for breaking the treaty to respect each other's borders that the two countries had signed. Between discussions, they broke into partisan songs, singing quietly so as not to reveal their presence. "Come on, Juri, sing along with us."

"I don't know the words," I said.

"Well, then, just hum along."

I did and began to feel like one of them. The melodies and lyrics, portraying the lives of partisans, were very emotional. They carried our souls along and imbued us with patriotism.

The movements of the partisans, and of myself, were restricted to going to the barn to relieve ourselves. The young man who had picked me up was the only person who went out and drove away. I believe that he was a native of that town. We had plenty of food, and we all slept in our clothes on the bedded floor. Two partisans always remained on duty.

The partisans knew about the *lagers* and the suffering we had endured. They encouraged me to continue on. "The Red Army will defeat the Nazis soon," one of them said. "We'll all be liberated and be able to go home." I felt safe and enjoyed being with them but hoped they would leave sooner than they planned so I could be on my way. One night, they bid me farewell as though they were leaving an old friend behind, took their guns, and disappeared into the darkness. They left food for me to take on my journey.

I started out early the next morning. The sore on my foot had not healed, continuing to bother me. After walking for a while, I got a ride on a wagon for a short distance. I then continued on my way, encountering a few military vehicles as I slowly limped along. My clothes served their purpose and acted as camouflage, but for some reason the closer I

came to Stepanki, the more tense and frightened I became. I was afraid
that I would be caught so close to home. Walking became more difficult,
and I had to remove one of my boots; it had rubbed into my flesh,
making any movement painful. I hopped along until a wagon pulled up
and the man told me to get on. As we drove off, he asked me where I
was going. I was happy to hear him say that he was going past Stepanki.
He told me he was a manager in a *kolkhoz*. He seemed to have had quite
a few drinks, but this did not stop him from periodically reaching for a
bottle hidden in the hay. He offered the bottle to me, and I pretended to
drink. He spent most of the time singing patriotic Russian songs and
occasionally whipping the two brisk horses as they galloped along.

As we reached the vicinity of Stepanki, my heart started to beat
faster. I was uneasy; I was returning to Stepanki with mixed feelings –
there was joy in arriving in the village that I hated to remember. It was
some time in the afternoon when the manager stopped to let me off. As
I jumped down, I tried to avoid putting pressure on my foot and ended
up twisting my ankle. It started to ache as I walked to Marusia's house.
As I went in the door carrying my boot, I saw Marusia and her two children sitting at the table. I became frightened when I did not see Avrum;
it was cold outside, and I had expected him to be there. Marusia quickly jumped up from the table.

"Where have you been?" she asked. "I was worried about you. I'm
so glad to see you." Her worried face revealed her concern.

"I've been working in labour camps," I said, and with dread in my
voice asked, "Where's Avrum?"

"He's staying at Messiah's now. He'll be thrilled to see you." Those
few words instantly allayed my fears and revitalized me. "Every day when
Avrum returned from work, he asked if you were back. He often became
depressed and I tried to cheer him up. Fortunately, Messiah was a frequent visitor and comforted him. Sit down. What's wrong with your
foot? Why are you limping?" She gave me a thick rag to tie around my
ankle but, being anxious to see Avrum, I immediately left for Messiah's.

It was a slow, painful walk. I opened the door and walked into the
room. There sat Avrum at the table. In that split second, my brain
received two separate sensations. First, my eyes registered a skinny-look-
ing Avrum; then my heart filled with happiness. My dream had finally
come true. He ran toward me; I did not know whether the tears pouring out from my eyes were tears of joy or tears of sorrow. At last, we were
together. We embraced each other and held tight, neither of us willing

to let go. Nor would our eyes dry up; they kept flooding with tears that seemed to come from inexhaustible reservoirs. As I held Avrum close to my chest, I could feel that there wasn't much flesh on his bones. My own body may have fooled Avrum as it was shielded by the oversized parka I was still wearing.

When we finally let go, neither of us could talk. We just continued sobbing, wiping away our tears, and looking at each other in disbelief. We had a lot to talk about – if only we could restrain our emotions. Messiah came toward us with tears in his own eyes and embraced us both.

"I have some good news for you," he said. "Avrum, along with some other orphans, is leaving for Romania tomorrow morning."

"Good," I said. "We'll finally leave Stepanki for a normal life. I just hope I'll be able to walk."

"No," he said. "You can't go. You're not registered, and they won't accept you. I was told there are orphans still left in other ghettos. Hopefully they'll be able to leave later."

"We're not going to separate," I said. "We'll wait for the next group."

As soon as Avrum and I sat down at the table and started talking, he began to cough. I did not think too much about it; I thought he just had a cold. But as we kept on talking, his cough intensified. Long spasms periodically shook his entire body, and he could barely catch his breath. I became very concerned. His physical appearance had worried me from the first moment I saw him. My memories of other children with similar conditions were still fresh and the images were still with me.

Avrum started to tell me how he had coped alone and about his sleepless nights wondering what had happened to me. He never gave up hope that one day I would suddenly appear. His life was lonely; he had no one to talk to or to curl up with to provide some comfort and warmth when the nights turned cold. Marusia had not kept the fire burning in the stove as she tried to save as much wood as possible for the winter. He had kept his job herding the cows until the farmer decided that there was not enough grass to make it worthwhile pasturing them.

Avrum had continued to stay at Marusia's until Messiah came and brought him the news about the orphan program. Messiah had been informed by a Jewish emissary from the Kopygorod ghetto that the Romanian government had agreed to repatriate orphans from Transnistria to Romania. The Jews in the provinces of Romania who had not been expelled and had been allowed to remain at home during the war had agreed to be totally responsible for the support of these orphans. It was Messiah's responsibility to inform the orphans to register. He invited Avrum to stay at his place until his departure.

There were only five orphans left in Stepanki to register. Avrum had hesitated; he could not forget our disastrous experience in the orphanage in Mogilev, and he was still hopeful that I would return soon. Finally, after much prodding by Messiah, Avrum was convinced that he should register.

The hours flew by as we sat at the table and talked. We were both anxious to hear about each other's experiences. We tried to condense five months of separation into a few hours of rapid talk. Most of our stories were unpleasant, but we were still happy just to sit across the table, hearing each other's voices. Smiles started to appear on our faces. Avrum was particularly happy that I had returned that day because it relieved him from the burden of making a difficult decision. He was glad that he would not have to go and we could be together again. But seeing Avrum's condition, I was not convinced that staying would be the best choice for him. I was very concerned by his appearance and his frequent coughing spells. It appeared to be more serious than a common cold; he had been suffering with this cough for some time. The only medicine that Messiah was able to get for him was herbal tea, but it had not helped.

My presence strengthened Avrum's belief that everything was going to be better now that I had returned. But the longer we were together, the more I realized how sick he was. I became convinced that he should leave with the other orphans where the opportunity to have his illness taken care of would be greater. I was afraid to take a chance with his life. He had suffered both physically and emotionally far too long to lose the opportunity to be a free man, which might now be within his reach.

Time was running out. The burden of decision-making had shifted to me and left me wrestling with my thoughts. For the past five months, my only desire had been to be reunited with Avrum. I had put my life in danger many times to reach him. Now, after being together for such a brief time, I was torn between my selfish desire not to separate again and the best interests of my little brother whom I dearly loved. How could I rob him of the brief happiness he had enjoyed since my return and convince him that it was best for him to leave?

It was very late at night, and the time to tell Avrum had come. His first reaction was tears. I tried to comfort him and to explain the reason without scaring him with my deep concern for his health. After some discussion, he said that he understood, confessing that he really wasn't feeling well. He finally came to the conclusion that, for his own good, he should leave. We would reunite in happier times after the war. We were both so tired we could barely keep our eyes open. We went to sleep, curling up to each other as we had in the past.

Dawn seemed to come earlier than usual. We knew it was our last time together in Transnistria. It was time to get up and prepare ourselves for the most difficult and saddest separation in our lives. Even though we knew it was for the better, we were being torn apart again.

Memories had started to come back to me. Before our family was uprooted, we were six happy people with a future. As time went on, our number dwindled. Now we two remaining brothers were going to be separated, and, if something were to happen, there would be only one of us left. I started to have second and third thoughts about letting Avrum go, but one look at his face overcame them. Messiah had risen by then and was preparing food for us. He told me that he had received written permission from the local police for two adults to accompany the five orphans to Kopygorod. The orphans who had registered were to gather at Messiah's. In Kopygorod, they would assemble for their journey with other orphans from the surrounding area. They would then travel by train to Romania and, once there, be taken care of by Romanian Jews.

My ankle had swollen overnight, but this did not deter me from trying to find some way of accompanying Avrum; maybe I could convince the authorities in Kopygorod to let me leave with him. I asked Messiah for some rags, and I tied them around my feet; I thought I could walk in them instead of wearing my boots. However, each time I put my foot down, the pain intensified. Messiah begged me not to come along – it would only slow them down, and I would certainly have to turn back shortly. I walked back and forth across the room, reluctantly arriving at the same conclusion. Avrum and I sat down to eat, but he just nibbled. When I asked him why he wasn't eating, he told me that he had had no appetite for the past month. We tried to stay as calm as possible and restrained our emotions until I saw the first two orphans enter the room. Realizing that Avrum's departure was imminent, the gates opened up once more, flooding us both with tears. The two orphans, who appeared to be Avrum's age, just stood, their faces expressionless. Shortly thereafter, a man escorting two younger orphans walked in. He and Messiah were going to accompany the orphans. They were all warmly dressed – Messiah had recently obtained clothes from the Jewish committee in Kopygorod.

The other man was anxious to leave and did not want to waste any time. Messiah and Avrum got dressed; it was time to say good-bye. Avrum and I were still in tears as we embraced each other. Our emotions were high, but this time not from the happiness we had experienced the previous day, but from sadness and distress. It was the first time that we ourselves had willingly agreed to part – the bond between us was strong, and this added to our pain. Even though we thought it was for the better, doubts remained deep in our hearts. Were we doing the right thing? The room was quiet and filled with sadness, broken only by the words "let's go."

As they started to leave, I could not resist grabbing my parka and following them. I got hold of a stick for support and hung onto Avrum. After we had walked a short distance, Avrum begged me to turn back. We said good-bye again, and I watched as he slowly distanced himself from me. He kept looking back and waving, ignoring the ruts he had to negotiate in the road ahead. I waved back until he disappeared into the hilly terrain. I was left standing alone on the dirt road, numb and broken-hearted. It was a short-lived happy reunion that ended in an abrupt, heart-rending separation. I slowly limped back to Marusia's to ask if I could stay with her once again. She promptly agreed to let me stay.

I was alone once more. The drive that had sustained me until now drained from my body, leaving me with only emptiness. The will that had propelled me to keep on fighting to return to Avrum was gone. Depression overtook me, leaving me feeling like an empty shell. I kept wondering if I had done the right thing in letting Avrum go. Some days I felt happy for him that he was gone, and other days I was troubled by the hasty decision that I had been compelled to make. Did I have the right to tell him to go? The nights were especially difficult, lying on the same floor where Avrum and I used to sleep. We had whispered to each other until we fell asleep, awaiting the morning with hope. Now I awoke each morning with feelings of guilt. What had I done to my little brother? Would his chances have been better if he had remained with me? He had always put his whole trust in me without ever questioning my motives.

One of my main concerns was the length of time he would have to wait for medical attention to lessen his suffering. It was an abnormal time where events moved at a snail's pace and circumstances made every day unpredictable. The whole situation looked bizarre to me. The Romanian government, which had chased healthy and productive Jews out of their country during a time of need – when they could have been used as slave labour – suddenly decided to accept sick and malnourished children back into the country. I was left with doubt and a great deal of suspicion.

During the time I was immobilized by my painful foot, Marusia was kind enough to supply me with food. Messiah also brought me food, but more important to me were his visits and his moral support. He encouraged me, trying to assure me that I had done the right thing by letting Avrum go. "Don't be so discouraged," he said, "Avrum's going to be all right."

"Do you really think so?" I asked. "I'm concerned about his health."

"Don't worry, he'll be taken care of. You did the right thing letting him go. There are many orphans in other ghettos who weren't as lucky and had to remain behind. They have to face another blistering cold winter."

"I miss him so much. I wonder where he is now."

"He's probably in Romania by now," Messiah said, "trying to adjust to a normal life."

As soon as I was able to get around with an improvised cane, I went to visit my parents' graves in the forest. When I got there, I could see some dried-up branches anchored by stones on the graves, as well as frozen imprints of a child's feet in the mud around the graves. Avrum must have been a regular visitor while I was away. Before I was caught and sent to Tulchin, we had frequently visited our parents' graves. Now that Avrum was gone, the graves were the only physical objects that could identify me as having belonged to somebody who loved me. As long as the weather permitted, I would go to the graves, lean against the big tree that I used as a point of reference for my parents' burial place, and cry my heart out. This either had a therapeutic effect or just plain tired me out. Afterward, I felt relieved and too exhausted to even think.

Whenever I returned from these visits to Marusia's and she was home, she could see the sadness in my face and would ask if I had been to my parents' graves. My eyes could not lie. She tried to comfort me by telling me that things were going to improve. Rumours were circulating that the Red Army was getting closer and closer and that one day soon we would all be liberated.

Life without Avrum was very lonely. Even though we had not played or joked around since we were chased out of our home, just being together breathed life into us and saw us through each day. We shared a state of mind that carried us along. Now I worried about his health and whether he had really been taken to Romania as promised. There weren't any rumours to alleviate my worries and lift my spirits.

Another depressing factor was the miserably cold weather which kept me in the house most of the time. Marusia's young children were full of life, wanting me to play with them all day long while their mother was away at work. I was not much in the mood to play. I told them I was tired and had to lie down. I would close my eyes, pretending to sleep. They continued playing, their shrieks piercing my ears. As I lay on the floor, my mind wandered around, thinking about the past, the present, and the future. Life seemed so hollow; there was nothing positive I could latch on to. I was no longer the boy who always saw the light at the end of the tunnel. But I realized that I could not let pessimism overtake me, and I struggled to resist it.

When there was a break in the weather and my ankle had healed, I went with Marusia to gather wood in the forest. It felt good to be mobile again and to be able to get around easily. I visited the few farmers who previously had been helpful to me. I also met the Steinhauers, a Jewish family who always offered me a bowl of soup and listened to my sorrows. Mobility helped me overcome my state of depression which had put me down and nearly destroyed me.

I tried to keep myself occupied to avoid having too much idle time to think. An opportunity to go to the nearby village of Ivashcauts presented itself one day. While returning to Marusia's, I met a farmer driving a sleigh who stopped and offered me a ride. "Where are you going?" he asked.

"Not too far," I said as I got on the sleigh, "just to the last house on the hill."

After learning I was Jewish, he said, "I'm from Ivashcauts. I know a Jewish family living in my neighbour's house. The man is a shoemaker."

Hearing the name Ivashcauts, I immediately recalled one of the men I had met in Tulchin. He also was a shoemaker who had originally been deported to Ivashcauts. He had told me that there were a few Jewish families living there and suggested that if I was ever in that village again, I should come to see him. It was a more prosperous village than Stepanki and I might find it easier to survive there.

I decided to seize the opportunity and go to Ivashcauts for a short visit. It might help get me out of the depressing rut I had slipped into. The driver let me off at his neighbour's house. I walked in, and it turned out to be a different Jew. The couple were very friendly, inviting me to join them for dinner. I told them the reason for coming and asked if I could spend the night at their place. They let me stay and asked if I'd like to remain in that village; he said he might be able to find me a job. An elderly woman whose husband had passed away lived nearby and would probably keep me in exchange for doing her chores. The next morning, we went to see her; she agreed to give me room and board in exchange for helping her. As soon as the man left, she showed me around, telling me what my chores would be: mainly chopping wood and feeding the pigs. She made me feel comfortable, and I quickly adjusted to the new surroundings. I had total freedom in the house and all the food I could eat.

It was a two-room house, but only the kitchen was heated, and it was used for all activities, including sleeping. There was a small cot next to the wall for me; it had a cushion and worn blankets on it. When it was time to go to bed, I was at a loss – I did not know what to do. I did not want to give the old woman the impression that I was uncivilized by going to sleep in my clothes. This was my first opportunity to return to some normalcy, but I found it difficult to undress. Normal behaviour became a challenge.

The stressful life that I had endured for so long had taken a sudden turn for the better, literally overnight. Materially, I started to live a more normal life. I now had a home, slept in a bed and had good food available without having to endanger my life. I also gained a devoted friend – the cat always sat close to me because I did a lot of nibbling between meals. The work was not difficult and was in fact a blessing for me. It gave me a feeling of accomplishment that put me back on track, allowing me to envision a future.

After I completed my chores each morning and came in from the cold, the old woman prepared a mug of hot milk for me. She was a very compassionate soul who pitied me and treated me with respect. She could not understand why we had been sent to the Ukraine. I had been asked the same question by other people who had helped me. I had a simple answer: we were Jews.

I imposed my own restrictions not to wander out of the yard except to visit the Jewish family nearby. I spent a lot of time with them, especially at night, talking about our lives and discussing the daily rumours they had heard from farmers bringing shoes for repair. The rumours that the Red Army was advancing rapidly and pushing the Germans back with great success were welcome and buoyed our spirits. The old woman also told me that she had heard from her neighbours that the Soviets would arrive soon and liberate all of us. The partisans in the vicinity became more active, and Romanian soldiers looking for them were more visible. We sometimes heard shooting in the distance.

After a couple of months in Ivashcauts, I decided to return to Stepanki to visit my parents' graves. I was discouraged by the Jewish family from going and risking my life. But I wanted to go and, after completing my chores one day, told the old woman that I was leaving for Stepanki to visit the graves. She did not object and gave me food for the road. On the way, I was stopped by Romanian soldiers. They spoke to me in Romanian, and I pretended not to understand. My clothes disguised my identity, and they let me go. I went straight to Marusia's, this time planning to stay only a few days. "Welcome back," she said. "Where have you been?"

"In Ivashcauts," I replied. "I'm planning to go back."

"You know you're welcome to stay here," she said. "Messiah came a few times to see if you'd returned. He's concerned about you."

"I'll see him after I've gone to my parents' graves," I said.

The next day, as I walked on the road to the graves, I encountered a teen-aged boy. Whenever our paths had crossed previously, he had always chased me, and after I was caught he frequently beat me. For some reason, this time he just greeted me and kept on going. Maybe fear of the imminent Soviet return prevented him from attacking me.

When I reached my parents' graves and started to clear away the snow, I broke down crying. I did not leave until the cold penetrated my body. As I turned back, I bumped into the Steinhauer's son, Mokie. "What's the matter?" he asked. "Where have you been? We wondered what happened to you."

"I'm just coming from my parents' graves," I said. "I've been in Ivashcauts for the past couple of months."

"Come home and have supper with us. My parents will be happy to see you."

Mokie's father told me to visit them anytime I wanted; I was always welcome there.

"I'm planning to go back to Ivashcauts," I said. "I have a good place to stay there."

"That's not a good idea," Mokie said. "You might encounter hostile soldiers on the road. You shouldn't take any unnecessary risks now that liberation is imminent."

They talked about the rumours circulating in the village that the Red Army was rapidly advancing. It was not only the rumours that encouraged Mokie's family – they had actually felt freedom for the past month when Mokie had moved around the village unhindered. Some people who had harassed him previously started to act differently, happy to share the good news that we would soon be liberated and able to go home.

Mokie and his parents convinced me to stay. The next day, I went to visit Messiah. He was very happy to see me, embracing me heartily. His wife's attitude toward me never changed; she ignored me. After discussing the situation, Messiah also suggested I remain in Stepanki.

Within a short time, through Mokie's initiative, we became good friends. Even though he was in his late teens and strongly built, and I was barely fourteen and small for my age, he gave me the feeling that we were friends and had things in common. This friendship was the beginning of my adjustment back to normal life. He took me along whenever he returned repaired pots and pans to farmers, and we stopped at other houses inquiring whether they had any leaky pots to repair. In one of these houses, a woman whose husband had hurt his back asked if either of us would like to help her with chores in return for food. I jumped at the offer. Every morning, I walked to the farmer's place, had breakfast, and after I finished my chores was given lunch. Even though there was only enough work for half a day, I also received food to take home for supper.

My future was starting to shape up differently from that which the Nazis had envisioned for me. I was alive and able to walk during daylight hours – within Stepanki, at least – in relative safety. But even though my eyes perceived some early evidence of freedom, my mind had difficulty accepting the possibility that it could be real.

SPRING 1944

One morning on the way to do my chores, I saw low-flying German airplanes, easily identifiable by their markings, in the skies. They were in flying formation, all heading in the same direction. Soon after they disappeared, I heard explosions in the distance. These activities continued, with intermittent lulls, for a couple of days. I did not know if they were bombing partisans or the regular Soviet army. On the ground where I was, everything was quiet except for a few horse-drawn wagons passing by.

While doing my chores a few days later, I heard rumbling noises. I left the barn and walked onto the road, where I could see military vehicles heading in my direction. I got scared, ran back into the barn and crawled up into the small hay loft. It was not long before the noise intensified and the barn shook from the movement of heavy vehicles. I was too frightened to go down to see what was happening. There was no window through which I could look. After a while I got an idea. I took a stick and pushed it through the straw roof to make a hole. With my hands, I pulled out some straw to enlarge it. As I looked through the opening, I could see all types of German trucks and tanks moving slowly bumper to bumper on the muddy, cut-up dirt roads, as well as on the field next to the road. Some trucks with soldiers were pulled along by tanks, and other soldiers were sitting on top of tanks. Everything appeared to be in disarray.

After several hours, the noise subsided as the last tank passed by. I descended from the hay loft and ran into the house, which was next to the road. The farmer and his wife were just as frightened as I was. Even though they had a bird's-eye view from their window, they were hiding in the corner so as not to attract the soldiers' attention. As we sat down to eat, our disposition changed from fear to joy; we realized we had lived to see the day that we had hoped for. We started talking about events during the war and memories came back.

"I remember when the Red Army pulled back three years ago," the man said. "I wondered if they'd ever return and if we'd be reunited with our two sons who retreated with the army."

"Yes, things were certainly different," I said. "I remember when we were in Otaci waiting to cross the Dniester. The Nazi trucks and tanks were parked along the road next to the forest, not like they retreated today. Then, the soldiers were cleanly dressed and laughed as they abused us. They sure looked different today, ploughing through the mud."

"I guess the Soviets will be here soon," the man said. "What a useless war."

I completed my chores and returned to Marusia's. On the way, I could hear explosions and saw low-flying German planes again.

It was very quiet the next morning. I went outside to see what was happening. When I reached the top of the little hill, a mass of people marching shoulder to shoulder across the fields was visible as far as I could see. I could not make out who they were – German or Russian. At the same time, I saw four or five people mounted on horses galloping on the road toward me. I turned around and ran back to Marusia's. As I reached the yard, so did the horses. I was relieved to see that they were Russian soldiers. One officer dismounted and walked into the house. I followed him in. He told Marusia that they were part of the Red Army and that we were liberated. Out of joy, she grabbed and kissed him. He asked her if there were any German soldiers hiding in the village. Marusia said she was not aware of any.

A little later, the swarm of soldiers reached the village. Some marched through the village but the majority remained in formation and marched over the fields in pursuit of the retreating German army. Marusia grabbed me and said, "Joil, let's go and celebrate with the people." As we reached the road, all the villagers, young and old, were dancing, hugging and kissing each other. Their faces glowed with joy and laughter. The few soldiers in the crowd were mobbed. As I stood watching, I envied the people – they had reason to celebrate. For me it was a sad moment – emotions started to surface. It seems that, in times of peril, human nature sorts out priorities by blunting the emotions and emphasizing survival. Fighting the daily battle had hardened me and only the hope of liberation had kept me going. Now even liberation could not put a smile on my face; it had the opposite effect. It felt like I was waking up from a bad dream, but as I looked around I realized that reality was worse than the dream.

I left the festive crowd and sadly walked away to my parents' graves. Where else could I go? As my eyes focused on the graves, my mind was full of bitter memories, and I had nothing to be joyful about. I had thought the end of the war would be a time to rejoice, but this was not the case. Feelings for parents were not something one could push aside and deal with later. I remained until nightfall and then returned to Marusia's. As I entered the house, she hugged me with joy. "Joil, wipe away your tears and cheer up. We are liberated. I hope my husband is alive and comes home soon."

Lying down for the night's rest, my thoughts focused on one question — where do I go from here when I get up in the morning? I no longer had a place I could call home, nor did I have the desire to return to my birthplace where I was not wanted because I was Jewish. Being Jewish was seen as a crime punishable by death, an attitude shared not just by a few ignorant people but by heads of state and millions of so-called civilized people. The battle for me was not over yet. The soul-searching struggle of adjusting to life without my family had just begun. The road ahead would be lonely and unpredictable.

After a couple of days, the peace and quiet of the village returned. The rumbling of the tanks and the military activity ceased just as suddenly as it had begun. The only signs of war were the carved-up terrain and roads created by the heavy armour.

Several days later, the Soviet authority mobilized every able-bodied male, including survivors, into the army. I went along, thinking that maybe I would find a home in the army. My hometown was still far from liberation, and I had no desire to remain in Stepanki. There wasn't one place with a happy memory for me to revisit. After we were assembled, we were told that we were going to be taken to a military camp and that we might be attacked by German planes on the way. If that should happen, we were to run for cover and hit the ground. They ordered us to follow the soldiers at the head of the column.

As we began marching, there was no panic, and people walked along at a normal pace. At nightfall, the column stopped on the outskirts of a village. The officer in charge told us to go into the village to get accommodation and food, but not to place more than four of us to a house. He warned us to stay on the road and not to take any shortcuts as the fields could be mined. Without understanding the consequences, we all ignored his warning, running like sheep across the field. We all wanted to be the first to reach the village and grab the best accommodation, which we judged by the outer appearance of a house. Fortunately, no one stepped on one of the deadly mines.

In the morning, we assembled again on the main road. As we

marched along, two German planes flew over us, and we all ran for cover. One plane dropped two bombs: one missed the target, and one wounded several people. When we reached the military camp, it was already full of recruits. We were given food and a place to sleep. After breakfast the next morning, we were told to assemble in rows. Officers walked between the rows, picked out individuals who were not fit for duty, and told them to go home. As one approached me, he barely glanced at me before motioning with his hand. "Kid, go home," he said, and continued down the line. My hope of finding a temporary home in the army was dashed. Among the group who were rejected were a number of survivors; they showed their happiness by congratulating each other. For me, it was a letdown – my first attempt at representing myself as a free man was a failure. From my physical appearance, they saw me as unfit. I felt dejected at a time when I was entering a new era, trying to fit in as an equal with a stream of people and in need of moral support.

The recruits were split up into smaller units and military training began immediately. Urgency seemed a priority. The ground around me vibrated with all the activity. The air was filled with shouted commands. I found myself lost amid thousands of people, not knowing what to do with myself or where to go. We were not given any assistance or told how to find our way back. I hung around for a while like a stray dog, not wanting to leave. The army would have been a refuge; a barrier against loneliness and isolation. Having no choice, I left the camp. On the way, I caught up with the survivors from other ghettos who were also discharged. They walked along slowly, returning to their ghettos to be reunited with the remnants of their families.

As I walked along with the group, we encountered military trucks. We tried to flag down those going our way, but they were all full of soldiers who cheered us on. One truck stopped, and the soldiers gave us some of their food. Some time later we came to a junction that had a military checkpoint. I asked for directions to Mogilev-Podolsk, where I intended to cross the Dniester River on my way to the place I used to call home. I left the group, continuing on my way alone. I envied the people who went back to the ghettos – their thoughts were focused on being reunited with family members and on making their way back home. My thoughts jumped from tragedy to tragedy; I did not have one happy thought or plan on which to focus and rest my mind.

At nightfall, I approached a town and found accommodation for an overnight stay. I told the people I was Jewish and on my way home.

"Jewish families lived in this town," the owner said. "But as soon as the Nazis occupied it in 1941, they rounded up all the Jews they could find and shot them. Others retreated with the Red Army."

The next morning, I continued on my way. I came across scenes where skirmishes had taken place – German and Soviet tanks and guns, recognizable by their markings, were scattered on the road and fields. As I walked up a hill and reached the plateau, I saw bombs on a primitive airfield next to the road. My curiosity took me off the road and onto the field, thinking I might find something of value. I could see hundreds and hundreds of different-sized bombs, with a variety of coloured markings, neatly arranged in rows. I was surprised that there was nobody there to guard them or anybody else hanging around. The only thing I found was a German military coat amidst the debris in a collapsed bunker. I pulled it out and took it with me. Walking alone, I had more luck and was picked up several times by Soviet military trucks. I rode with them short distances until they turned off in various directions. They gave me food – mostly canned military rations – and some bread. It was the first time I had ever eaten canned food.

On the last day before reaching Mogilev, I encountered a group of survivors heading back home to Bukovina or Bessarabia. I joined the group. As we walked along, we were surprised by very low-flying German planes skimming over treetops of the forest and coming toward us. Some of us hit the ditch; others just stayed on the road and looked up. "Run for the ditch," I yelled as I lay there and looked up, expecting to see bombs coming down. The planes angled sideways and were so low I could see the pilots. They circled several times to look us over, probably searching for soldiers. If they had wanted to, they could have decimated us in seconds. Maybe it was our fate to survive; maybe they mistook us for Ukrainian refugees.

When we reached Mogilev, I saw hundreds of survivors mingling on the streets. I wondered why they were not anxious to go home. The group I was with headed straight for the bridge to cross the Dniester River into Bessarabia, the province I would have to pass through to reach my home town in Bukovina. As I walked, I heard the name "Joil" shouted in a clear loud voice. I stopped. To my surprise, it was my second cousin Clara Sussmann standing in front of a burned-out building. It was the first time I had seen her since the late fall of 1941, and it made me feel good that I was still recognized after all the hardship I had been through.

She embraced me and invited me to stay with her family. She told me I would not be able to cross the river. They had come from Shargorod a few days earlier and had to remain in Mogilev; only military traffic was allowed to cross for the time being. I entered their temporary home; only a small section of an upper floor was left, acting as a roof. The sky was clearly visible. Her parents and her brother Marcus were there. Marcus, with whom I'd worked in the Tulchin labour camp in 1943, had told them about my family. They were happy to see me and expressed their sorrow about the tragedies that had befallen me. Considering their three years' internment in the Shargorod ghetto, to me they looked relatively good. Marcus's father Keeva was my father's first cousin. He and his family had lived in Berhomet where they had a grocery store. I was happy to see that they had all survived; it raised my hopes that other members of my family were still alive.

They were in the process of preparing for supper, picking pieces of wood debris off the floor and breaking up some of the floor itself. A fire was built between two big stones in the middle of the room and a pot was balanced on top of the stones. It was a setting that one could not forget. We sat on the bare floor around the fire, waiting patiently for supper to cook. "Where is Avrum?" Keeva asked.

"He left with other orphans for Romania late last fall," I said. "I haven't heard from him since. Do you know anything about the orphans who left for Romania?"

"No, I don't," he said. "Don't worry, I'm sure they'll be taken care of."

"What happened after you left Tulchin?" Marcus asked.

"I ended up in another work camp in Zhmerinka," I said and told them what happened.

"What about you, Marcus? Did the train go to Mogilev?"

"Yes," he said. "From there, I went back to Shargorod."

We continued talking until long after supper. Without warning, a sudden barrage of gunfire was heard coming from all directions. Some sounded like cannons – we could not tell if the shells were coming in or going out. One anti-aircraft gun must have been placed right outside our wall. The rapid fire was so loud it was deafening. I hoped that, after everything we'd been through, a bomb wouldn't take our lives now.

"This happens every night," Marcus said. "German planes come back to bomb the bridges to slow down the Soviet advance." Most of the anti-aircraft guns were placed close to the bridge in the area where we had found shelter.

As I lay down for the night's rest, I might as well have slept outside; I could see the stars directly above me. The only advantage of being inside was a feeling of safety.

The next day when Keeva came back from the market, he brought a small bunch of tobacco leaves. He said he had heard that tobacco was a valuable commodity in Bukovina. I had no money, but an idea crossed my mind: I could barter my German military coat for tobacco. The best deal I was able to get was two kilograms of dried tobacco leaves. This was my only possession of value with which to start anew. What irony – the Nazis stripped me naked, and now I used one of their coats to start my new life.

Mogilev became a bustling city of survivors from all over. It was one of the few crossing points to Bessarabia that we were aware of and through which tens of thousands had crossed into Transnistria in 1941. During the day, most of the people were out on the street with one purpose in mind – to see if they could find a relative or friend who might know what happened to some of their family members. Some carried photographs and stopped strangers on the street to ask if they had seen that person. Older people who had lost their families and were left alone were so confused they didn't know what to do with their new-found freedom.

Some people, myself included, became impatient sitting around in Mogilev. I desperately wanted to reach Czernowitz, the capital of Bukovina, in hopes of finding Avrum. I thought that he might have been sent there from Stepanki. I tried to cross the Dniester twice in one day but was turned back each time. Others were not anxious to leave because they had heard that the fighting was still going on in the regions they wanted to return to or the Soviet army had not yet reached their home towns. After several days' delay, I finally was able to cross the river.

The first Bessarabian town I set foot in was Otaci, which brought back bitter memories of the atrocities committed there. The local population had not only robbed, beaten, and shot the local Jews but had also committed crimes against the tens of thousands of transients who made their way through Otaci on the way to Transnistria in 1941. I doubt if any of us could ever forget Otaci.

It took me four or five days to reach Czernowitz, in a series of short rides with military trucks. The soldiers supplied me with food and boosted my morale. Once I reached Czernowitz, I was let off at the railway station, where military personnel and civilians mingled. As I walked among them, I was surprised to hear a couple of well-dressed civilians speaking Yiddish. "When did you come back from Transnistria?" I asked them.

"We were never in Transnistria," one of them replied. "Thanks to the Queen of Romania and the mayor of Czernowitz, we were saved at the last minute in 1941. Their intervention stopped the last transport of about 12,000 Jews from being expelled to Transnistria."

"I just returned," I said, "and I'm anxious to find out if a group of orphans from Transnistria came to Czernowitz in the fall of 1943."

"We've never heard about them, but we'll take you to a man who's involved in Jewish affairs and might know."

This man told me that he had heard about the orphans but none of them had come to Czernowitz. They were all sent to Old Romania (the provinces in Romania from which the Jews had not been expelled and had been allowed to remain at home during the war). I spent the night with one of these men.

The next day, I hitchhiked on a military truck to Storojinet, the city where I was born. It was about twenty kilometres away. As we reached the top of the hill and started to descend into the city, scenes from the day we were force-marched up this hill came back to me. A sudden shiver gripped my body, and I began to sob. With no other place to go, I had returned to Storojinet in desperate need of finding some close relatives. I was so alone I had to latch onto someone to be able to identify with my roots. I had no identification papers, not even a birthmark; the only proof that I was Jewish was the fact that I had been circumcised.

The military truck let me off in the centre of the city. The beautiful buildings that I remembered lining the main street were all burned-out shells. Only some walls sticking up into the air were visible. The once-clean sidewalks were cluttered with debris. Few people were walking around. I looked for a familiar face but did not see any. I did not know what to do or where to go. I felt lost in the small city where I had lived before my family moved to Berhomet. I used to love to walk with my friends on the sidewalks and in the parks. Our favourite ice cream and chocolate store was razed to the ground. Everything seemed strange to me now. I went to see the house in which we had lived; only some walls were left. It was not a pleasant homecoming; there was no one awaiting me. I felt uncomfortable going to our former Christian neighbours to ask if I could stay with them for a while. I did not want to go through the agony of explaining what had happened to my family. As evening progressed, the streets became deserted except for military traffic. It was

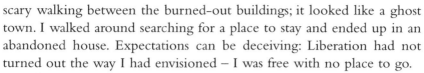

scary walking between the burned-out buildings; it looked like a ghost town. I walked around searching for a place to stay and ended up in an abandoned house. Expectations can be deceiving: Liberation had not turned out the way I had envisioned – I was free with no place to go.

The next morning, I walked along Panca Street, the road that would lead me back to Berhomet. A few kilometres out of the city, I was stopped by a Russian patrol and asked where I was going. Not satisfied with my answer and having no identification, one of the soldiers told me to get into the jeep. They took me to their commanding officer who interrogated me. He had no idea what I was talking about when I mentioned Transnistria. After a short conversation on the telephone, he told me I could not go home to Berhomet. The area to which I was heading was part of the front line, and I would have to turn back.

I walked around Storojinet and recognized a few Gentiles, but I avoided them. I was so resentful that I had no inclination to engage them in conversation, even to find out if any Jews had returned. I finally recognized a young couple as being survivors by their appearance and dress. They said they had come from Transnistria and were also on their way to their home town before being turned back by soldiers for the same reason I was. "We're living in an abandoned house on the Neue Weld Gasse," the man said. "Come stay with us. There are several other survivors living on that street." Many Jews had lived on that street before the war.

None of us had any money to buy food. "I have tobacco leaves," I said. "I'll try to barter some for food." I went to the market and discovered that it was a much sought-after commodity. For a few leaves I was able to get good value from the farmers who came to the city to sell their produce. I sold some of the tobacco for rubles, the currency used in the USSR, and the remainder I kept to trade for food.

Within days, Jews originally from Storojinet and surrounding towns and villages started to trickle back from Transnistria. Those from the surrounding areas had no desire to go back home and resettle there because very few Jews from their home towns had survived. Some had been massacred in pogroms at the outbreak of the war. Instead, they found shelter, several families together, in abandoned houses containing only pieces of old or broken furniture. We had great difficulty adjusting, both emotionally and financially, to this new life, which had no resemblance to the life we had left behind. Not only did we not get any help rebuilding our lives or finding work; we didn't even get any sympathy. Many people were simply surprised to see us alive. One day I bumped into a distant

relative, Sammy Schauber, an electrical engineer who managed the station supplying electricity to Storojinet. I believe that he was one of the few Jews allowed to remain in Storojinet during the war.

My daily routine was to walk the streets searching for relatives and asking returning survivors about the orphans who were sent to Old Romania in late 1943. One told me they had heard that the orphans were split up and sent to different cities. I went to ask the recently established Soviet civilian administration for permission to go to Old Romania to look for Avrum. I was told that the war was still raging and the area I intended to go to was not yet conquered.

The couple with whom I was staying got jobs with the new administration and received work permits. This was very important because Russian soldiers were grabbing young men without permits and sending them to Russia to work in the coal mines in Donbass or recruiting them into the army. One night, there was a knock on our door and a couple of soldiers walked in and asked to see permits. The couple showed theirs. "Who's sleeping under the table?" one of the soldiers asked.

"A young kid," the man said, and the soldiers left. Men who did not have permits were now hiding from these night raids.

The Sussmann family had also arrived in Storojinet and found shelter on the Neue Weld Gasse. The house was shared by two other families. Each family occupied one large room and shared the same kitchen. Marcus invited me to stay with them. All five of us slept in the same room; Marcus and I shared a bed. Shortly after I moved in, soldiers awoke us during the night and asked Marcus and me for our work permits. Not having any, and ignoring my age, they took us to the city centre and placed us in the courtyard of a bombed-out building. People kept arriving; by morning, there must have been several hundred of us. Marcus and I paced around, trying to figure out a way to escape. We made our way to a pile of debris and hid, waiting for an opportunity to elude the sentry and make our getaway. Meanwhile, Clara had come to see what had happened to us and hid behind a pillar. She spotted us and waved her hand, giving us the all-clear signal. We quickly escaped and made our way back home. That night we slept in the attic.

The next morning, I went to see Sammy Schauber at the electric station, hoping he might get me a work permit. He gave me a job going house to house, checking the number of light bulbs and telling the people that it was against the law to use more than one small light bulb per room. Even though I now had a permit, I was afraid to go back to the Sussmann's and slept at the station. The noise from the generator was deafening, but at least I felt safe.

After a few weeks, Sammy told me that a Russian officer was recruiting boys under the age of seventeen to send to a military school in Czernowitz to be trained as sappers. Marcus and I registered. We were given permits and told to assemble in a few days for our trip to Czernowitz. The ten who showed up included two other survivors whom I had known before the war, Isiu Schneider and Paul Dermer. We made our way to Czernowitz where we reported to a Russian major. He took us to a hotel that was occupied mainly by military personnel. There we met about thirty other boys from different areas in Bukovina and Bessarabia who were also going to be trained.

AT WORK IN THE MINEFIELDS

The next day, we were assembled in a column and marched to a class-room. There, we were addressed by a Russian officer who told us the reason we had been brought there was to learn how to remove land-mines. This would allow the seasoned sappers to remain with their units and continue fighting the German army. Once we had finished the course, our responsibility would be to remove the thousands of land-mines that had been planted in the countryside by both the Germans and Russians.

We had two officers as teachers, a captain and a lieutenant. In our first class, we were drilled and taught a Russian military song to sing while we marched to school and back. Isiu was picked to be the lead singer. The real education began the second day. We learned how explo-sives were made and what mechanism it would take to blow them up. They showed us the different types of landmines, both foot and vehicle mines, that were used by the Soviet and German armies. We had to draw and learn the name of each type of mine and its component parts and understand the function of each part. Some trigger mechanisms were very tricky, especially the German ones. Compared to the more sophis-ticated German mines, the Russian ones were relatively simple. Most of their mines were enclosed in wooden and other non-metal casings and their trigger mechanisms were less complex. They were, however, just as effective. In fact, since only the mechanism, a very small component of the mine, was metal, they were more difficult to detect. The most sophis-ticated mechanism was the one used in the German tripwire foot-mine. When the wire was tripped, the mine would jump about a metre into the air and then explode, sending shrapnel in all directions. They showed us how to defuse mines and how to deal with booby-trapped mines. We were taken out of the city to get experience and the feel of igniting det-onators and blowing up 100-gram sticks of dynamite. We also learned how to use mine detectors.

After about six weeks of long hours in the classroom and studying late into the night, we finally made it to the exams. The following day, we assembled in the classroom for the last time and were given our certificates.

The captain who had taught us called me to his office and told me that I had finished at the top of the class and would be the only one to be given a rank and receive a salary. I was proud of my accomplishment and regained the confidence I had lost when I was rejected by the Red Army. On my return to Storojinet, I was to report to Captain Zubkov, whose command I would be under. Because I was too small to fit into the standard uniforms, he gave me a permit to go to the local military depot to get fabric for a coat and two military uniforms and leather for a pair of boots.

Upon my return to Storojinet, I contacted Captain Zubkov. He had a regional map on the wall of his office and pointed out the villages from which the populations had been evacuated. "Before the civilians can return, the mines have to be removed," he said. "There's a group of young recruits waiting to be trained. You'll have to teach them how to defuse and remove mines before we can move out to the minefields." The other nine boys from our area who had trained with me were to work alongside the new recruits.

After the training was completed, I finally was able to make a day-trip to Berhomet, the town from which we had been forced in 1941. As I came close to our home, I recognized former Gentile neighbours sitting in their front yards chatting or tending to their flowers. Their lifestyle had not changed; it was just as I remembered it before the war. They ignored me – I don't think I was recognized, dressed as I was in a military uniform. Kids were playing on the same grounds where my friends and I used to play; some of the Gentile kids I saw that day had been in my class in school and had played with me before the war. Their natural childish instincts were still with them. To me, it seemed that childhood had passed ages ago. A neighbour's vicious German shepherd, which I'd named Hitler and which had always scared me, was still on a chain and barking just as loudly.

When I reached the house, I paused for a while. It appeared to be inhabited because the broken windows had been replaced. I opened the gate and walked into the yard, slowly making my way to the entrance. I did not know what to expect. I knocked on the door, but there was no answer. I opened it and walked in. Dead silence greeted me. My body was gripped with emptiness, and I froze. It seemed as if it had been occupied and the residents had left in a hurry. The odd piece of furniture remained, and there was clutter all around. As I started to tour the house, scenes from my life there began to flash in my mind, especially when I entered the kitchen. In the place of the aromas that had always emanated from there when I came home from school was only stale, hot air. Almost everything had been removed. Only through my imagination was I able to replace the furniture to fill the empty spaces. I visualized the table next to the window where we had each had our special place. Memories of the life my family had shared around that table came flooding back – playing games, doing homework, meal times, minor arguments among us children, telling our parents what we had done in school, and sometimes all of us talking at the same time. There was never a quiet moment in the kitchen. Now through the silence I could hear the voices and the laughter: a portrait of a happy family frozen in time. My eyes started to tear, especially when I saw King Michael's picture hanging on the wall where my parents' wedding picture used to hang. I took it down and smashed it to pieces. I was too upset to hang around or stop to ask the neighbours who had lived there. Returning to the place that had held happy memories filled me with bitterness. I regretted my trip and never returned to Berhomet after that.

The following day, Captain Zubkov brought Sergeant Lionka, who had earned decorations for bravery as a sapper fighting against the Germans, with us on our first mission in order to oversee our work. As we arrived at the village where we were to begin, silence greeted us. It looked peaceful. The fruit trees, with tall weeds all around, were loaded with apples, plums, and pears just begging to be picked. My favourite fruit, cherries, were dried up but still hanging on the branches. It was all very tempting, but we had been warned not to go off the road. We had been told repeatedly to use extreme caution, as a sapper cannot afford to make a mistake. Carefully, watching out for booby-traps, we made our way into the empty homes where we would live until the village and surrounding area had been cleared of mines. We would then move on to another village.

During the first week, we continued to be supervised by both the captain and the sergeant. The practical work was much more dangerous than the fun we had had blowing up 100-gram sticks of dynamite during training. Here, we were involved in a deadly game: men against mines; any wrong move could kill. My aim was to work slowly with casualty-free results. The tall weeds that had grown unhindered for months in the open fields were cleared by setting fire to them to allow us a clear view of the terrain. The heat caused some mines to blow up. The biggest problem we encountered was when the villages themselves were mined and booby-trapped and the tall weeds surrounding homes could not be burned away.

A fatal tragedy occurred in one of these villages. Sergeant Lionka, who had come back to see how we were progressing, stepped on a foot-mine and was killed. We were all shaken, realizing that these were not toys we were playing with; they could kill even the most experienced and decorated expert. He was taken to Storojinet and was given a hero's burial in the city park where other Russian military men lay buried.

Our mission was to investigate the whole territory. We had a scouting group to locate uncharted minefields who walked on roads and surveyed each area. Dead animals were frequently an indication of mines. River banks were always suspicious. Returning farmers sometimes informed us of minefields they had seen planted. Once minefields were discovered, red-flagged posts were stuck into the ground around them. Another group would set fires to clear the area of growth before they walked in with mine detectors and special steel-tipped sticks to probe the ground, looking for mines. After probing new terrain and locating minefields, we always removed the foot-mines first. Mines were usually set in a pattern. After the initial mines were removed, the pattern was revealed. Once the mines were defused by removing the mechanisms that induce a mine to explode when triggered, they were collected and put in a pile for the military to haul away. Mines that required any degree of force to be removed were left and blown up on the spot.

One reason clearing minefields was so dangerous was that one could not be trained on the job as in other professions except with mines that have been disarmed. Very few sappers survive their first mistake. While in the minefields, I did not think much about the danger. Even though I knew the job well, I always concentrated on safety. I approached each mine as if it were the first one. Overconfidence could kill.

We had another enemy to deal with, the Banderovczs (an anti-communist organization) who were hiding in the forest and randomly attacking Russian civilian authorities and isolated soldiers who were easy targets. I had to report the site of our work to the NKVD (police) or to the military authority each time we moved to another location so that they would know that explosions in the area came from our group and not from the Banderovczs.

Obtaining food was not a problem. The empty houses had basic supplies, and we did our own cooking. We took flour to a nearby village that was free of mines and had someone there bake bread for us. We requisitioned animals for slaughter from farmers who were paid by the government at a later date. If a deer was spotted, it was shot.

Evenings were spent in rooms lit by kerosene lamps, reviewing problems that we had encountered that day and planning the next day's work. To enliven the group, Isiu always started with a song, and we all joined in. Occasionally, Marcus, Isiu, and I would spend part of the evening outside, talking about subjects unrelated to work.

We moved from village to village, staying in empty houses. Once an area had been cleared of mines, I went to Storojinet to report our progress to Captain Zubkov. He informed the authorities, and the local residents were then allowed to return. On several occasions, we were surprised when Zubkov and another officer from the regular army, along with army sappers, came to check the areas which I had reported to be free of mines. Captain Zubkov was very pleased with my work and promised to help me get papers to allow me to go to Old Romania to search for Avrum once winter set in.

On one of my trips to Storojinet, I arrived late at night and noticed candles burning in Jewish homes on Neue Weld Gasse. I did not know the occasion until I walked into the Sussmann residence. It was Yom Kippur eve, the holiest of Jewish holidays, a time when families are always together. At the conclusion of services and after the traditional lengthy fast the following day, I walked out of the synagogue, which had miraculously escaped destruction, and experienced the saddest day since liberation. I realized again how alone I was and how much I missed my family. I visualized our whole family walking home after services to a festive dinner and a room filled with vibrancy as we children, dressed in our new clothes, ran around with joy. I could not hold back my tears and burst out crying. I stayed behind in the darkness, sitting on the synagogue steps, crying my heart out late into the night before returning to the Sussmann's. Family bonds meant everything to me, especially at holiday times when loneliness is magnified.

Every time I returned to the city, I walked the streets in hopes that maybe I would spot some of my relatives. One day I was lucky and ran into cousins of mine, Abrascha Wecksler and his sister Bertha. My joy was short-lived, however, upon learning that they were the only survivors of their large immediate family. They were not aware of any other survivors of our extended family. They lived with their uncle in a two-room house. It was another place I could visit. Bertha was a good cook and made a point of preparing dishes that I used to like before the war. I enjoyed being with them, reliving happy memories.

It was now fall, and most of those who had survived Transnistria had probably returned. My hopes of reuniting with my uncles, aunts, and other cousins were slowly fading until one day, on a return trip from the minefields, I was told by a neighbour that he had seen my Uncle Simon walking with friends. I became very excited and went searching for him. I knew where an old friend of his, Karl Weiner, was living. I ran over there and was overjoyed to see Uncle Simon. At the same time, I couldn't help but notice how he had aged.

To my surprise, cousin Regina was also there – Uncle Simon's niece, who was several years older than me. I was shocked to see what had happened to a beautiful, vibrant young girl. Perhaps one does not see oneself in the same light as one sees others; I probably didn't look any better in their eyes. Regina had witnessed the deaths of her parents and four siblings. I remembered how much I had enjoyed staying at their home in Berhomet during summer vacations. She introduced us to new games, always keeping us occupied. They had a swing in their backyard, and we kids would all take turns seeing who could fly higher. Regina was full of life; she had a beautiful voice and entertained us with her singing. Now she was broken-hearted and looked as if the whole joy of life had left her.

Uncle Simon told me about his experiences in Bershad, the camp where he lived during the war. His wife had perished, and now he was alone. Upon liberation in the spring of 1944, he was drafted into the Red Army but released in the fall due to illness. He then returned to Storojinet to search for relatives. He had always been very family-oriented and was devastated to hear about my family. After we sat down and talked, we realized how our extended family had been decimated. Some branches of the family had no survivors at all. Long gone were the happy times when members of our large family would gather for Sabbath and holidays, as well as for family functions.

However, Uncle Simon's presence lifted my spirits. He was the youngest of my mother's siblings and my favourite uncle. He always kibitzed around with me. A soccer player, he introduced me to the game at an early age. Whenever I was out of school, he took me along to local games. Once, when the team played out of town and travelled in the back of a canvas-covered truck, he took me along, hiding me under the bench. Uncle Simon was very sociable and had an out-going personality. He was a slender man who had belonged to an amateur theatre group that raised funds for charity. He travelled throughout the province as a fabric salesman. He was married and his wife was pregnant when the war started. Now that I had found him, I returned to Storojinet more often to spend time with him. He was concerned about my work as a sapper and was always happy to see me.

My dangerous work walking the minefields was drawing to a close as it got colder and snowflakes started to fall; it must have been sometime in November. Most of the minefields that we were aware of had been cleared, luckily with only one casualty. Captain Zubkov told me to dismiss all the boys. It was too dangerous to work in the cold, especially once the snow began. They were all happy to leave and return home in one piece. I stayed behind another day to make sure that the few minefields that had to be left until the spring were properly marked with red-flagged posts.

I was particularly concerned about a big field planted with foot-mines several miles from the village, next to a river. I approached the minefield very carefully, slowly walking along the riverbank. I saw a mine next to my foot, and without thinking I carelessly picked it up before defusing it. I was terrified to see that the safety pin was missing. It must have fallen out, and rust probably prevented the spring from being released and exploding the mine. I could not put it down or throw it away; any little movement would cause the mine to explode. I was paralysed. Luckily, I was standing at the edge of the riverbank. The only solution I could think of was to kneel down slowly, extend my arm over the edge of the steep bank, turn my head away and let the mine fall by its own gravity.

It exploded in the air, leaving me dazed and bleeding. The bank absorbed most of the force of the explosion and certainly saved my life. I came away bleeding from my left forefinger and from my right eye. I could only see with my left one and thought that I had lost an eye. I took a handkerchief and pressed it against the socket to stop the bleeding. I made my way back until I reached an area of the bank that was slightly sloped and descended to the river. I washed my wounds in the ice cold river and covered my eye again. I also wrapped something around my finger. I walked to the road and caught a ride back to town. The driver let me off at the makeshift medical unit. There were no doctors, only a nurse. I told her that I had lost my eye and needed medical attention. I removed my handkerchief, and she examined me. She picked up a piece of skin that hung from my eyebrow and suddenly I could see again. What a relief! The skin had been blocking my vision. After she stopped the bleeding, she bandaged my wounds and put my hand in a sling. I left for Storojinet to get further medical care.

Captain Zubkov recommended I go to Czernowitz and gave me the address of someone to contact. I was sent to a hospital where most of the patients were military. After the doctor examined me and I explained what happened, he told me that I was extremely lucky to be alive. About a week later, I was discharged and returned to Storojinet with a bandage around my head and eye and a hand in a sling. Uncle Simon became frightened when he first saw me as my appearance was worse than my condition. To this day, I have the scars to remind me of that accident.

I spoke to Zubkov to see if he had arranged yet for me to go to Old Romania. He was not successful but promised he would keep trying after New Year's when he returned from a long-awaited visit to his family near Moscow. I was extremely disappointed and went to see the government official in charge of the region. He was sympathetic but could give me only more promises. I became very upset and planned to cross the border illegally once my wounds healed. I had the necessary army documents that allowed me to be in the vicinity of the border to look for mines. And having worked fairly close to the border, I was familiar with the terrain and thought I would have no problem crossing it.

Uncle Simon was concerned about my plan and gave me all sorts of reasons to wait for permission instead. In the meantime, he got a job as a clerk in an army store where only military personnel with coupons could purchase items. Many of the goods found there were not available in government-controlled civilian stores. He had also found a better place to live and insisted I stay with him. Even though the Sussmann's treated me like one of their own and Marcus was like a brother to me, I could not refuse my favourite uncle. Abrascha and his sister Bertha lived nearby. Regina stayed with friends until the following year when she married a Jewish Russian major by the name of Arinovich and they moved to their own quarters. As far as we knew, these few people represented all of our once-large extended family that had survived the Transnistria Holocaust.

I had always been happy to see my relatives, and now, after the war, they became even more important to me. I considered them as my immediate family, and they treated me as such, giving me a feeling of belonging. Storojinet was a relatively small city, and we got together as often as we could to keep up our spirits. We already knew each other's sorrows and, not to subdue our get-togethers, tried to steer clear of topics that would lead to discussing the tragedies that had befallen us.

But as a human, I needed a release from my sorrows and found it more comfortable discussing them with my friends.

In a material sense, life for me was good. My injuries were healing well, my salary was adequate, and I had access to inexpensive good food in the military restaurant. I had gained a lot of weight and grew a few inches; I was now probably the appropriate weight for my height. But living in the small city in which I was born was difficult. I was surrounded by scenes from my carefree childhood and memories would always come back. The only thing that could brighten my life and relieve me of my feelings of guilt for letting Avrum go was to be reunited with him, but I took Uncle Simon's advice and waited for permission. When Zubkov returned from his leave, I approached him again and pleaded with him to secure a permit for me. He took me to see a friend of his, Major Velichka, who was in charge of the recruiting office in the region and carried a lot of influence. I came away from the meeting feeling optimistic. Some time later, he told Zubkov that he wanted to see me. He told me that the war was winding down and all he could do was to secure a permit for me once it was over. I kept track of the war by watching the big billboard that had been set up in the city. It had a map posted on it with big, red, movable pinheads showing the locations where the fighting was still going on. The pins were frequently moved, closer and closer to Berlin.

One day, Velichka asked Zubkov if he could spare me until the weather permitted me to go back to work in the minefields. He wanted me to give two-week courses to small groups of seventeen-year-old cadets. I was to familiarize them with the basics of mine removal before they were drafted into the regular army. Zubkov thought it was a good idea – I would maintain my skills and have something to do over the winter. I started the training, and, after having taught several groups, Zubkov told me that he had another job for me. He had been asked by the local civilian authority to break up the ice that jammed the two bridges spanning the Siret River in Storojinet. We blasted the ice with dynamite, allowing the river to flow freely.

Once the snow was gone, Zubkov told me to take the new trainees into the countryside to remove the remaining mines. The first stop we made was the minefield where I had nearly lost my life. The terrain was rugged, and the mines had deteriorated to such an extent during the winter that it was too risky to attempt to remove any of them. We blew them all up on the spot. After all the minefields had been cleared, the cadets were elated, and a few high-spirited ones, having removed some tank mines and hidden them, blew them up to celebrate the end with a bang. The boys were released and went back to their homes. I returned to Storojinet. Newspapers and loudspeakers on the streets were announcing the imminent defeat of Germany.

While walking through the park one day, the loudspeakers stopped playing music and an announcer came on. "Citizens," he said, "The war is over." Who could forget that moment? It was May 8, 1945.

Valichka's promise to get me a permit to go to Old Romania turned out to be nothing more than a promise, or perhaps he really was not able to secure one. But he said he had some good news for me: he had made arrangements to send me to a military officer school. I refused, giving the excuse that I did not want to be separated from my uncle and cousins, the only family I had left. I would now have to revert to my old plan of making my way into Old Romania illegally.

For the survivors, life in Storojinet took on some semblance of normalcy. They managed to find jobs in state-controlled operations. Everybody found shelter in former Jewish homes, most of it inadequate but good enough to call home and to be able to get together in the evening with new and old friends. There was no shortage of topics common to all of us to discuss. The Jewish community was small compared to the pre-war population, even though all the Jews from surrounding towns and villages now lived in the city. Young people got married, and the rooms in which they lived in the daytime became the ballrooms in the evening, with one or two musicians providing entertainment.

People talked about the future, but with fewer expectations than before the war. We had to adjust to a communist system: there was no private enterprise allowed, and incentives were taken away. Communist propaganda was delivered by the barrel-full, whereas news from the free world was fed to us periodically by the teaspoon. For entertainment, good sports facilities were provided free to all. A large church was converted into a dance hall and a military band provided music twice a week. Young and old went to dance or just to listen.

Because of our disrupted lives, none of the teenagers knew how to dance. So a small group of us, both boys and girls, would gather in a home to learn how, accompanied by our own whistling or humming or occasionally by Marcus playing a fiddle. Once we'd learned, we were invited to a few weddings to liven up the evening. We danced and participated in the singing along with the other guests. An especially happy event was my cousin Bertha's wedding. She married a young man by the name of Chaim Tennenbaum. The wedding, which took place in her uncle's house, was overflowing with guests. There was good food and vibrant music for dancing. I was in charge of dispensing beer from a big barrel and was told the next day that my eyes revealed I had had my fill.

One day in the military restaurant, I was given advance information by an official that a distillery was going to be opened and needed empty bottles. They were going to exchange one bottle of vodka for five empties, half-litres and litres. I asked Zubkov for my two weeks' leave, which he granted. I searched abandoned houses, including attics and basements, and bought some bottles from people in their homes. I must have collected more than 250 bottles. After the plant was opened, I exchanged the bottles for vodka and sold it. By then, I had my escape route planned and told Uncle Simon that I had made up my mind to leave for Old Romania. He begged me to delay my departure.

What stopped me from leaving was the sudden appearance of another uncle of mine who we thought had perished along with his wife in Transnistria. It was Uncle Schlomcu, Simon's older brother, who was liberated in Kopygorod by the Red Army in the spring of 1944 and was immediately drafted into the army. His wife Betty had returned to their home in Czernowitz. After a short training period, Schlomcu was sent to the front to fight the Germans. Upon his release from the army, he stopped in Czernowitz for a few days to be with Betty and then came to Storojinet to look for surviving members of his family.

It was a happy and unexpected reunion, but a great shock for him. He had had no idea of the extent of our family's losses. He was still dressed in his uniform and appeared relatively unchanged, except for his thinning hair that had turned grey. As a soldier, he was adequately nourished and regained the weight he had lost. Unlike Uncle Simon, Schlomcu was a reserved, quiet person. He was not interested in sports but in politics. Whenever he came to visit us in the old days, he'd always discuss the political situation with my dad. A neat dresser, he liked to socialize and had a dry sense of humour. He was a heavy smoker and, by accident, I once saw him smoking on the Sabbath in a secluded spot outdoors. His first reaction was to tell me not to tell my grandmother; he bribed me with money for a chocolate bar. After that, I made a point of hanging around him whenever he visited us on Saturdays.

Uncle Schlomcu told us about rumours circulating in Czernowitz that all the Jews from Bukovina and Bessarabia would be allowed to leave for Old Romania. He returned to Czernowitz and, shortly after, registered. He was allowed to leave at the end of 1945 and settled in Timisoara, a city in Transylvania.

In Storojinet, we anxiously awaited the opportunity to register. Meanwhile, my training as a sapper seemed applicable to different types of dangerous work, and I was assigned to another job. I was responsible for using dynamite to break burned-out tanks into pieces small enough to be loaded onto trucks or horse-drawn wagons and hauled away to a smelting foundry.

Finally, the news we were all awaiting reached us. Any survivor who wanted to leave could register. Some people who registered were fired and looked upon as enemies of the state. People with good jobs delayed registering for as long as possible to remain on the payroll. Others were afraid they might lose their jobs and then emigration would be halted. In the end, with few exceptions, all registered. Cousin Regina was refused on the grounds that her husband was born in Russia and was a major in the Soviet army.

One day in late fall when Zubkov returned from Czernowitz, he brought me material for a winter coat and two uniforms and leather for boots. He had been told to put in a request for medals to give to the sappers who had done outstanding work. He asked me how many I would recommend; I told him six. I hesitated to go to a tailor as I planned to register at a later date and was afraid I might be viewed as having taken advantage of the state and be punished. I delayed going until one day when Zubkov told me to make sure my new uniform was ready as I was to be decorated with a medal for the outstanding work I had done. He also requested the names of the six sappers whom I had recommended. He wanted to inform them about their medals and the date they were to present themselves to receive them. Among the sappers who received medals were Marcus and Isiu Schneider.

The year 1945 was drawing to a close, and I was afraid that, if I did not register, I might lose the opportunity to leave the country legally. I told Zubkov that I was going to register to look for Avrum. He allowed me to continue with my work and kept me on the payroll.

We started hearing rumours that everybody who had registered would soon be able to leave. These rumours persisted for weeks. We were finally notified and given documents allowing us to go. Everybody had to make their own arrangements to get to Siret, a border city used as a crossing point. Some people got together and hired horse-drawn wagons; others bribed state-employed truck drivers. Before crossing the border, we were searched by Soviet soldiers for foreign currency and Russian gold coins. If any were found, they were confiscated. Two years after liberation, we were finally on the move again – but this time with less pain. We had nothing to leave behind except bad memories. As soon as I crossed into Old Romania, I came face to face with one of those bad memories, the Romanian border police. As they greeted us, I got the shivers. I saw the same Nazi faces in different uniforms.

But I knew my stay in Romania would be brief. Before I left Storojinet, I had one goal in mind: to find Avrum and make my way to Palestine. Some of the people had a planned destination, and others just followed along. Uncle Simon planned to go to Timisoara where his brother Schlomcu had settled.

We remained in Siret for a few days until transportation could be arranged. During this time, I bumped into Isiu Schneider and gave him my uncle's address in Timisoara so he could keep in touch with me. Our plan was to make our way as soon as possible to a country where a Jew had the right to live in peace – and that was not Romania, but Palestine.

For a sum of money, part of which went for bribery, Uncle Simon and Karl Weiner arranged with the railway station manager to get a boxcar hooked up to a freight train with a bill of lading for Timisoara. The Sussmann family and other friends occupied the car. It was a slow train, which frequently stopped in towns, sidelined for hours at a time. We used the facilities in the railway stations and bought food whenever we had the opportunity. Once we reached the city of Ploiesti, our boxcar was unhooked and was sidelined for several days. We had to resort to bribery again so that we were finally hooked up to a fast train. Our trip to Timisoara, which normally would have taken less than two days took almost two weeks.

SPRING 1946

We all found shelter in Timisoara. I stayed with Uncle Simon and several of his friends under one roof. Uncle Schlomcu and Aunt Betty lived with her brother and his wife. The Sussmann family found shelter about ten blocks from us. At the first opportunity, I went to see a member of the local Jewish community to ask if he could help me locate Avrum. He promised that he would try, and I gave him Uncle Schlomcu's address.

Several days after our arrival, Uncle Simon and his friends were offered short-term jobs baking matzos for Passover. I went along, hoping I could also work there. The pay we received was enough to buy food. On the way to work, the Russian uniform I wore was both a help and a hindrance. I was able to move about freely without being harassed by the Romanian police but had to be on the lookout for the Russian military patrols, in their red armbands, who were checking all the Russian soldiers for passes. Having registered to leave the Soviet Union, I no longer had the legal right to wear the Russian uniform; I would have been arrested if caught. I was impatient and went again to inquire about Avrum. The man was unable to find out anything and encouraged me to go to Bucharest.

A couple of weeks after our arrival, I was at Uncle Schlomcu's for Passover lunch when the postman walked in with a postcard addressed to me; it was from Isiu Schneider. The contents were brief: "I am leaving for Bucharest. The address where you will find me is Radu Vodu #7. See you soon." Uncle Schlomcu, who had become very religious after having his life spared during the Holocaust, had not yet returned from services at the synagogue. I told Uncle Simon that I was going to the railway station to find out what time the train was leaving for Bucharest. He thought I was crazy making such a rash decision and came along with me, trying to convince me not to leave. I had seven hours until the train left. On the way back, I stopped at the Sussmann's to say good-bye and ask Marcus if he wanted to come along. He was ready to go, but his family, especially his mother, was against his leaving. Marcus accompanied me to Uncle Schlomcu's. Both uncles tried to persuade me to change my mind, but finally realized that I was determined to leave.

"What are your plans?" Uncle Simon asked. "How are you going to cross all the borders without any documents? What about money? How are you going to manage?"

The truth was that I had no plan – I just wanted to get out of Europe and make my way to Palestine by any means, legally or illegally. The only things I had in my favour were my age, chutzpah, and determination. All my belongings could fit in a briefcase. I saw no future for me there, and the only things of importance that I would leave behind were the remains of my dear family.

The clock kept on ticking – it was time to go and pack. We all went back to Uncle Simon's place. I grabbed my empty rucksack, put in one military uniform, a few pairs of socks, underwear, and two shirts that Uncle Simon gave me. My coat did not fit, so I carried it. Uncle Schlomcu gave me some Romanian currency, which he could ill afford to spare; I gave most of it back. Most of the money I had made selling vodka was used to help Uncle Simon get medicine. He had developed a painful stomach condition in Transnistria, and the only way we were able to get the prescribed medicine was to bribe the pharmacist. My remaining rubles were traded on the black market for ten American dollars, which I had smuggled across the border. Uncle Simon bought the train ticket and insisted that I take part of the money that he had smuggled across. I took five dollars.

They all accompanied me to the train. I did not want to stay on the platform longer than I had to because we could see the Russian soldiers in their red armbands patrolling. After we hugged each other, I stepped onto the car. I sat next to the window, and we just looked at each other as the tears started to appear once again. This time, it was I who was responsible for the separation, the cause of their distress. It was a sad moment for me, but I never doubted for even a second that I had made the right decision.

Passengers kept boarding the train, but, seeing me dressed in a Russian uniform, bypassed the empty seats across from me. I sat alone until a Russian officer stepped into the car, taking one of the seats. I immediately reached for my handkerchief and pressed it against my jaw, feigning a toothache. I wanted to avoid any conversation with him that might expose my masquerade. He started talking to me, and I just nodded and mumbled. My prompt reaction probably saved me from being arrested. Fortunately, he got off at a military base about an hour out of Timisoara. I started to think that posing as a Russian soldier was not such a good idea.

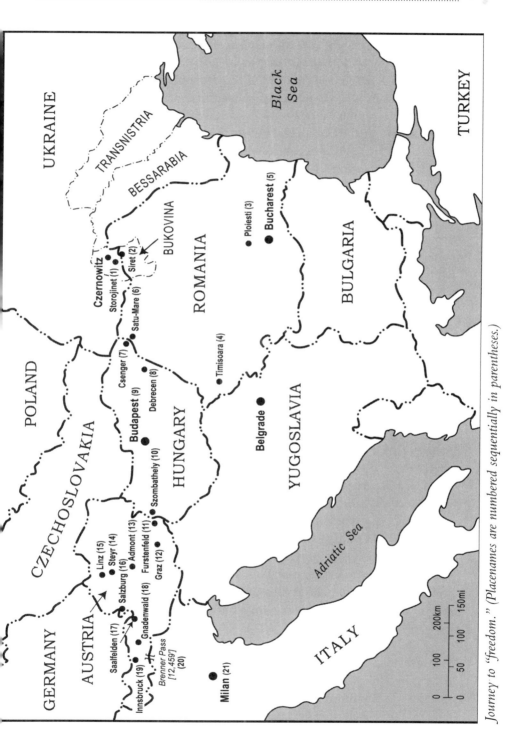

Journey to "freedom." (Placenames are numbered sequentially in parentheses.)

After an overnight ride, the train arrived in Bucharest. As it slowly pulled into the station, I was overwhelmed by the size of the city, wondering how I would ever find Isiu. Russian patrols were all over the platform. I hid between the masses of civilian passengers and got out of the station. Once on the street, I took the first available public transportation to get away — it did not matter where. After a short ride, I got off and asked pedestrians for directions. I must have walked for several hours until I found someone who knew the street I was looking for. I offered him money to guide me there, finally arriving at Radu Vodu #7 where Isiu awaited me. Radu Vodu #7 was a large private house that served as a transit point for Betar, one of the many Zionist organizations that helped Jews get out of communist-dominated countries into western countries. The process was done illegally through the use of bribery. Eventually, we were to go to Palestine.

Isiu and I had become close friends after the war. We had worked together in the minefields and spent many of our evenings together. He was a very sociable, lively person whose mind never seemed to rest; he always brought up interesting and stimulating topics to talk about. When we finally obtained our permits to leave Storojinet, we had arranged to be in touch with each other and make our way out of Europe together.

I had high hopes of finding Avrum in Bucharest. I was so convinced I would be successful that my mind skipped ahead. How would we react when we saw each other? How close would he appear to my mental image of him? How would I look to him? After a joyful reunion, we would make our way to Palestine together.

The next day, I asked the leader of the organization where I could inquire about Avrum; he told me whom to contact. They had no record of him but said that I had come to the right place. They would investigate and be in touch. I also left my uncle's address and walked away dejected, fighting my fear that something had happened to Avrum. It had been more than two years since our separation, and I had not been able to find out anything about him or his whereabouts. I did not want to give in to despair and tried to block out the unthinkable, continuing to live with hope.

I was to be among the next group to depart. Our group consisted of young males, many of whom were teenagers. The majority were originally from Bukovina and Bessarabia and had lived through the Nazi persecution in Transnistria. Our time was spent singing Hebrew songs, talking about our past, discussing our future, and listening to lectures.

Current events were of interest, particularly the British opposition to allowing homeless Jews who had barely escaped their graves to achieve their dream of reaching their homeland. I believed that only in Palestine could our roots take hold deep enough to be immune from the dreaded disease of anti-Semitism; only there could we live like our former Gentile neighbours who were never persecuted or uprooted regardless of the political party in power.

While the group was anxious to leave, I was still in doubt. I again went to inquire about Avrum, but they had nothing new to tell me. I told them what I had planned and asked them for advice. "If you have the opportunity to leave, you should," they said. I sensed they knew that they would not be able to locate Avrum.

The group was ready to move at a moment's notice. But discouraging news caught us by surprise: all activities related to departure had to be halted for the time being. The leader of the organization had no idea how long it would take to open the illegal channels again; we were to prepare for a lengthy wait. We were all frustrated.

During our stay, however, Isiu and I made many new friends, among them Max Reger from Vatra Dornei, southern Bukovina and Sasha Balaban and his friend Mischa Kaufman from Noua Sulita, Bessarabia. The five of us were compatible and spent a lot of time together. We had similar aspirations, sharing the same ideology and outlook on life. We were determined to leave, so instead of waiting, decided to make it on our own. We started to make plans. Sasha told us that before leaving Bessarabia he had managed to obtain a *komandirovka* – a transit pass allowing soldiers to travel to another unit – from his employer, a Russian officer. It had an official stamp on it and space for names and dates to be filled in. He had foreseen the need for such a document to assist him and his friend in their flight out of Romania.

We talked to the leader of the organization, explained what we had in mind, and sought his advice. "It's not a good idea to go on your own at this time," he said. "Bribery helped before, but for some reason the Romanian border guards are now strictly enforcing the law by tightening the border to prevent the flow of illegal crossings. If caught, you'll be arrested and put on trial."

"We're willing to take our chances," one of us said, and asked him for the name of one of the border towns that had been used previously as a crossing point.

"Satu-Mare, a city in Transylvania," he said. "It's close to the

Hungarian border. From there, you'll have to cross the border illegally on foot and make it to Budapest on your own. In Budapest, you'll be taken care of by another Jewish organization."

We went to the railway station to inquire about departure times and the cost of tickets to Satu-Mare. They told us the fares for both first- and second-class accommodation. We returned to our residence to pool our resources; some of us had a few American dollars that had to be exchanged on the black market for Romanian currency. I had a difficult time exchanging my dollar bills. I was told that they were old bills no longer in circulation. They were considerably larger than the current ones. One man showed me the smaller bill and offered me half the value for mine. Not being familiar with American bills and being in need of immediate money, I accepted his offer. I also traded my Russian military coat for a used civilian jacket and some Romanian currency.

We managed to gather enough money to buy tickets, with some to spare. We decided to go first class to ensure that all five of us could be together in one compartment. Dressed in civilian clothes, we planned to travel as Russian soldiers on leave, returning to Budapest. Sasha filled in the *komandirovka,* showing Budapest as the destination and listing our names. He signed it, using the name of a fictitious Russian officer. With a Russian stamp on it, it looked authentic. We thought the *komandirovka* would serve to get us to Satu-Mare in the event we were checked by Romanian police. But without supplementary documents to verify its authenticity, it was inadequate to allow us to remain on the train and go through passport inspection by the Hungarian border guards or by Russian soldiers who might be present. We planned to get off the train at Satu-Mare and cross the border into Hungary on foot during the night.

JOURNEY TO "FREEDOM"

After we were satisfied with our detailed plan, we made our way to the railway station. We were relieved the moment we felt the first jolt of the train as it began to pull out. Happiness was reflected in our faces. We were on the first leg of a long and unpredictable journey, but this time it was a journey of our own free will. We were determined to shape our own destiny. Out of joy we started to sing – not in Hebrew but in Russian, hoping to conceal our identity from Romanian police or secret service. After all, we were not entirely free yet and travelled under false pretences. The singing attracted a Russian officer who happened to walk by our compartment. He opened the door and asked if he could join us. We invited him in and he took the empty seat. His uniform, decorated with a chest full of medals, aided our charade. Following a visit with his family in Russia, he was returning to his unit stationed in Hungary. Without thinking, Sasha told him that we were on our way to Budapest to report for work. The officer was happy to hear that we would continue our trip together. He joined us in singing and, after a while, left to get a bottle of vodka from his belongings to toast our friendship.

In his absence, we had to make a quick decision – how to break loose from him in Satu-Mare where we had to get off the train. Being a border town, Satu-Mare would mean a lengthy stop before crossing into Hungary. We decided that Sasha would invite the officer for a drink at the bar in the railway station. Once they were gone, the four of us would take our rucksacks, including Sasha's, get off the train, and leave the station. While in the bar, Sasha would excuse himself from the officer and go to the washroom. From there, he would leave the station and join us.

As the train approached Satu-Mare, we became uneasy. None of us had ever been there, and we had no idea what to expect or how to proceed from there. Once the train stopped and passengers started to leave, we waited impatiently for the officer and Sasha to get off the train. After they left, we grabbed the rucksacks, quickly walked a short distance away from the station, and looked out for Sasha.

People walked past us without paying any attention. While waiting, we stopped a young Orthodox Jewish man, recognized by his long

side-curls, and asked his advice about crossing the border. He told us
he could help and invited us to stay at his place overnight. By then,
Sasha had joined us, and we all went home with the man. In the morning, he was going to contact someone who was familiar with the
border and, for a fee, took people by horse and wagon to a remote
crossing where there were no guards.

After contacting the man the next day, our host came back with
some disappointing news. The driver had advised him that we should
wait in Satu-Mare for several days before taking our chances at crossing the border. For some reason, the borders had been very tightly
patrolled during the past few weeks; his most recent attempts at taking
people to the border had been unsuccessful. Our host generously fed
us and let us stay at his place until our departure. He empathized with
us – he himself had lost part of his family in Auschwitz and, along
with his new bride, planned to make the same journey in the near
future. He was the first person we met who had been in Auschwitz.
When questioned about his experience, he was reluctant to talk about
the past.

A few days later, we met the driver after dark in the outskirts of
Satu-Mare and paid him in advance. After riding for a distance, he turned
off to a narrow dirt road. "Keep quiet," he said as he slowed the horse to
reduce the noise. "We're getting close to the border; I'll let you off soon."
We rode a bit farther, and he let us off. Pointing to lights in the distance,
he said, "That's Hungary," and told us how to bypass the town.

Walking on the road, we were surprised by two Romanian gendarmes who suddenly appeared out of nowhere and told us we were
under arrest for trying to leave Romania illegally. As they marched us to
the Romanian border crossing point, their attitude toward us reminded
me of Transnistria. I was once again under the threat of a Romanian gun,
but this time under different circumstances. My vision of freedom was
now so strong it suppressed my fear. I was a stateless person trying to
cross borders illegally, and yet I felt it was worth the risk to obtain my
goal. When we arrived, the gendarmes on duty told us that we would be
kept there until morning, then taken to the gendarme compound to be
interrogated by the officer in charge of the borders in that region. We lay
down on the grass and went to sleep.

In the morning, we were escorted to the compound. Upon our
arrival, one of the soldiers on duty took us to a room, and, as we entered,
I was surprised to see an Orthodox Jew and two attractive young women

sitting on the bare floor. "This is going to be your sleeping quarters until the officer in charge returns," the soldier said.

The man got up and started to argue with the soldier. "You have to put them in a separate room," he said. "I'm a rabbi and these are my daughters. It's against the Jewish religion to have an unmarried woman sleep in the same room with men." The soldier ignored his request and told us that we were allowed to walk outside as long as we stayed within the fence surrounding the compound.

Walking around, we found the compound kind of strange – everything was quiet, and there were only a few soldiers around. This gave us the idea to try to escape during the night. As we continued walking and surveying the surroundings, the rabbi and his daughters went to the soldier guarding the entrance and insisted that we be put in a different room. His being there turned out to be a lucky break for him and for us. A man with a horse and buggy drove by and noticed the rabbi. He stopped, came to the gate and spoke to the soldier on duty, who seemed to know him. He told us in Yiddish not to worry, he would get us out. Because it was the first of May, he could do nothing that day; the soldiers and officer in charge were on parade and would probably party all night. The next morning, he would speak to the officer in charge. The rabbi was relieved, but we were a bit skeptical and did not waver from our plan to escape.

The rabbi continued to be less concerned with his captivity than he was with his daughters having to sleep in the same room with us. He nagged us to persuade a soldier to put us in a different room, but our request was denied. At nightfall, as we all sat on the bare floor and waited for the right time to make our escape, we told the rabbi of our intentions. He thought we were foolish as we could be shot and suggested that we wait another day. We did not heed his advice. Around midnight, we no longer heard soldiers' footsteps in the corridor, and, with the windows kept open to allow fresh air in, everything seemed right for us to make our move. Max Reger volunteered to be the first to crawl out. He no sooner let himself down to the ground than two big German shepherds came running and barking. He barely had time to make it back through the window unscathed. We were caught by surprise; we had not seen any dogs around the compound. Two soldiers came running into the room to check on us. When everything appeared normal, they left.

The following morning, the compound came alive; soldiers were everywhere. One of the gendarmes who had caught us told us that we were going to be taken to jail and put on trial. Later that morning, the Jewish man came to visit and informed us that he had spoken to the officer in charge who was his friend and with whom he had business dealings.

"Everything is arranged," he said. "The rabbi and his daughters are coming back with me. You five will be released after a mock trial. You'll be called into the officer's office at sundown; the gendarmes who caught you will lay charges against you for trying to leave the country illegally. Your story will be that you were headed in the opposite direction, from Vienna, through Hungary to Bucharest. When questioned, speak only German." That was no problem as we were all familiar with the language.

As planned, we were taken to the officer's office at sundown. The officer was there, along with four or five soldiers and one of the gendarmes who caught us. The officer asked the gendarme why we had been brought to the compound. After the gendarme told him the reason, the officer blasted us in Romanian for committing a criminal act against the communist state. He told us that we would be transferred to the state police for punishment. He asked us if we had anything to say before we were taken away. Pretending not to understand what he said, we started speaking in German. One of the soldiers spoke German, and he was asked by the officer to interpret. The gendarme who caught us interrupted and told the officer that we spoke Romanian. He was ordered not to interfere. We told the interpreter that we were coming from Vienna and going to Bucharest. The officer said that it was illegal to cross without papers and became enraged and started cursing us. He told two of the soldiers to immediately take us to an obscure place on the border and make sure we cross back into Hungary. Infuriated, he burst out of the room.

We were escorted to the border and crossed into Hungary. While bypassing the nearby town of Csenger, we were caught again, this time by Hungarian police. It appeared as if they knew we were coming. They took us to the police station where the officer in charge told our captors to take us back to the Romanian border. While walking back, a man caught up with us. Isiu took a chance and spoke to him in Yiddish, asking for help. We continued walking and the man told us not to worry, the border crossing was closed from 8 p.m. to 8 a.m. and he would come to get us.

As promised, he came shortly after. The Hungarian border guards seemed to know him well. After chatting with them for a while, he took us back to his place. For his and our safety and due to the nature of his business, he put us up in the attic. He did not want to arouse suspicion amongst his Christian neighbours who frequently stopped by. By bribing the border guards, this man was able to smuggle goods across the borders. He knew the person who had rescued us from the gendarme compound the previous day. They both made their living the same way, assisting each other whenever the need arose. After the war, bribery was a way of life in communist countries.

It was extremely uncomfortable in the attic during the day due to the hot weather and high humidity. We sat around in our underwear, except after dark when the host told us we could come down the ladder, one at a time, to go outside to relieve ourselves. We were supplied with sufficient food and drank copious amounts of water to try and keep cool. It was difficult to hold back when nature called during the day. We could not find a suitable container until someone opened a chest containing Passover dishes and utensils. We hesitated, but had no choice. The empty wine bottles served our needs! Sasha, with his sense of humour, kept us in stitches.

After several days in Csenger, our host told us he had made arrangements with a truck driver who was going to Budapest. We were to meet him in a local cemetery that night and bring American money to pay him. We had very little money to scrape together until Max confessed to having hidden ten American dollars for just such an emergency. When it got dark, our host took us to the cemetery. On the way, Isiu spotted some large denomination Hungarian bills scattered on the ground and became excited, thinking they would help us on our journey. After we made it to the cemetery and hid among the headstones, a truck covered with a tarp arrived. Our host spoke to the driver, gave him the fifteen dollars we had managed to pool together and was told to tell us to remain quiet until we arrived in Budapest.

We all fell asleep and were awakened suddenly by the noise of a blow-out tire. While the driver was changing the tire, we peeked through the tarp and could see a well-lit area nearby. After the tire was changed, we passed in front of this area and saw a brightly lit archway indicating, in Russian, that this was the Debrecen military camp. We were fortunate that no one from the camp had bothered to come out to see why a truck had stopped so close to a military compound in the middle of the night.

Once we arrived in Budapest, the truck stopped at an intersection to let us off. As we jumped off and grabbed our rucksacks, a policeman must have noticed us. No sooner had we started to walk then he confronted us and spoke in Hungarian, a language none of us understood. We spoke to him in German, which he did not understand. He motioned us to follow him and we ended up at another police station. A police officer who spoke some German questioned us, wanting to know our names and where we came from. We told him we were from Vienna, and we all gave fake names, mine was Moishe Zichmich, which means, in Yiddish, "Look for me."

With an air of indifference, he spoke in Hungarian to a policeman and then told us to follow him. We were taken to a school housing Jewish refugees. The following day, the police came and showed the man in charge the names of five people they were looking for. The refugees were assembled, and one of the police called out our names. Nobody responded. When my name was called, everybody started to laugh. As none of us identified ourselves, they told us they were not looking for us; they were looking for the truck driver. They wanted to know where the driver had picked us up and where he was going after he let us off. They left without any information.

The school, Erzsebet Iskola, had been converted into a transit camp and housed many Jewish refugees from eastern Europe. They remained there until they could be smuggled across the border by the Bricha, a Jewish organization helping survivors reach western coastal countries from which they could sail to Palestine. Everything was done illegally. We were all taken care of and awaited our turn to be smuggled out. We made new friends with whom we had many unpleasant memories to share. I heard first-hand about Auschwitz and other camps where people were gassed and burned in crematoria. Even after everything I had been through, as a human I was horrified; my brain went numb. It was only after the war that I became aware of these atrocities. Similarly, few who had been in those camps had heard about Transnistria.

While waiting, Isiu wanted to share some of the fortune that he had found in Csenger. The five of us walked into a coffee house, anticipating some delicious pastry and coffee. We were enjoying ourselves in the nicely decorated gathering place, with its relaxed atmosphere, until the waiter brought us the menu. We could not read it but could see the zeros following the numbers. We burst out laughing and left in a hurry. Items were priced in the hundreds of thousands of pengo; the currency had become almost worthless due to rampant inflation.

Avrum was never far from my mind. Had I done the right thing leaving Bucharest? It put me out of range of people who may have had some connection with the orphans from Transnistria. Maybe they could have given me some leads to finding Avrum on my own.

After staying in Budapest for a couple of weeks, some of us were taken on a picnic hosted by the Budapest Betar organization. It was my first social outing since leaving Storojinet. One of the hostesses was a beautiful young girl by the name of Magda. Isiu spent a lot of time with her and, on parting, asked for her address.

Shortly after, the leader of the camp told us on short notice to get ready to leave. Our group of about sixty people, mostly young males, filled two trucks. We arrived at the border town of Szombathely during the night and were stopped by a Russian patrol. Not having any documents, we were taken to their headquarters. The officer in charge, who happened to be Jewish, told us not to be frightened; he asked if we could spare some money for a few bottles of vodka to give to the soldiers who had brought us in. Our leader gave him the money, and he let us go. After a short ride, we were let off on a back road and walked across the border into the British-controlled zone of Austria. (After the war, Austria was divided into four zones: British, American, French, and Russian.)

We continued walking until dawn when we were caught again – this time by British soldiers, who took us to their compound in Furstenfeld. After a long wait, an officer appeared and asked those who could speak English and German to identify themselves; they were to act as interpreters. After five or six people, including Max, identified themselves, they were told to leave the group and were taken away. It turned out that these individuals were taken to jail and interrogated.

The rest of us were taken by truck to Graz and placed in an overcrowded camp holding people of many different nationalities. Rumour had it that some of these people were Nazi murderers masquerading as refugees. We were all happy to see Max when he rejoined us a few days later and had a few laughs at his expense. "Let's hear some words of wisdom, Max. What did you learn in jail?" Sasha asked. Max, who was several years older than me, had surprised us when he indicated he could speak English. At first, he had seemed serious and always deep in thought, but his personality lightened up when he got to know us better.

After several more days, our group was sent by train to Admont, a town in the British-controlled zone. While waiting at the train station, I was impressed by the nurses, dressed in white with Red Cross armbands, tending to refugees with cuts and wounds. As I watched them, a nurse noticed an open wound on my arm; she offered to clean and bandage it free of charge. It was an unprecedented experience for me – having a stranger show concern for my health. Only a Holocaust survivor could fully appreciate the significance of such an act of kindness.

In Admont, we were taken to a large Austrian military base which had been converted into a Jewish refugee camp. The small town was surrounded by mountains and forests. The setting was beautiful and gave us the feeling of being in a resort. The camp was supported by the International Refugee Organization and supplemented with food and clothing from the American Jewish Joint Distribution Committee. Individuals were assigned to specific barracks housing people with the same political ideology. It was a well-thought-out plan that had a positive psychological effect on us. Although we were amongst total strangers, we felt at ease as soon as we walked into the barracks. Our political views were the same; even the songs we sang reflected our shared vision and hope for the future.

The five of us went to the barrack occupied by members of Betar, the Zionist organization, where we met Judith, the person in charge. She was a born leader with a strong conviction, based on historical events, that the only place for European Jews was in Palestine. Her mild manner and soft-spoken words were deceiving; she was a former partisan who had fought the Nazis in Lithuania during the war and had shown courage under fire. She made us feel like part of a family and asked us why we had picked that barrack. We told her that we had all participated in Betar before the war.

We were shown to a small room with only four military cots for the five of us. Having been together for about six weeks, our friendship became very close. None of us felt comfortable putting the odd man out; we brought another cot into the already crowded room. This was going to be our home until we left the camp, and we decided to make the best of the situation. There was frequent laughter emanating from our room. No matter in what situation we found ourselves, Sasha always saw humour in it and made us laugh. He had a perpetual smile on his face and enjoyed kibitzing around. The tallest among us with thick black wavy hair, he was easy-going and quite a character. Mischa, in contrast, was quiet, reserved and seldom smiled. Sasha and Mischa were long-time friends from before the war.

Sasha liked to play practical jokes on us, and one day the four of us decided to retaliate. We placed two raw eggs under his blanket and waited for him to go to bed. He must have suspected something and checked his bed before lying down. He removed the two eggs and, without any expression of surprise, casually made holes in the shells and sucked out the contents. He then politely thanked us. What a disappointment!

The majority of the people in our barrack were young single males from eastern Europe, and we all got along like a big family. We had a lot in common to talk about and the same goal for the future – to make it to Palestine. We frequently went together on morning outings to the nearby mountains, taking along our allotted breakfast of one quarter of a loaf of white bread and butter. Time was spent singing Hebrew songs and listening to speakers, one of whom was Tzemach. He was barely five feet tall, but his dynamic style of presentation and the topics he spoke on captured our attention. He brought us up to date with current events and filled us in with happenings against Jews during the war. He told us about a ship crammed with Jewish refugees from Europe that was turned back from the coast of Palestine by the British navy during the war and then sunk, presumably by German torpedoes. He also told about the sinking of a ship with many orphans on board that had left Romania for Palestine before the end of the war. Hearing of this particular tragedy made my blood surge and sent flashes through my mind. Avrum was in Romania at that time, and he could have been on that ship. It was hard to shake off my thoughts or alleviate my fears.

We were given adequate food, and anyone in the Betar barrack who wanted to earn extra calories in the form of sweets could participate in a work group two to three hours a day. We gathered inside the fence surrounding the camp and were told to dig a large rectangular hole about one-half metre deep. They did not tell us the purpose, and it became a guessing game. We spent more time fooling around than digging. After completion, we were told to refill the hole. It turned out to be a plan to keep us occupied and was repeated several times during our stay for those who wanted the extra sweets.

The Organization for Rehabilitation through Training (ORT), an international Jewish organization that helped survivors learn a trade, sponsored a variety of courses. I took the auto mechanics course and learned the basics of how a car engine operates. Some of us participated in various sports; I played on one of the camp's soccer teams. Others just hung around the camp, visited friends in other barracks, or wandered into town until one day when a serious incident occurred. Two boys from our barrack showed up late one night with swollen, bloodied faces, barely able to speak. They had gone into town the previous day and decided to spend the evening there. While returning to the camp, they walked past a house that had an apple tree with branches hanging over the sidewalk. They reached for some and were severely beaten by a number of young Austrians who were gathered in the yard. They were left bleeding, lying on the sidewalk. After struggling back to the camp, they told us what had happened.

Later that morning, a group of us, including one of the injured, returned to the house where the incident occurred. We wanted to show the beaten-up face of our friend to the occupants and warn them that we would no longer tolerate vicious attacks on Jews. While we stood on the sidewalk deciding how to proceed, two men walked out from the house, cursing and hollering at us to keep moving. They came toward us and, without provocation, started pushing us; a fight quickly erupted. Neighbours walked out of their homes and joined in. A young boy from the camp happened to be nearby and saw what was happening. He ran back to the camp and told them that a group of Austrians was beating us up.

We were outnumbered, and, as we retreated, we could see people from the camp running to our rescue. More local people joined in the fight, turning the small incident into an ugly riot, resulting in broken windows and cuts and bruises on both sides. The small contingent of four or five local police in their office were caught by surprise. They were overwhelmed by the sheer number of refugees entering their station. Carried away by the violence of the moment, we disarmed the police and locked them in their cells. Someone must have called the British military authority in a nearby city for assistance. The riot lasted for several hours until British soldiers on trucks arrived and chased us back to the camp. We were ordered to line up for inspection, but those with visible injuries for whom they were looking hid in the nearby forest. Following the inspection, and after hearing the barracks leader's version of what triggered the riot, the soldiers left. Those who required treatment went to the infirmary in the camp.

Having survived the Holocaust and made my way to the western countries, it was frustrating for me to linger in the camps and wait until the British rescinded their policy of restricting Jews from entering Palestine. So far, they had shown no signs of doing this; on the contrary, the Royal Navy was stopping ships on the high seas that carried Holocaust survivors on their way to Palestine. The ships were diverted to Cyprus under escort, and the refugees were interned in barbed-wire-enclosed camps guarded by British soldiers. The only crime that had been committed by those survivors was to dream of reaching their homeland and, with their bare hands, of rebuilding their shattered lives.

I must have been naïve to think that once I escaped from communist countries I would be a free man. How wrong I was! My perception of what it meant to be a "free man" in western countries was rapidly changing. I began to feel like an undesirable commodity being shifted from camp to camp and from country to country. We were kept in camps and treated as unproductive, stateless people living on hand-outs in countries where we were not wanted, particularly in Austria and Germany, where it was painful for us to even breathe the air.

Our pent-up bitterness became part of our baggage, and we tried to cope as best we could. For some, relief came when we joined one of the Jewish underground organizations that were recruiting young people who were willing to fight and die for their homeland. This gave us purpose and brought us hope. We had three choices: the Haganah, the Irgun Zvai Leumi, or the Stern Group, a small more militant offshoot of the Irgun. Of the three, the Haganah was the largest. It was established in Palestine after World War I as a defence force against unprovoked Arab attacks on Jews. The Haganah was under the control of the Mapai political party. Because the organization conformed to a policy of restraint and appeasement, it was tolerated by the British authorities. The Jewish Agency, which acted as a liaison to the British Mandatory Government on Palestine Jewry matters, believed that such a policy would lead to a favourable outcome.

I joined the Irgun Zvai Leumi, the fighting force of Betar. As a young boy, Betar had appealed to me for its social and sports activities. Now, I was in dire need of regaining my identity and having a home to go to. I felt the road to reaching my objective was through the Irgun. As I placed my hand on the bible to be sworn in as a member, I had a hard time keeping my eyes dry and my trembling hand steady. Scenes from the past flashed by, and both happiness and sadness gripped me as I repeated the words pledging my allegiance to the Irgun Zvai Leumi. The Irgun came into being in Palestine in the 1930s. Their goal, opposed by the Haganah, was to create a military force in which Jews would be trained and prepared to fight for their homeland. Their policy was to use political means when possible and force when necessary to oust the British from Palestine.

I was still young, but adventure was not what attracted me to the Irgun. Rather, I was attracted as a Holocaust survivor with a vision for the future. I had sharp memories of Hitler ranting at the top of his lungs about destroying the Jewish people and forcing us into ghettos in broad daylight. I also remembered how the world watched as we marched toward our death and only a few bothered to ask why. A total lack of concern for Jewish lives had kept us corralled within easy reach of the Nazis. I felt that England, as the custodian of Palestine, had a moral obligation to give us part of the desert where Moses and the Jews he had led out of bondage from Egypt survived for forty years. We, too, deserved the chance to survive in that same desert. But politics mixed with oil was a deadly concoction for European Jews.

As a survivor, I felt that I would have betrayed the spirit of the ancient Maccabeans if I did not join an organization whose philosophy was to stand up and fight for our own country. Nobody else had done the fighting for us in the past or would in the future, and, if we had to die to prevent another Holocaust, we would die for a cause and not on the heaps of ashes where millions of innocent and defenceless Jews had perished.

We were to train in secret as underground fighters while in Europe, and once we reached Palestine we would join the struggle there. The Irgun Zvai Leumi breathed new life into us and awoke our pride in belonging to a people with a long history of civilization. It gave us a sense of security and raised our morale. At last, we would be counted in the ranks of fighters; not just as numbers tattooed onto arms. My experience as a sapper was put to use, and I became an instructor, sharing my knowledge and skills with other members of the Irgun.

Sometime in August, our close-knit group started to break up when Mischa left for Colombia in South America. He had previously been in touch with his two brothers who had left Bessarabia before the war. They arranged for the necessary documents and transportation for him to join them. Shortly after, Sasha made his way illegally to join a relative in a transit camp in southern Italy.

As summer was drawing to an end, Isiu, his girlfriend Magda (with whom he had corresponded and who had joined us in Admont), Max, and I, along with a couple of new friends, decided to go to a camp in Linz, in the American zone, from where illegal movement to Italy was proceeding. Rumours about our leaving spread through our barrack and more people wanted to join our group. Judith, the person in charge, persuaded us to take them along, causing us to alter our plans for bypassing the British checkpoint into the American zone. The undertaking became a logistical nightmare. Instead of taking a difficult but secure route through rugged mountains that some of us were familiar with, we had to take an easier but riskier route to accommodate about twenty people, including two pregnant women.

Judith gave us a contact in Linz and assisted by making arrangements with a trucker to drop us just inside the British zone after nightfall. We had to be extremely quiet; the short path through the mountains leading back to the road was very close to the British checkpoint. In the event the train conductor checked tickets shortly after we boarded on the American side, we had bought tickets in Admont and punched holes through them to make it look as though we had actually been on the train and crossed the checkpoint legally. The pregnant women and those who had difficulty walking were told to wait for the train at the first station after the crossing. The remainder walked to the next station so as not to arouse suspicion in the small station.

The train was late, and the group at the first station panicked when an Austrian policeman approached them. He asked them where they were from and how they got there. Without realizing the consequences, a young boy of about twelve told him that the leader of the group was going to board at the next station. The policeman allowed them to board the train. When our second group reached the next station, we spread out, boarding the train by different cars. One of the men in our group went to look for the others already on the train. He was made aware of what had happened and came back to warn us to be on the lookout.

As we reached the next stop, which seemed to be a bigger station, daylight was breaking. I could see police on the platform entering the cars. I immediately left the car and jumped off on the opposite side of the platform. I wanted to run across the tracks into the nearby bush but was stopped by an oncoming train and was caught by a policeman. I was asked for identification and, not having any, was taken into the railway station and placed in a room guarded by a policeman. Two from our group plus one stranger were already there; shortly afterward, two more from our group were brought in. The six of us were taken to the police station where we were individually interrogated by an officer. I was asked to what organization I belonged, where I got the pistols and ammunition that were found on the train, and where I was taking them. My face expressed surprise, and I showed him my ticket that was bought in Admont. I told him I was on my way to the camp in Linz to get my teeth fixed. To gain his sympathy, I opened my mouth and revealed my chipped and broken teeth, a result of malnutrition in the concentration camps.

He ignored my plea and told me I would be put on trial for transporting arms illegally. I had lost much of my fear and learned to live with threats and more serious encounters in Transnistria, so I was concerned but not panicked.

We were taken by truck to jail in Steyr and locked behind bars in a small room. After a lengthy wait, we were separated. I was treated like a hardened criminal, led between two guards to a cell. The solid door was opened, and they motioned for me to walk in. The clanging of the heavy metal reverberated in my ears as the door slammed shut behind me. It was a nightmare – the cell was dimly lit with one tiny light bulb peering down from the centre of the ceiling; it gave off more of a glow than a light. The cell had dark grey walls, a small window covered with iron bars, an open toilet in one corner and a number of narrow cots. There were about ten people of different nationalities, mostly in their twenties and thirties. They surrounded me like bees; some of them spoke German and started questioning me, wanting to know what crime I had committed. They were a rough-looking bunch sentenced to jail for assorted crimes. One in particular frightened me, a heavy-set bearded man who did not say much but kept staring at me. He appeared to be mentally deranged. As we went to bed, I tried to stay awake with my eyes focused on him, but sleep eventually overtook me.

After a restless night, I was awakened early in the morning. One of the men showed me how to make my bed – it had to be neat and uniform, the blanket folded in a certain way and placed at the foot of the bed. We were let out into the courtyard for a brief walk. Marching in column formation around the courtyard was my only chance to see and wave to my friends, but we could not speak to each other. The remainder of the day was spent in the crowded cell, listening to prisoners' conversations in German and in Slavic languages. The only prisoner with whom I felt comfortable enough to converse was from Transylvania, supposedly an artist. I also had ample time mentally to retrace my journey out of Admont and how it ended up in jail. I kept wondering what had happened to the rest of our group and what was going to happen to me. My main concern was my inability to contact anyone to make them aware of my presence in jail.

Some of our group had made it to Linz and informed the leader of the Betar that others had been arrested. Within a few days, a female lawyer who had been contacted by a Jewish organization came to see me. She told me that I would be taken to court where she would plead my innocence; she thought that my age would be a factor in getting me released prior to trial.

The following day, I was escorted to court where the lawyer awaited me. We were shown to a room, and as the judge entered I was called up in front of him. A policeman displayed some of the evidence that was used against me. Upon being questioned I denied any involvement. After some discussion between the judge and the lawyer, I was released. She bought me a train ticket to Linz, and I promptly left.

Upon arrival at the Binderminchel camp in Linz, I had a happy reunion with my friends from whom I had been separated. We were all anxious to talk about our different experiences. Some who had run away from the railway station were caught but then managed to escape from the police station. Isiu was not caught and, after hiding for a while, walked on the highway hoping to catch a ride. After many unsuccessful attempts at flagging down a vehicle, a small truck stopped and told him to hop on the back. To his surprise, he found both Magda and Zvi, who had managed to run away from the railway station, sitting there. It was a happy reunion for them.

After a short stay in Linz, part of our group joined about fifty members of another Betar group and, after making brief stopovers in camps in Salzburg and Saalfelden, we finally arrived in Gnadenwald (Wiesenhof) in the French zone. This was the last assembly point in Austria before crossing into Italy. We were housed on the outskirts of town in a building run by the Bricha, whose function was to smuggle refugees across the Alps through the Brenner Pass into Italy.

By coincidence, most of the transients in Gnadenwald at that time were members of Betar. Sami, the leader of the Bricha as well as the person in charge of the camp, belonged to the Haganah. Like many other Jews in Palestine, he had voluntarily joined the British army and served as an officer in the Jewish Brigade. After the end of the war, he remained in Europe to work with the Bricha. He was still dressed in his military uniform and drove around in a jeep. He was aware of our political affiliation and, upon our arrival, made us feel somewhat less than welcome. It was the first time I felt the friction between political parties. To aggravate the situation, Sami fed chocolate to his dog. When one of our members asked him why our rations did not include chocolate, he told us that we were not as worthy as his dog. That night, we decided to break into the supply room and remove all the chocolates. Some of the people who had filled up their rucksacks with chocolates were afraid they would be confiscated and went into town early the next morning to sell them. The next few days in the camp were tense. One evening, three canvas-covered trucks arrived to take us to the border. Sami was as anxious to be rid of us as we were happy to leave.

On our way to the Italian border, we were stopped by Austrian police during a routine check. Not having any documents, we were taken to police headquarters in Innsbruck. While the trucks parked on the street, our leader was escorted into the police station. After a short wait, he returned and told the drivers to head back to camp, which they did. No sooner were we out of view of the police then we headed back toward the Italian border via a different route. We were let off before the border and led by members of the Bricha away from the road and into the Alps to cross the Brenner Pass illegally.

It was a rugged and difficult terrain to walk, especially at night. In some areas, there was no path and we had to wend our way between the trees. In other areas, the path skirted the edge of a cliff overlooking a deep ravine. The reflection from the snow on the ground illuminated our trail. We were all tired and sleepy until the sound of gunfire startled us and we hit the ground. Once the shooting ceased, we resumed our trek. The leader told us that we had made it into Italy. We continued walking until dawn when we were led out of the woods onto a road where trucks awaited us.

Having made our way through snow at high altitude, we were all cold and anxious to get under the canvas covers of the trucks. I jumped on and ran all the way to the back to grab what I thought would be the warmest spot. As the truck started to descend from the mountain, however, the cold wind created by its movement rushed through the small openings in the canvas and penetrated the thin layers of my clothes. I felt the cold as my body became a wind-breaker for others and switched places with Isiu whenever one of us got too cold.

MILAN, OCTOBER 1946

After a long ride, we finally arrived in Milan. We were all in high spirits; we were getting closer and closer to realizing our dream of reaching Palestine. As the truck slowly made its way, we could see the beauty of the city through the opening at the rear. We were amazed at the size of the city, which we thought would never end. The truck made its last turn into a narrow street and finally stopped at Via Unione #5.

We were let off and walked under a large, enclosed archway with heavy metal gates, opening into a big courtyard surrounded by a large, three-storey stone building. Located in downtown Milan, the building served as headquarters for the Bricha and as a stopover for Holocaust survivors who were brought into northern Italy illegally. There, they were fed and housed and, after a couple of days, were sent to camps in different cities in Italy. Milan itself had two such camps: Scuola Cadorna, a transit camp located in a school in a working-class neighbourhood, and Adriatica, a holding camp on the outskirts of the city that housed people in barracks.

The day after we arrived, Isiu, Magda, Max, Beno Grobstein (our new friend whom we had met in Gnadenwald), and I went for a stroll in the city. The streets were lined with beautiful stores displaying the latest fashions on mannequins that could be mistaken for real people. Coffee houses packed with people were inviting, but we were penniless. As we walked past restaurants, we looked through their windows and could see tables elegantly dressed in white tablecloths and covered with neatly arranged place settings of sparkling glasses and china.

"Which restaurant should we go to?" Beno asked. We couldn't help but start laughing.

"Yes," Max joked, "and what are we going to use for money?"

"Does anyone have scissors, a needle and thread?" Beno asked. "I have 500 American dollars hidden in my shoulder pads. I'll take some out, if one of you can sew the rest back in."

We were astonished that he had so much money. Having just recently met him, it was surprising that he would reveal how much he actually had. To us, it sounded like a fortune. Beno told us that he had made

his money in Romania after the war by acquiring merchandise that was in short supply, then selling it at a substantial profit.

True to his word, he took the five of us out for dinner that evening. Not speaking any Italian, we communicated with the waiter by pointing to a neighbouring table where a meat dish was being served and all ordered the same thing; we found out later that it was veal milanese. That particularly enjoyable evening stands out in my mind. Together with friends in a relaxed atmosphere, pampered by waiters, our hands and eyes to communicate with them – it all added up to a delicious meal and an unforgettable experience.

Having lived in a communist country, the freedom and democracy I was observing acted as an incentive for me: to work hard and earn enough money to be independent and afford the joys of life, not just to work and save to create wealth, which I had seen taken away overnight. We left the restaurant in an upbeat mood and walked back to Via Unione. We were all captivated by the city.

Disappointing news came the following day, however, when we were told that our whole group would be sent to a camp in Crugleasca, a suburb of Turin. We were determined not to leave, and, with the help of a member of Betar, the five of us bluffed our way out. We were taken to Scuola Cadorna, where we were shown to a room in which there were about twenty other people. Cots were assigned to us and we were each given a D.P. (displaced person) card and tickets entitling us to three meals a day. Being a transit camp, the population varied, and with it the length of the line-ups for food.

After a week, we were offered jobs as security guards by a member of the committee running the camp. It was no coincidence – he was a member of the Irgun and knew of our affiliation. He wanted to have members of his party on the security staff. Isiu, Max, and I promptly accepted; Beno had different plans – he was interested in pursuing a career in business. The three of us moved out of the crowded room into spacious quarters occupied by twelve other young men working with security.

We were given uniforms and told what our responsibilities would be. They ranged from orienting new arrivals, patrolling the grounds, to keeping order. Periodically, cigarettes, chocolate, and clothes were handed out. Line-ups quickly formed with a lot of jostling as everyone wanted to be first. Other duties included working in the control booth to keep out local people who didn't have permission to enter the camp and to prevent refugees who had turned into entrepreneurs from smuggling out and selling new boots, cigarettes, and canned goods they bought from others in the camp. This measure was taken to prevent them from getting into trouble with the law in a country where they already were residing illegally. There were only a few who were involved in these transactions; the odd one did it for excitement, to prove to himself he could function on his own in a free society. Other than these restrictions, all the refugees were allowed to come and go as they pleased. Our uniforms were more symbolic than threatening; no one was arrested or reprimanded. We were all Holocaust survivors and understood each other's needs.

We always worked in pairs, and for the first month we were each teamed up with an experienced worker to get to know the place and how to handle different situations that arose. The area that created most of the problems for us was the gymnasium – it was a unique place. It slept more than 150 people, male and female, young and old, in bunk beds that also served as sofas in the daytime. The only way to have privacy was to drape a blanket over one's bunk. Most of the people did not know the neighbours in the surrounding bunks. Disputes frequently arose in the evenings because there was only one switch to control the lights. Some would be in the mood to sing or socialize late into the night, while others were depressed or tired and wanted the lights out early to be able to sleep. There was constant bickering about the lights and the noise level. No sooner were we able to calm down the people in one area of the gym than we were called back to settle another dispute. We did not encounter the same problems with people who were assigned to sleep in the classrooms.

The gymnasium was a real and lively community – various activities were going on in different areas of the room at the same time. Some would-be entrepreneurs were hawking herring and deli food, which they had bought at the store; others were selling wine and liquor by the glass. Barbers were offering to cut hair for whatever a client was willing to pay and fortune tellers were trying to attract customers to predict their futures. In another part of the room, one could hear the sounds of an instrument being played or a comedian trying to make people laugh. Others made themselves look silly by strutting around pretending to be models. Cheered on by young spectators and booed by older people, there was no shortage of amateur talent willing to perform and have fun. All the activities after hours placed the security staff in a difficult situation. We felt sorry for them, but we had to follow orders and enforce the law. When we tried to stop them, they argued that they were not rowdy and were only trying to turn a bad situation into an atmosphere of fun and laughter to keep up morale.

Being a transit camp, refugees were moved on short notice, and no activities were planned. For the younger people, boredom was hard to combat. They had the energy but no way to release it. Most of the refugees in this camp led an inactive life; the only things they did were to line up for food, mingle with other refugees, or have an afternoon siesta. Few ventured out into the city for fear of getting lost and finding themselves unable to communicate with the local people. Those who did go out made good use of their hands to find their way back to the camp. They then discussed their adventure with their friends. For those who liked to watch soccer, Italian amateur teams could occasionally be seen playing behind the school. There were also soccer teams made up of camp staff who played against each other. Players ranged in age from seventeen to fifty. We were quite a sight: some were fast enough to train for the Olympics, and others could barely run.

After we had settled into Scuola Cadorna, Isiu, Max, and I decided to visit the city. Beno, having already explored on his own, was our guide. We went by streetcar to the Piazza del Duomo, where we got off and walked around. Passers-by could tell we were strangers – not only by the clothing we wore, but also by the way our heads were constantly turning around to admire the surroundings.

We were attracted to the tall, impressive cathedral with its huge marble pillars. As we walked in, we were approached by a guide but could not understand what he was saying. He took us to the elevator, indicating with his hands that it cost money to get up to the top. When he saw we were not responding to his request, he led us to the stairs and motioned for us to go up. As we climbed the hundreds of narrow spiral stairs, we could see carved on the walls names, dates, and origins of the many people who had made the same trek. We decided to do the same and left our marks there with a pocket knife. We continued climbing, and after what seemed like forever, finally reached the top, out of breath. As we walked around, we could not help but admire the artwork of hundreds of statues and spires that lined the edges of the roof. It left us guessing how this tall, ornate structure could have been built hundreds of years ago with only primitive manual labour. Its height gave us a good view of the beautiful city. After we had negotiated the last few steps of a long descent, we were all tired and hungry and once again Beno came to our rescue, treating us to a meal. Even though we'd only known Beno for a relatively short time, it felt as though he'd been a long-time friend. He was an outgoing, friendly person who enjoyed being around people and didn't mind picking up the tab until we were able to pay our own way.

Going back to catch the streetcar, Beno took us to see a public bathhouse that he had recently discovered. It was next to Piazza del Duomo in the Galleria, a building that had a huge tunnel-like archway leading to another street. Boutiques and fancy cafe houses were located on the street level. Beno led us down the staircase to the lower level to show us the bathhouse. It may seem strange that, with all the beautiful things we saw and admired, a visit to the bathhouse was more important to us, but it was something we needed. It consisted of two long rows of cubicles, each containing a bathtub. It was for men only, and entrance was by ticket that most anyone could afford. It entitled one to thirty minutes and included a sparkling clean bathtub, soap, and a large towel. From then on, it became a ritual for us to go to the bathhouse every Friday afternoon.

After several months in Scuola Cadorna, my work became routine and enjoyable. My co-workers were a friendly and lively group; we had a lot of laughs together, kibitzing around and playing tricks on each other. Nobody took any offence, and we always helped each other out. There was no problem switching shifts or working double shifts, allowing us to have longer stretches of time off to visit the many interesting sites in the city. Isiu, Max, and I had learned enough Italian words to feel comfortable during our frequent trips downtown. The streetcar stopped next to the school, and the fare was cheap. Our token salary and fringe benefits were sufficient to allow us to visit the neighbourhood coffee house, see a movie, buy the odd piece of clothing, have our laundry done, and to pay for miscellaneous expenses.

Encouraged by an Italian barber who serenaded his customers, we went to the famous opera house La Scala just for the sake of having been there. We struck it lucky: Samson and Delilah, the story from the Bible with which we were all familiar, was being performed. The opera house had a limited number of tickets at an affordable price in a standing-room-only section of the top floor. As we made our way up the back stairs, the surroundings in the stairwell were rather disappointing, but, once we opened the door to the actual theatre, huge glittering chandeliers and a sea of red velvet surrounded us. It was truly magnificent. Even though we did not understand the words, it was easy for us

to follow the story. It turned out to be an unexpectedly enjoyable and memorable evening.

During the winter, there was less activity in the camp, giving us more free time. But the cold and dampness discouraged many of the staff from going downtown. Some of my co-workers spent a lot of time in our room playing cards or shooting dice, activities that didn't appeal to me. I preferred spending time in a small reading room containing newspapers, mostly month-old Jewish papers from New York, or going to a nearby coffee house. The local people always seemed to have enough patience to engage us in conversation. This helped me learn the language.

Isiu, Max, and I frequently met with members of Irgun inside the camp and sometimes at a rented farmhouse not far from Milan where some Irgun leaders resided. At these meetings, we were informed about the latest happenings in Palestine. Of the topics discussed at these meetings, one in particular troubled me. I could not understand the hatred of the Haganah leaders in Palestine toward the Irgun. They were both fighting against the British for the liberation of Palestine, and yet the Irgun had to be as guarded against disclosing their identity to the Haganah as to the British. Even in the camps, we were told not to let members of the Haganah know of our affiliation. It was difficult for me to comprehend the Haganah's attitude and activities during a time when both parties were struggling to reach the same goal.

We weren't even a country yet and couldn't afford the luxury of acting as though we were. It appeared as if the main objective of the Mapai, which controlled the Haganah, was to grab power at the expense of our common goal. Even though they were both trying to build a democracy, the Mapai and the Betar had differing ideologies. The Mapai was based on a socialist system and placed a lot of emphasis on agriculture, whereas the Betar, forerunner of the present-day Likud party, was based on a free-enterprise system like that found in other industrial countries. Its goal was to secure the country first and then proceed with free parliamentary elections where the people would determine the type of government to run the country.

Spring finally arrived. The turnover of refugees that had slackened off during the winter months started to pick up again. One particular group that stands out in my mind arrived by bus. Its passengers were all young children, mostly toddlers, accompanied by several mothers who took care of all of them. We helped them off the bus and placed them in a room where they were well taken care of. Some had short outbursts of crying but settled down after being given food, including chocolate and candy.

Later that day, I was approached by one of the attendants to see if I could understand a little boy who was constantly crying and mumbling something. They had tried to quieten him down with more sweets, but nothing helped. As I approached him, he was still crying and mumbling in Romanian: "apa, apa." I told the attendant that all he wanted was water, but she doubted if I had understood him. When he was given a mug of water, he grabbed it with both hands, not letting go until he had drained the last drop.

This busload was somehow allowed across the border on humanitarian grounds, whereas the parents had had to cross the Brenner Pass illegally on foot. Once in Italy, they were brought by truck directly to Scuola Cadorna, where they were reunited with their children. As soon as the children saw their parents, their tearful eyes gave way to happy, smiling faces. Many of these parents had themselves experienced separation from their families during the war and were left only with images of their parents.

Yes, the war was officially over in 1945, but not for Holocaust survivors. After liberation we had hoped to walk as free men, never again to be interned in camps. But our freedom was only superficial. Two years and, for some of us, three years after liberation, we were still homeless, scattered throughout western Europe, moving illegally from country to country. We were not even allowed to travel to different countries to search the camps for family members. We felt stripped of our rights as humans; ironically, what the war to defeat the Nazis was all about.

The only place we could call home was our refugee camp. Our only identification was a piece of paper the size of a business card that showed our name, the date of issue, and the label "Displaced Person"; dogs had a more personal description on their dog tags. It was not a dignified or encouraging description for people trying to rebuild their lives. Many of us were already disadvantaged, having had our education curtailed during our formative years.

We felt neglected and abandoned while some countries debated, at a snail's pace, our future. This was in contrast to the British Royal Navy which, with its modern warships on high alert, moved with great speed, searching for old unseaworthy boats carrying Holocaust survivors to

Palestine. It appeared as though we were doomed to live out our lives in camps unless we took control of our own destiny.

Few countries were willing to let Jews in unless they had sponsors. Some of those who might have been eligible to leave the camp did not know or could not remember their relatives' surnames or where they lived. Most had left Europe long before the war started. There were a few who became so desperate to leave the camps that they would grab the opportunity provided by some South American countries that issued visas to those who converted to Christianity. Among the few who did was a young man I befriended in the camp. He suggested that I do the same. How could I? My parents and siblings had paid with their lives for being Jewish. I would have betrayed my heritage and everything my parents believed in and wanted me to be; my conscience would haunt me the rest of my life. Besides, my only desire was to go to Palestine, never to be uprooted again.

One day in April 1947, distressing news reached us. Several members of the Irgun, including Dov Gruner, were hanged by the British in the Acre Jail in Palestine. They died for a cause they believed in – to oust the British and regain our homeland. People in the camp walked around in anger and disbelief; they thought that the killing of Jews had stopped and that justice would prevail. Some Haganah members who ran the camp expressed indifference and referred to those who were hanged as terrorists. This attitude infuriated me; to me, they were heroes. Those courageous young men had sacrificed their lives to open the gates to Palestine and empty the camps of Holocaust survivors all over Europe. This unfortunate event accentuated the rift between the Mapai and the Betar, the only two parties that had credible underground military forces in Palestine.

There were also many other political parties in Palestine; they all had affiliations abroad. Based on various ideologies and beliefs, they could each be placed in one of four different categories: socialism, capitalism, religion, communal living. Most of the parties leaned toward either the Irgun or the Haganah and had their own preference under which system the Jewish state, once created, should operate. The majority of Holocaust survivors found and belonged to a party that embraced their views and gave them the feeling of belonging to a family, something all of us yearned for. The largest and most powerful party was the Mapai (socialist), backed by American Jewry. It was the party to which they had been most extensively exposed.

The multiple parties have continued to cause problems in present-day politics in Israel. Since the creation of the nation, no political party has ever succeeded in coming even close to winning a majority in parliament. Small parties with similar ideologies, varying only slightly to the left or right, can exert enough pressure to topple the government.

As the weather improved, more people arrived at Scuola Cadorna, at times causing overcrowding. Notwithstanding all the hardship, life went on. People fell in love and got married, undeterred by crowded living conditions, an uncertain future, and a lack of privacy. They bought a few bottles of wine, sought out a rabbi from among the refugees to perform a ceremony, and got married. Their honeymoon suite consisted of a bunk bed draped with double blankets – a dream world of their own!

Isiu and I always did things together and even shared the few items of clothing we had managed to buy. But he started spending a lot of time with Magda and, whenever he and I were alone, always brought her into the conversation. I could see he was in love, and he finally admitted it to me. "Isiu," I said, "she's a lovely girl. People are going to envy you."

Changes were made in the security staff; Isiu was transferred to the distribution centre, handing out clothing, cigarettes, and chocolates to new arrivals. I had learned the Italian language well enough to converse and was temporarily transferred to Via Unione #5 to join their security staff.

My new job was different and at times challenging. In addition to coming by trucks, refugees started arriving by train at the Central Station. They were transported by the Bricha from German and Austrian camps to the Brenner Pass and made their way illegally on foot into Italy. Once in Italy, they went by train and were instructed to follow each other when they got off in Milan. My job was to be at the station several hours before the train arrived and arrange with the streetcar supervisor to sideline one or two cars, depending on how many refugees were expected. I went onto the platform to meet the refugees and my co-worker watched the exit gate in the unlikely event that I missed them. I had no problem spotting them by their appearance and clothing, as well as by the line they formed. I approached the lead man and asked him in Hebrew: 'amchu?' (one of ours?) He, along with the others, followed me to the streetcar. As they entered the car, the conductor counted them, and I paid for the tickets. He followed the regular route but did not stop to pick up any other passengers. We were let off at a regular stop less than one block from Via Unione.

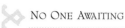

My other duties, besides working in security, included doing chores for Issachar, the man in charge of the Bricha. One of these was to take his business correspondence to the post office and have it sent by registered mail. Most of the letters were addressed to Palestine. He was a man who had connections and carried a great deal of influence. I took advantage of my position and asked for his assistance in tracing Avrum. He renewed my hope; until then, all my inquiries since arriving in Italy had been futile and had left me discouraged.

Standing in front of the building one day, watching people go by, I noticed a black man dressed in an American military uniform walking into a nearby restaurant. The Shirley Temple movie I had seen as a child came to mind. Out of curiosity, I walked into the restaurant and took a seat facing him at the next table. I ordered an inexpensive meal and sat there, eating very slowly. Seeing him convinced me that there *were* black people; my brother Shimon had been right. After the soldier left, the waiter told me that he occasionally came to the restaurant. I went back and told my co-workers; they had never seen a black person either. From then on, we made a point of looking through the window of the restaurant to see if he was there. One day, we saw him, and a couple of us went in. He was eating a salad plate. It looked tempting, and we ordered the same thing. It consisted of prosciutto with tomatoes, potatoes, and onions, all evenly sliced, sprinkled with a touch of vinegar and garnished with black olives. I still eat the same salad today, minus the prosciutto.

While I was on duty one day, a new group arrived, adding to the already crowded conditions. A noisy quarrel turned into an unprecedented incident in the camp – a fight among half a dozen people. A father and son who were separated in 1941 and had not seen each other for six years were involved in the scuffle. In the confusion, the son did not realize whom he was hitting until his father cried out his name. As they grabbed each other and embraced, the brawl ceased as if on cue. Some onlookers shed tears of joy. I felt so happy for them that while father and son were sitting on the stairs, tears streaming down their faces, I ran to the store to buy two bottles of wine to celebrate the reunion. I hoped that one day such a miracle would happen to me.

An ongoing problem of mine, my teeth, kept on bothering me. After having had two teeth pulled out without any freezing in Scuola Cadorna by a survivor who was a dentist, others started to act up, sometimes causing unbearable pain. I went to see the dentist in the building where I worked, who pulled some more broken teeth and made me a bridge. He was more like a mechanic than the dentist he claimed to be.

In the summer of 1947, heartbreaking news reached Holocaust survivors. *Exodus,* the ship that had sailed from France with 4,500 refugees on board, had reached the shores of Palestine only to be prevented by the British Royal Navy from entering the port of Haifa. After ramming the ship and rendering her unseaworthy, British soldiers boarded, and a fierce battle erupted, resulting in many casualties on both sides. The damaged ship was brought into the port of Haifa, and the refugees were transferred to three ships and returned to France. After refusing to disembark, they were escorted to Hamburg in the British-controlled zone of Germany. They were forced off with tear gas and placed in camps. The survivors in Via Unione and Scuola Cadorna became extremely upset. Though few of them could read the Italian newspapers, the picture they saw told the whole story, and their eyes filled with tears. After Auschwitz, how could this happen?

Despite the setback, the work of the Bricha continued unabated. People were moved from camp to camp, awaiting their turn for embarkation. Even though they were aware that they would likely be intercepted on the high seas by the British navy, it did not deter them from trying to edge closer to Palestine.

Shortly after the *Exodus* incident, Isiu, Max, and I were assigned by the Irgun to stick posters, printed in English, on foreign consulates or, if that was not possible, on nearby buildings. The posters protested the action of the British as well as their refusal to open the gates to Palestine. Late at night, we were caught by two detectives. They asked for identification, and we showed them our D.P. cards. Looking at the posters, they questioned us about the meaning of the symbol of a raised right arm grasping a bayonetted rifle, the emblem of the Irgun Zvai Leumi. We pretended not to know and said that we were being paid to post them. One of the detectives was able to read the poster and told us that we could be locked up in jail for such activities, but they let us off with a warning and confiscated our remaining posters and a can of glue. This was typical of my experience with Italian people during my stay in Italy. They were friendly and helpful to us in many different ways.

The tragedy of the *Exodus* dramatized the plight of the refugees before the United Nations, where the debate regarding the partition of Palestine was taking place. Britain still had its mandate over Palestine and under its quota system allowed only a limited number of Jews to enter.

We followed the proceedings with keen interest, hoping that recovering our homeland would open the gates to freedom and help us regain our identity. It was our only hope of leaving the crowded camps without having to shed more blood fighting the British in Palestine.

Cheerful news awaited me one day. "Joil," Isiu said, "I've got some good news to tell you. Magda and I have decided to get married and you're going to be the best man." I wasn't surprised, I had seen it coming for some time.

"Mazel tov," I said as I congratulated him. "You deserve the best. She's a wonderful girl. You'll be very happy together." She always had a smile on her face and was very friendly to everyone she met.

"Are you going to use our sleeping quarters for the ceremony like Ferst did or have it outside in the garden?"

"No," he said, "I want something a little more memorable. I'm going to arrange with a rabbi to have the ceremony downtown." After the ceremony in the rabbi's study, to which Isiu's close friends were invited, we all went to a restaurant to celebrate. I thought I had lost my closest friend, but, in fact, I had gained another.

Following the party, I returned to Via Unione. As the days passed, I spent more of my free time in the office. Listening to conversations, I could not help but become aware of the fact that members of the staff either belonged to Haganah or were Haganah sympathizers. I went along with their political ideology, keeping my affiliation with the Irgun under wraps to protect my job. But the longer I stayed in Via Unione, the more I became aware of the animosity of the Haganah toward the Irgun. They frequently referred to the Irgun as a terrorist organization. The name-callings had a demoralizing effect on me. I strongly believed that it was a time to put aside individual party ideologies and fight together for a common cause. I was young and patriotic and could not understand the difference in priorities between patriots who were willing to fight and die for their country and politicians who were more interested in establishing a power base. I suspected that it was no coincidence that the top positions in the Bricha were held by Haganah members – they came from Palestine and must have been appointed by the Mapai.

After the Holocaust, a new breed of Jew surfaced, loaded down with images of atrocities. Their motto was "Never Again." I was one of them. In the fall of 1947, I was approached by a senior member of the Irgun and asked if I was willing to volunteer for a top-secret mission. I asked him what the mission would involve, but he did not give me an answer;

I didn't really expect one. I suspected that my expertise with dynamite might have something to do with it. The *Exodus* episode and feelings of frustration over being a stateless person three years after the end of the war reinforced my willingness to participate. I did not hesitate to accept and was given a week to transfer back to Scuola Cadorna, where it would be easier to cover my tracks. Upon being contacted again, I told him I was ready to go. I didn't consider myself a potential hero but, as a survivor, I felt it was my duty to do whatever was required to regain our homeland. He accompanied me to Mestre, a town close to Venice. We went to a private farmhouse rented by the organization, and there I met eight young men. We were told that it was a dangerous mission and that we still had an opportunity to change our minds. None of us did.

Accompanied by our leader, we made several trips to Venice – it was fascinating to see a city where canals and waterways replaced noisy, paved streets. Everything moved on water, from motorboats to rowboats to gondolas rowed by gondoliers serenading their passengers. While overlooking the Grand Canal, we could also see ships, including those of the British navy, anchored in the calm sea. After exploring Venice and walking our feet off, we always sat down for a drink in St. Mark's Square and watched the pigeons as they were being fed by tourists. We wondered why we had been brought to Venice, continuing to be kept in the dark about the goal of the mission. For some reason, it kept being delayed. One of the guys jokingly said, "The British Navy might sail before we have a chance to complete our mission." We all started to laugh. But after a couple of weeks the mission was called off. At approximately that time, the United Nations voted to partition Palestine and establish a Jewish state.

I returned to Scuola Cadorna and resumed my job. Refugees were more jubilant, knowing that their dreams were about to be realized. Only patience and time separated them from the coastline of Palestine and life in a new era where being a Jew would no longer be a curse; on the contrary, it would be a blessing to return home after 2,000 years in the Diaspora. They would be proud to walk the streets where the Star of David would shine on the fluttering flags instead of being sewn on their clothes to identify them for slaughter.

Most of the refugees were penniless. For some, this did not matter because they belonged to one of the Zionist organizations whose ideology was to live off the land in communal farms *(kibbutzim)* that had been established many years ago. Upon their arrival in Palestine, they would be taken to one of these *kibbutzim,* where they would participate as equals in a lifestyle of their choice. Communal living, however, was not everybody's preference.

One of the refugees I knew was luckier than most; he had a brother in Palestine who had emigrated from Poland in the early thirties. They had established contact after the war, and in one of his letters, the brother asked him to find out the cost of purchasing and shipping a truck to Palestine. He would make the necessary arrangements for payment. A truck would ensure my friend self-employment and the ability to earn a good living.

Word spread in Scuola Cadorna that the Canadian Jewish Congress had persuaded the Canadian government to allow them to sponsor a number of orphans, eighteen and under, to emigrate to Canada.[18] Within weeks, registration started. Not all who were eligible registered; their goal, as well as mine, was to go to Palestine.

Even though the atmosphere in the camp was joyful, however, the friction between the Mapai and the Betar did not abate. News came back from Palestine that anyone who belonged to Betar, particularly those suspected of belonging to the Irgun, would find it difficult to get a job. It was advantageous to belong to the Mapai (Labor) Party since it controlled the federation of trade unions (Histadrut) and gave preferential treatment to its members when it came to securing jobs. Having recently returned from a mission where I had voluntarily offered to risk my life for a common goal, I became disillusioned and started to have second thoughts. An Israeli state was imminent, and my training to help fight for independence was no longer needed.

Being penniless and wanting to build my future without depending on any political party, I wondered if going to Palestine at this time was the right decision. I began thinking about registering, but I wavered, hesitating to make a decision. I was ashamed to admit to my friends that I was considering going to Canada, even though my stay there was to be temporary: only long enough to earn sufficient money to buy a small truck. Like my friend, I too, wanted to ensure my financial independence once I got to Palestine. I had many sleepless nights wondering whether I should go to Palestine to search for Avrum. I went to see Issachar again with the hope of hearing some encouraging news, enough to tip my indecision in favour of going to Palestine. But his answer was disappointing – he was unable to provide me with any information.

CANADA, MARCH 1948

I delayed registering for as long as possible. When I finally told my friends I was leaving for Canada, they did not believe me; they were so convinced I was being sent on a secret mission that they did not even try to talk me out of going.

Isiu, Magda, and Max remained in Scuola Cadorna, planning to leave for Palestine. Beno had fallen in love with Milan and planned to remain there. The only obstacle he had to overcome was getting a residence permit. Following a lengthy period of trying, he finally succeeded. After a successful start as a merchant, he went into the import–export business in the 1950s and developed a thriving enterprise. He remains in Milan to this day.

Those of us who applied for permits had to pass a thorough medical examination before being accepted for immigration. Having lived through the war on the edge of starvation, I was concerned about my health, but before long I was informed of my acceptance and given a departure date. Until the last minute, I remained ambivalent about going, continuing to think about Avrum. Travelling to Genoa for embarkation was a sad day for me, even though I was planning to stay in Canada for only a few years.

Following a rough sea voyage on the Greek liner S.S. *Nea Hellas,* with about eighty other orphans from various Italian camps, we were all happy to see land once again. As the ship slowly approached the port of Halifax on March 21, 1948, I still had mixed feelings; I felt I had betrayed my homeland by not going to Palestine to participate in the historic event of an Israeli state coming into existence. After disembarkation, we entered a bleak-looking building and lined up for processing. As I waited, I became apprehensive; this was my first experience entering a country legally, and I did not know what to expect. I was relieved once I reached the customs officer, who was polite and welcomed me to the new country.

Members of the Jewish community in Halifax greeted us and put us up in private homes for the night. Our group was assigned to different cities, mainly Montreal, Toronto, and Winnipeg. I asked to see a map of

Canada and decided to go to Winnipeg because it was situated in the centre of the country. Its location would facilitate moving either east or west, should I choose to do so. The Canadian Jewish Congress had arranged with the Canadian National Railways to allocate sleeping cars to our group. As the train pulled out of the station, I had no idea of the size of Canada. We travelled for a number of days and nights through miles and miles of uninhabited wasteland and forest and arrived in Winnipeg. It was very different from the densely populated European landscape, where towns and villages were so close that one could walk from one to another. Every little piece of land there was utilized for growing grains, vegetables, and fruits. The train ride gave me ample time to think about my new home: I knew no one there, could not speak the language, had no money, and, of utmost importance, had no schooling or trade to rely on.

Even on this distant prairie, however, Winnipeg had a vibrant Jewish community offering a diverse cultural and religious life. Jews from central and eastern Europe had started to arrive in Winnipeg in the late nineteenth century to escape pogroms, persecution, and racial discrimination, and to better their lives. By 1948, there were approximately 20,000 Jews living in Winnipeg, a city with a multi-ethnic population of 234,000. Most of them resided in the north end of the city, except for a small number who had relocated to the south.

We were welcomed by members of this community and taken to the Young Men's Hebrew Association (YMHA). There, we were greeted by more people, including some orphans who had arrived several months earlier. After lunch, we socialized for a few hours and were taken to private Jewish homes where we were given room and board, paid for by the community until we were able to support ourselves.

My roommate, Ben Blum and I were shown to our room in the attic of a three-storey house in the north end of the city. It was sparsely furnished with a double bed, a small table, and two chairs; an old dust-covered gramophone sat on a pedestal in the corner. After dinner, we returned to our dimly lit room, not a particularly welcoming setting for my first night in Winnipeg. I hadn't expected an elaborate room, but my indecision about going to Canada in the first place was not helped by these surroundings, which magnified my loneliness. I walked up to the gramophone and played the record that was on it. I thought it would cheer me up, but instead it had the opposite effect. It was a sad song sung in Yiddish. I'm not sure why, but I kept on playing it over and over again until late into the night.

My first impression of the city itself was also rather disappointing. It was the end of March, and partially melted, dirt-covered snow lay everywhere. Only when spring arrived a little later did the bleakness of the surroundings lift. It turned out to be a beautiful city with cloudless blue skies, clean streets, lots of trees and parks, and well-kept, small houses surrounded by colourful flowers and neat lawns. In the evenings, people sat outside on their front steps or on chairs, enjoying the fresh air. Everything was so unlike Milan. And having lived in a pig barn and in overcrowded rooms since 1941, I was impressed by the standard of living. Every house had a living room, a kitchen, and sufficient bedrooms so that only one or two people slept in each one; many had refrigerators and, to my astonishment, telephones.

We were each assigned to a social worker; mine was Miss Schreiber, a pleasant lady with whom I could communicate in German. She understood our needs and was helpful to us. The Jewish community was also very supportive. We were taken to a clothing wholesaler, where we were outfitted with everything from underwear to an overcoat. We were also given free membership at the YMHA. Even though I received a weekly allowance until we found a job, I was anxious to start working.

The garment industry was flourishing in Winnipeg and needed workers. I was told that cutters were in demand and that I would be able to work a lot of overtime hours. I soon got a job at 35 cents an hour, which was automatically increased to 40 cents when I joined the union six weeks later. I worked hard and was determined to learn the trade. Miss Schreiber suggested I go to night school to learn English, but, after attending a couple of sessions, I decided I would rather earn the overtime money to fulfil my goal of going to Palestine.

Less than two months after my arrival in Canada, on May 14, the Jewish state of Israel was proclaimed. The following day, five Arab states (Egypt, Jordan, Iraq, Syria, and Lebanon) attacked Israel. No country came to their rescue. They stood alone; lacking in manpower and modern arms, they fought against overwhelming odds. The hastily organized army included Holocaust survivors who had barely enough time to unpack their rucksacks before being rushed to the front. I went to see Miss Schreiber and asked if she could arrange passage for me to Israel as I wanted to participate in the struggle. Her response was that that would be impossible. Seeing my reaction, she tried to lessen my disappointment by pointing out that, since I was the only one left from my family, I should not put my life at risk by going to Israel at that time.

She meant well, but, not knowing of my past affiliation with the Irgun Zvai Leumi and my feelings as a Holocaust survivor, she could not realize how much it would have meant to me to be in Israel during its time of need. I followed the war with keen interest while the fighting raged on. The Jewish state held its own and gained some ground. Within a short time, the United Nations called for a ceasefire, and all combatants complied.

I was not happy living in my first home, and after a short while I was fortunate to be recommended to Zalman and Zlote Chisvin, a couple who also lived in the north end. They agreed to give me room and board for twenty dollars a month, but I was not to be concerned if I could not afford this; any amount would be fine. When I moved in, they, along with their children, Phyllis, Jack, and Al, made me feel like part of the family. Family meant a great deal to me, and it had been a long time since I had a place I could call home. The children made a point of introducing their friends to me, and I was often invited by Jack to go on double-dates he arranged.

In addition to being a superb cook, Mrs. Chisvin served plentiful dishes of food at the table. Each evening she would ask me what kind of sandwiches and how many I wanted to take to work the next day. I was free to have friends over to visit and was told to invite two or three friends for holiday meals. Once my wages increased, I offered to pay more, but she refused to accept it. I felt so much a part of the family that, when I got married years later, even though I no longer lived with them, I asked the Chisvins to sit next to me at the head table.

After working for a few months, I asked for a raise, but was refused. I went to another garment factory and told them that I had more experience than I really had. After they saw my work, they agreed to pay me 50 cents an hour. I soon realized that the only way to get a raise within a relatively short time was to move to another factory, as cutters were in demand. I moved several times.

The people I got to know were very friendly and welcomed me into the community. I was frequently invited to the lake for weekends where I was introduced to canoeing and to the game of tennis. I was also invited to play "football," which I thought was my favourite sport. I was anxious to play and show off my skills. When I reached the field, I saw boys kicking a ball in the air and others trying to catch it. The ball seemed to have an unusual shape; I thought some air had leaked out. They kicked the ball toward me. I tried to use my foot soccer-style to keep it under control, but it bounced away. When I caught up to it, I saw that it had an odd shape. They explained that it wasn't a soccer ball but a football and how the game was played. I decided that "real" football was my game, however. That summer, I joined a junior soccer league and our team won the city championship. Each of the players received a leather jacket with the team emblem.

I enjoyed my work and was happy to get the overtime hours. I inquired about a truck and was told that the cheapest place to purchase one would be in a port city, such as Montreal or New York, to avoid taxes and double transportation costs. Based on my potential earnings, it would take me several years to save the required amount of money. It was more than I anticipated, but I wasn't discouraged. The only thing that kept troubling me was my inability, for more than four years, to find out anything about Avrum.

An accident brought me to my first encounter with democracy at work. Riding my bicycle to work one day, I was crossing an intersection with a green light indicating my right of way. A car made a right turn and was about to hit me, and only my quick reaction in jumping off the bike saved me from serious injury. The front fender and a pedal was damaged, and I sustained bruises on my left thigh. The driver stopped the car and came out hollering at me. Even though I knew I was in the right, the fact that he drove a big car scared me; he had the power and could say that I was at fault. A policeman standing across the street saw the whole incident and came toward us. He asked if I was hurt, and I said "No," afraid to get involved with a wealthy man who, I thought, would wield the same degree of power he would under the system in which I grew up. Instead, the policeman gave him a ticket and gave me the telephone number of the police station in case I did need medical attention. I realized then what democracy and equal rights are supposed to mean.

The first time I had reason to cry from happiness was in July when I received a very emotional letter from Avrum. He was alive and well in Israel. I re-read the letter many times and absorbed each word like a sponge. He never doubted that I was alive and that the day would come when our dreams would be fulfilled and we would be reunited as we had promised each other in Stepanki. I felt proud of my kid brother – he was the one who had succeeded in getting in touch with me. Included with his letter were two photographs, one of him and one of Mother, which had been given to him by Mrs. Rudich, the wife of my father's former boss at the saw mill. Mr. and Mrs. Rudich had somehow managed to leave Romania for Palestine just before the war broke out.

In 1944, after the Soviet army occupied Old Romania, Avrum wanted to return to Storojinet to look for me and other surviving family members but was told that it was impossible to do so at the time. Later, when he might have been able to go, the Jewish organization that had taken him out from Transnistria dissuaded him from going. He was told that in the near future Transnistria survivors would be allowed to be reunited with their families in Romania.

His efforts to get in touch with me proved futile. He did not mention how or when he got to Israel. Once he was there, he approached new arrivals to Israel, inquiring about me and our extended family. One day, he was lucky and met a man from our hometown of Berhomet who had lived in Timisoara and knew Uncle Schlomcu and Uncle Simon, and Avrum had gotten in touch with them. Upon my arrival in Winnipeg, I had written to my uncles, and they had sent Avrum my address.

Unfortunately, the return address on Avrum's airmail envelope was smudged with dirt and "Post Afula" were the only words I could make out. I immediately wrote a letter addressed to Avrum in the town of Afula, Israel. Being impatient, I wrote several more letters, hoping that someone in the post office might recognize the name.

I did not hear from him again. Knowing that there was a war going on, I became worried. I wrote to Isiu, who had left Italy for Israel after the state was proclaimed and asked him to inquire about Avrum. After a long delay, a response finally came. As I read the letter, my hands began to tremble. I could sense Isiu was trying to soften the blow before he came right out and stated that Avrum had been killed fighting in the War of Independence.

My dreams and hopes for the day when we would embrace each other in happier times were shattered. Not having known for such a long time whether Avrum was alive, and then suddenly being contacted by him, had put me in a state of euphoria. It was belated joy that had eluded me at liberation when hope gave way to despair. I had stood alone on the road to freedom, gripped by sadness and fear and with nothing to celebrate – everything seemed so hollow. Now that I thought my hopes were going to be realized, the news of his death was even more shattering. To have struggled so hard and gone through all the pain and suffering, losing Avrum in the War of Independence seemed so unfair and was more than I could bear.

Throughout the war, we had spent many hours talking about how we would proceed with our lives after liberation. We must have looked to the future with our hearts as there were no visible signs to the naked eye that the Soviets would one day liberate us. No matter how difficult and horrendous conditions were, life to Avrum and me still had value and we both looked forward to sharing it one day. Even though we had worked as a team, it was our individual efforts trying to beat the odds that helped us live to see liberation. These steered us away from negative thoughts and guided us to a vision of hope on which we lived from dawn to dusk. Maybe our youth had something to do with our positive outlook; our only memories were those of a child eager to get up each morning and experience the joys of life – a life without worry, protected by parents in a loving environment.

Now, all I was left with were bitter memories and unanswered questions. Had I done the right thing persuading Avrum to leave Stepanki? Would he have been better off staying behind with me? These are thoughts I have continued to live with. I was left broken-hearted and, for years, feeling guilty, would not talk about my sorrow to my friends, who would have tried to comfort me.

Later, when I received Avrum's belongings, I was partially able to piece together what happened after he left Stepanki. His passport indicated that he left Romania and arrived in Palestine in October 1945. For some unknown reason, his passport with his picture in it identified him by a different name and different date and place of birth. This probably was the reason that I was unable to trace him.

The many photographs included with his belongings were heart-breaking to look at. Taken at different times throughout the years, they gave me an overview of his life from his journey to Romania to his arrival in Palestine and his participation in the war. He looked relaxed and seemed to be enjoying his work on the *kibbutz*. They showed how quickly he grew up within a few short years from a youngster to a confident young man training his comrades to use a machine gun.

I later received commemorative books from the Israeli government, two of which included his picture and a brief history of his life from his arrival in Palestine until his death. After his arrival, he received schooling at Nave Amiel near Sde Yaacov and then took part in a military course of the Gadna (an army youth program). He became a corporal and was in charge of training exercises at Nave Amiel during 1946-47. He moved to Sde Aliyahu, in the Galil a few miles from the Jordanian border, where he worked on a *kibbutz*. From there, he was drafted into the army, sent to an officer school and became a lieutenant. He belonged to the Palmach, the elite force of the Israeli army, and he fell at Latrun on July 18, 1948. He was buried in Mount Herzl cemetery in Jerusalem among the fallen heroes who gave their lives fighting for a homeland, a land that brought hope to tens of thousands of wandering Holocaust survivors.

When I received the news of Avrum's death, I was torn apart. I lost my drive, and it affected my work. I started to make small but costly mistakes, which I had to cover up. This added to my stress. I felt a change would help, and I decided to move to Montreal.

I met some friends from Italy there as well as other newcomers. Most of them worked in the needle trade. Some found it difficult to adjust and planned to emigrate to Israel. But they received letters from their relatives stating that conditions were unfavourable: life was harsh, and accommodation and jobs were difficult to find. Many people were living in corrugated metal huts that were cold in winter and hot in summer. They advised them to stay in Canada until they saved enough money to be able to get into some small business. I received a similar letter from a friend of mine telling me that life was harsh, but he still encouraged me to come. The feeling you'll get knowing you live as a Jew in your own country will soften the harshness, he wrote. But he added that I should never mention that I'd belonged to the Irgun. This dampened my enthusiasm and, knowing Avrum's fate, I decided to remain in Canada until I could afford adequate housing and a bigger truck or some other business to support myself.

In 1950, after having worked in Montreal for about a year, I returned to Winnipeg. I had saved more than $1,000 and, wanting to be independent, decided that my chances to succeed in business would be better in a smaller city. I continued working as a cutter and looked for a business opportunity requiring only limited resources. I had a chance to buy a small corner grocery store that required little money, but it had to be open seven days a week with long hours and small profit. There was little chance of increasing volume as, like most groceries, it was a neighbourhood store. The other option was to go into the cattle business in a small way with friends of mine who had shared the same cabin crossing the ocean. I chose the cattle business.

On credit, we bought a truck that would hold eight big cattle or fifteen calves and, with some money advanced by a cattle commission firm through which we were obligated to sell, we went out to the farms to buy cattle. This restricted us to dealing with that particular firm, sometimes to our disadvantage. Gradually we were able to borrow small amounts of money from the bank, thus allowing us to sell through the firms of our choice. We drove from farm to farm, and, if the farmer had any cattle for sale, we made him an offer. Sometimes we couldn't agree on the price of the animals and we left. Our profit, or sometimes loss, depended on how closely we judged the quality and weight of the animals, since we bought them individually on the hoof and sold them by the pound.

After struggling for a couple of years and learning the business from our mistakes, we split up and my partners moved to a neighbouring province. I continued alone, trying to scratch out a living and make the payments on my truck. June and July were slow months when the cattle were grazing and putting on weight, and the farmers were too busy haying to waste time rounding up a few animals – unless they were in desperate need of money. I tried to recoup my expenses by buying discarded car batteries and copper radiators and selling them to a junkyard in Winnipeg. I also bought horsehair that farmers accumulated from combing out horses' tails and sold it to a dealer who made brushes; in those days, farmers still used horses for some of their farm work. During the summer when I didn't return to Winnipeg for the night, I'd sometimes sleep in the truck to save the cost of a hotel room. Whenever I went to a restaurant, I always looked at the right side of the menu before ordering. But I wasn't discouraged – I liked the freedom and the idea of being self-employed, something I'd always dreamed of.

After several more years, I had saved some money and felt I had learned the business well enough to buy at the auction markets instead of buying a few cattle directly from farmers. This, however, required a substantial amount of money and, with no backing and no references, getting it proved to be a difficult task. It took time to convince the bank manager that I was reliable and risk-worthy. None of my friends had any assets to qualify them to sign for me. People whom I got to know at the Winnipeg stockyards, the largest in Canada at the time, could have signed, but they were reluctant to do so because I would become their competitor. In fact, they discouraged me from starting to buy cattle at the auction market and advised me to continue buying in the country. But my instinct told me that I'd reach my goal sooner by leaving the life of a drover and buying cattle at auction markets where large volumes were available. This would allow me to ship out of province, the same as my future competitors were currently doing. Years later, I was proven right. Cattle auction markets sprang up all over the countryside, and farmers sold their cattle by weight to the highest bidder at the market of their choice. Drovers became a dying breed.

Bidding against seasoned professional buyers was a new experience for me and not as easy as I had thought. Competition was keen. But I was determined to persevere and, after some years, it paid off. Some cattle dealers work on a commission basis, but I always bought the cattle on my own. I shipped them by truck or train to auction markets in eastern Canada and, as I gained more experience and the bank increased my credit, to the United States. I sorted my cattle according to quality and weight and, being in daily contact with sales representatives, shipped them to different locations, depending on where I could get the best price. In the 1980s, conditions changed, and I sold many of my cattle at pre-arranged prices directly to feedlots, as well as the occasional load to packing houses for slaughter. I continued to sell others at auction markets.

I was happy with my accomplishments, but my happiness was tempered by what had happened to my family. Quite often, without warning, my thoughts would drift back to Transnistria. Once again, I was a boy wandering around and revisiting the countryside where I used to roam. I visualized what I did and what happened to me. My longest "visit" was at my parents' graves, trying to remember them the way they were before the war and the good life they provided for me. But the pig barn nearby reminded me of the suffering they endured. When I broke away from my trance, it always took me a while to adjust to the present.

During the early years in Canada, I felt more comfortable associating with other newcomers. We had things in common and didn't have to cope with a language barrier. A local bowling alley was a favourite meeting place on weekends – some of us bowled or played pool and others just went to socialize. In the summer, we'd frequently meet in the park. Gradually we integrated into Canadian society, becoming members of synagogues, developing friendships, and some through marriage.

Sometimes, at social functions, I met people my age who were born in Canada and the conversation would turn to happy memories of their teenage years. Regardless of their background, rich or poor, they all had pleasant memories and laughed as they recalled them. Some of the things they did were foolish, but they had fun doing them. I walked away or just listened, putting on a happy face so they would not feel sorry for me. It took me a long time to get adjusted to a normal life.

In 1957, I visited Israel and went to Avrum's *kibbutz*. I was told that he had been highly respected by the members and that his picture, commemorating him as a fallen war hero, had hung for years in the mess hall. I later received a medal and commendation signed by the prime minister in recognition of Avrum's heroic efforts in fighting for his country. Although these were things to be proud of, they were also bitter reminders that, of the more than eighty percent of our large extended family who were defenceless and driven to their graves simply because they were Jews, only Avrum had the opportunity to defend himself and died fighting for a cause.

EPILOGUE

After the war, many people were reluctant to talk about their experiences in camps. They dreaded re-opening old wounds which had only partially healed and were barely covered by a thin membrane. It required only a slight scratch on the surface to trigger a pain that would penetrate deep into their hearts and evoke the bitter memories all over again.

Writing this book and reliving my experiences and losses has been painfully difficult, almost as difficult as was the day-to-day struggle during the war when my only thoughts were on skirting graves and making it through another day. As I was living through it, the pain of seeing members of my family deteriorate from the first day they got sick until the last minute of their lives was always there, but it must have been numbed by the daily struggle for survival. Now that I have been fortunate enough to live in a free country, it saddens me to think of the joys and pleasures that were denied to my family, and to know that they were not able to fully live out their lives and realize their dreams.

Life in Canada has been good to me, but I feel that part of me is missing, left behind in Transnistria where my loved ones are buried. Sometimes horrific scenes suddenly appear before my eyes, especially in dreams at night when I have to relive them again and again. These scenes are so real I feel as though the war is still on and I'm fighting for my life all over again. The battle ends only when I wake up or am awakened by my wife gently tapping me to stop my body from shaking. Once awake, I spend the rest of the night thinking about them and wondering if there was anything else that I could have done to relieve the suffering of my family. In reality, I was in no position to do any more, but part of my mind assumes that I should have been able to. Little words like "if" and "maybe" pop into my mind and haunt me – "if I had done this" or "maybe I should have done that" are unpleasant thoughts locked deep in my heart that I have to live with all my life.

When I think back to that time, I'm not sure how I managed to remain so optimistic or from where the mysterious strength even came. Given the circumstances, I should have been overcome with despair and ready, even eager, to give up. But hope, quite literally, kept me alive. I don't recall ever praying to God for help, but maybe hope came from my belief in Him.

I have managed to maintain this positive outlook throughout my life in both personal and business affairs. I know that it has helped me succeed in life and has allowed me to see the good in everything. Luckily I inherited many of my parents' characteristics and beliefs and have tried to fulfill their wishes; these have guided me and helped me ease back into the mainstream of life. I decided long ago that I was going to live a normal life, in spite of my history, my hardships, and my nightmares, and I have done so. For me, life in any form, even when it is cruel and harsh and unforgiving, still has meaning and is still worth living.

Once I arrived in Canada, I knew what I wanted to do with my life: to live a life with a purpose, with a human face. Until then, I had sustained myself by stealing and begging, then lived under a communist system, and the last two years on handouts. Canada was my first encounter with a democracy where I was responsible for my own well-being.

Having no schooling, I had to sort out the possibilities that were compatible with my abilities, either in business or in a trade. I was determined to keep focused and persevere until I succeeded in whatever I chose to do. Being penniless was not an obstacle. I had learned long ago to block out negative thoughts, which are the biggest threat to one's ability to succeed in life.

I also learned a lot from listening to and observing those people who respected others – their behaviour was an education for me about the real world that I would have to face, and I tried to follow in their footsteps. I had to build my future on a reputation and on references that did not exist. I knew who I was, but it was also important that others should know who I am.

With time and experience and hard work, my relatively unusual pursuit in the cattle business proved to be a fascinating, challenging vocation. I have travelled hundreds of thousands of miles and have had the privilege of meeting people in the cattle industry throughout most of Canada and in the mid-western United States, places where my cattle were shipped. During the fall, the peak of cattle movement when I bought hundreds of cattle each week, I was often on the move for days at a time with very little sleep. I would leave Winnipeg for various auction markets in our neighbouring province of Saskatchewan, buy cattle at the markets during the day, and drive to other towns during the evening and well into the night. During the off-season, I spent many evenings with other cattle buyers, all of whom were Gentile, in hotel lobbies or in one of our rooms having a social drink. Invariably, I was asked what life was like during the Holocaust and how I managed to survive. Most of them knew little of what had transpired and took a keen interest in hearing of my experiences.

Throughout the war, I imagined the day when I would be able to walk out of the shadows of darkness and proudly proclaim my true identity. Once I began my life anew in Canada, I made a habit of doing just that. To this day, whenever I introduce myself to someone, I introduce my heritage as well. Everyone who extends his hand to me in business, friendship or in need, is told that I am Jewish. I do this for many reasons: so that people will see that we survived, so that they will see what a Jew is, and so that they will see that we are no different than anyone else.

For this same reason, I willingly answer the questions that my Gentile business associates have so often asked me. Through my story and my achievements in life, they can learn the value of optimism and the pain caused by intolerance. Besides, I believe that silence too often can be misconstrued as guilt. If I don't tell people about what happened to me, if I don't express my pain, which more often than not is accompanied by emotion, I feel I would be doing an injustice to all those who perished. Most importantly, silence also allows the perpetrators of repression to get away with their crimes and history to be repeated. It's easy to sway a person to one's point of view if they are ill-informed on a topic. Therefore, it is crucial to make people aware about events of the Holocaust. Just as knowledge can serve as a springboard for truth, a lack of knowledge can open the door to injustice.

Ironically, the early liberation of Transnistria by the Soviets in the spring of 1944 ensured that the rest of the world did not find out about our particular fate for some time. With the war still waging on the European continent, survivors were lumped together with and treated the same as the Ukrainians living in the area at the time. Many of us were drafted into the Soviet army. With Transnistria under communist rule, and foreign journalists either not allowed in or having no knowledge of our existence, our tragedies were overlooked. The mass killings of millions of Jews, uncovered by the Allied forces at the end of the war in 1945, dwarfed the Transnistria tragedy. It was only in the spring of 1999 that Transnistria was added to the list of Holocaust sites permanently

engraved in the Hall of Remembrance at the United States Holocaust
Memorial Museum in Washington, D.C.

Even though my major means of movement during the Holocaust was
by foot, I was twice forced into rail cars, both times unsure of the destination. These experiences occasionally resurfaced when I sorted cattle
into pens according to quality, size, and gender. After being fed and
watered, the cattle were chased into cattle cars or trucks. Some just went
in, others sensed something was wrong, hesitated, and turned back, and
the odd time an animal was so desperate to get away that it disregarded
the corral fence, ramming itself through by breaking a few planks.
Occasionally, an animal also succeeded in jumping the fence.

As I watched the cattle being loaded, I couldn't help but feel sorry
for them – they had been uprooted from their natural environment and
were under great stress. They were loaded into cars according to
Humane Society guidelines, but I always made sure that there were two
animals less than the allowed weight to give the other cattle more room.

Sometimes in summer, I walked along the platform next to a trainload
of cattle. While waiting to unload my cattle, I could feel the heat radiating
from the cars and see their eyes peering through the slats. Without intend-
ing it, my thoughts would suddenly shift, and I would be looking at Jews
being transported in cattle cars to their deaths. I had seen documentaries
where Jews carrying their belongings were assembled at railway stations –
men, women with babies, children, old people with canes, all in disarray,
forced into crowded cattle cars by German soldiers. I had also heard fellow Holocaust survivors talk about their suffering in the trains – travelling
for days in crowded cars without food or water. Surrounded by crying
children, dead bodies, and unbearable heat and stench, they never knew
when their time would come; depressed, sitting in fear, awaiting their fate.
Only when the train stopped or slowed down to enter a train station was
there any activity – every little hole in the boxcar now had eyes peering
out to catch a glimpse of where they were. When they finally arrived at
their destination, the situation became chaotic. As the car doors slid open,
they were greeted by vicious-looking German shepherds barking, attuned
to their masters' loud commands: "Get out! Get out!" They were forced
out and told to line up, men to one side, women and children to another,
and sorted: some to live and others to die.

I sympathized with my fellow Holocaust survivors. I remembered
the day in the summer of 1943 when soldiers caught me as I entered the

city of Shargorod. They took me to a gathering place where Jews were assembled to be taken to work. We were marched to a train station and forced into crowded boxcars. Even though we were all males, and everything indicated that we were going to a work camp, we were still in distress knowing that others had been taken to work in just this way and had never returned. We felt imprisoned, crammed together in the suffocating heat with barely any light. As I looked through a small opening in that boxcar, I realized that my movements up until then, even though they were illegal and perilous, had always allowed me a limited degree of freedom and the feeling of being in charge of my own life. In truth, it was only a mental exercise in self-delusion. Nevertheless, it suppressed the reality on the ground and allowed me to look toward the future, even though I had seen my shadow on the grave many times.

I've often been asked why the Jews didn't resist. Of course, the answer is not a simple one. For us, it was more a question of how to save our families by *not* resisting. We were unarmed, and, even if we had had access to a few guns, logic rather than passivity would have prevented us from taking any action that would endanger our families as well as the whole convoy. We faced well-armed soldiers with trigger-happy fingers who perceived us as targets rather than as people. The local population showed us no support; in fact, many displayed open animosity toward us, and some even assisted the soldiers. To resist would have been futile, or worse than futile, since it would have brought about the deaths of many. And besides, people's nature is to live in hope, and hope was still alive. We were lured into believing that we were going to be resettled; no one anticipated the possibility that the Nazis were planning to send us to our deaths. Destroying a whole people was a concept that was impossible to grasp. When reality finally sank in, we were malnourished, weak and sick; many were already dead; and with no sign of help from the free world, the human impulse to resist had vanished from many as life just lingered on.

I sometimes look back to the past to try to understand why Avrum and I survived. Maybe it had to do with Mother's last sorrowful words of advice. "Take care of Avrumale and yourself," she said to me in the moments before she died, our eyes focused on each other. I couldn't hold back the tears. Those few whispered words in the pig barn at Stepanki had a profound and lasting impact on me. They ignited my spirit and gave purpose to my fight for survival as I tried to fulfill her wishes. Avrum and I rebelled with power and purpose. We were so embittered after the loss of our parents that we found a true, if childish, determination to survive in order to spite the Nazis. We found the courage to keep on fighting and hold off despair. We were also emboldened by the boundless pangs of hunger which drove us to take bold measures without thinking of consequences. With nothing to lose and our lives to gain, we ignored the dangers and, with the help of luck, overcame the unavoidable risks of our lives as orphans in the midst of war.

I cannot revive the dead of Transnistria, but I can try to bring to light the struggles they endured in trying to survive. Maybe future generations can learn from history to let people live according to their beliefs and find ways to prevent humanity from destroying itself with lethal weapons, supposedly developed to prevent wars.

Transnistria left me with an imprint to cherish life in any form and not to lose sight of human values. Monetary gain has its rewards and satisfaction, but, for me, having parents would have been far more rewarding than any material achievements. It would have enriched my life in loving relationships, which are the only rewards that truly matter. Instead, I was left with only my imagination to envision how my life would have evolved, growing up a child embraced by loving parents, in a normal environment. The human mind serves one's desires – some through illusion and some through reality. Some people can find the richness and meaning of life even in an environment where life barely exists. Others have everything to live for, but life to them is hollow, their expectations beyond reality.

After the war, Holocaust survivors were homeless and travelled to different countries in our search for a place to plant new roots. But we were denied the pleasures that other immigrants take for granted. They looked forward to returning one day to their homes to visit family and friends and to pay their respects at the graves of loved ones. But few of us would dare to let our minds wander to such forbidden territory, which would evoke only bitter memories. Long gone are the days when, in the smallest villages to the largest cities, Jewish lives once flourished and dreams and aspirations could be realized in homes we called our own.

I believe in Jewish traditions and value strongly my Jewish heritage. Without keeping that heritage alive, our people's identity would have been lost after 2,000 years in the Diaspora. My wife and I belong to a Conservative synagogue and keep kosher at home, as our parents did. We do, however, enjoy eating out and thus eat non-kosher food outside the home.

My wife Ida's parents, Ira and Rosa Reiss, and her brothers Harry, Sam, and Ed came to Saskatchewan from Poland in April 1939. The Canadian government allowed a limited number of Jews to enter with the stipulation that they settle on the land as farmers. With the exception of Rosa Reiss's brother and his wife, all of her parents' large families perished in the Holocaust. In 1950, Ida's family left the farm and moved to Winnipeg. After attending the University of Manitoba, Ida became a dietitian, and for many years she held the position of Assistant Director of Dietetics at the city's largest hospital.

✳

From Winnipeg, I tried to reach back into the past to find the person who helped me more than any other, and that was Marusia. I wanted to help her materially and made several attempts to get in touch with her by mail. Unfortunately, I never learned her surname, and my letters, addressed to "Marusia in Stepanki," were never answered or returned.

Other communications with the past were more rewarding. In early 1954, I received a letter from my cousin Moishe Hoffer telling me that he, along with his mother and sister, had survived Transnistria and emigrated to Palestine. He got married there and then moved to New Jersey. It was happy news as I wasn't aware that he had survived, and I went to visit him for Passover. While having dinner with him and his wife Pepi, we started talking about Transnistria, and she told me that she had lived in Stepanki.

"How did you end up in Stepanki?" I asked her, surprised.

"My family and the other Jews in Vashkovits were ordered out in late fall 1941," she said. "We were each allowed to take whatever belongings we could carry. They forced us into crowded boxcars, and, after several days of travel, we reached the Dniester River. After we were chased out of the cars, we were force-marched across the river to Mogilev. Three or four days later, we reached Stepanki."

"Were you in the pig barn?" I asked.

"No," she said. "The pig barns were overcrowded, and through bribery and luck, my dad, who was a tinsmith, was able to acquire a small shack and support us. Even that was very crowded, because I had three sisters and a brother."

"What was your maiden name?" I asked.

"Steinhauer," she said.

"Was your brother's name Mokie?"

"Yes," she said, her eyes opening wide. "How did you know?"

"I used to come into your shack to warm up, and your mother always gave me soup and a piece of bread."

Moishe and I talked late into the night, reminiscing about the good times before the war and the happy visits to his parents, Uncle David and Aunt Dvorah.

My former comrades Max, Isiu, and Magda made their way to Israel after the state was created. Isiu adopted a Hebrew name, Israel Doron, and was elected mayor of Acco in the 1960s and 1970s. My two uncles and the Sussmanns, as well as Bertha and her husband Chaim, emigrated to Israel in the 1960s. Bertha's brother Abrascha was the only one of my relatives who had left Romania illegally in 1948 for Palestine. He married an immigrant from Bucharest, and they had two daughters. In the late 1970s, while shopping in a vegetable market in Jenin, he was shot by an Arab using a silenced gun. Regina and her Russian-born husband and son were not allowed to leave and remained in Storojinet until the early 1970s. Only by pretending to be Uncle Simon's sister was she finally allowed to leave for Israel.

On my first visit to Israel in 1957, I went to my brother's grave. It was heartbreaking to see the ages engraved on the tombstones; many among the rows and rows were so young. The country was beautiful, and I stayed for three months, investigating the possibility of establishing myself there. I had a limited amount of money, and, after talking to friends and looking around, I realized that my resources were insufficient to go into any kind of business that would support me. By then, the cattle business back home had started to grow, and I decided to postpone my move.

In the meantime, I had also met my future wife in Winnipeg. I had seen an attractive-looking girl at the lake on summer weekends. I inquired about her and was told that she was a sister of two men I knew. I phoned her, but she was hesitant to go on a blind date. She gave me some excuse to keep me on the line, however, and I suspected she was asking her brother about me. She came back to the phone and told me she would accept the date, and after about three weeks we became engaged – on October 1, 1963, her birthday. We got married two and a half months later. With her whole family living in Winnipeg, she was reluctant to move as far away as Israel, and we decided to remain in Canada. It was a short courtship that resulted in a long, happy marriage.

One of the joys of growing older is reaching the stage where one can choose to overlook the future and enjoy remembering the past, reflecting on happy events throughout the years. Another is to pass the time talking with friends and letting our memories wander. Memories have a life of their own; they are compartmentalized, and one can choose to recall any event any time and to relive it. For Holocaust survivors, however, our weightier memories sometimes intrude upon our more pleasant ones and shape the nature of our recollections. Even those of us who adjusted and were fortunate to live happy and comfortable lives after the war were left with scars. Each survivor has coped differently – how one copes is as personal as one's fingerprint.

Over the years, I frequently discussed with Ida my plans to write a book about my experiences in Transnistria. As the only survivor of my immediate family, I felt that I should somehow honour the lives and memory of my parents and siblings, and the thousands of others who also perished, almost unnoticed by the world, in or enroute to Transnistria. I had told her about only certain incidents, but, knowing me, she felt it would be too difficult emotionally for me to put it all down on paper. When I finally did start, I hesitated to write the most horrific truths and tried to soften my experiences. I thought that people might find them difficult to believe. But Ida felt that, if I was going to write, I should tell the whole story as I remembered it. Only with her continuous and unfailing support and assistance was I able to complete the book you hold in your hands.

NOTES

1 Anti-Semitism was particularly strong in Romania. According to Raul Hilberg, "The emancipation of the Jews had been a recent occurrence in most of Europe, but it was particularly recent in Romania. Most Jews had acquired Romanian citizenship after the end of World War I, in pursuance of a minority treaty concluded by Romania with the Allied powers as part of the price that Romania had to pay for its new-won territories. There was considerable sentiment in Romania against payment of that price, and in the 1930s the rise of the pro-Nazi and anti-Jewish Iron Guard cast a shadow on Jewish security in the country. In December 1937, when Romania acquired its first pro-Nazi regime under Prime Minister Octavian Goga, about 120,000 Jews lost their citizenship." Raul Hilberg, *The Destruction of the European Jews,* Vol. 2 (New York: Holmes & Meier, 1985), p. 761.

2 Goga's and Cuza's ideas continued to exert considerable influence on Romanian politics, partly because the civilian bureaucracy of wartime dictator Ion Antonescu's regime was staffed with many former Goga-Cuza adherents. David S. Wyman, ed., *The World Reacts to the Holocaust* (Baltimore: Johns Hopkins University Press, 1996), p. 229.

3 Romania acquired Bukovina and Bessarabia after the end of World War I. Nora Levin writes, "At Versailles, the Romanian Government had finally accepted a minority treaty granting Jews citizenship, but the minorities statute, incorporated in the peace treaty of 1919, was never fully honored in the newly acquired territories of Romania. In 1937, during the pro-Nazi regime of Octavian Goga, 225,000 Jews in the annexed territories were stripped of their citizenship and an additional 91,000 were classed as foreigners." Nora Levin, *The Holocaust: The Destruction of European Jewry, 1933-1945* (New York: Schocken, 1968), pp. 562-3.

4 The British Government issued its Palestine White Paper on May 17, 1939, fixing an upper limit of 75,000 Jews for admission to Palestine over the following five years. To enforce this policy, the British government put diplomatic pressure on Yugoslavia, Romania, Turkey, and Greece to prevent boats carrying "illegal" immigrants from proceeding toward Palestine. Martin Gilbert, *The Holocaust: A History of the Jews of Europe During the Second World War* (New York: Holt, 1985), p. 79.

5 "By early 1941, a formidable German Army of 680,000 troops was massed in Romania which bordered the Ukraine for 300 miles and put German troops within easy striking distance of the Soviet Union." Nora Levin, op. cit., p. 561.

6 This was part of the so-called Tighina Agreement, concluded between the German and Romanian military staffs on August 30, 1941. Transnistria was created as a temporary "dumping ground" for Jews from Bessarabia and Bukovina. Under the agreement, Romania was to assign the Jews to camps from which they would perform forced labour until military operations ended, and then to transport them "to the East." This plan was part of Hitler's instructions to Antonescu on how to handle the "Jewish question" in Romania. Nora Levin, op. cit., p. 573.

7 Martin Gilbert, *Atlas of the Holocaust* (Toronto: Lester, 1993), pp. 71, 73. The suffering of Romanian Jewry, however, was not distributed equally. As Nora Levin writes, "The 350,000 Jews in Old Romania, in the main, survived. In Transylvania, 150,000 were engulfed in the Hungarian deportations, while the 300,000 Jews in Bessarabia and Bukovina bore the brunt of Romanian destructive frenzy and the German *Einsatzgruppen*." Nora Levin, op. cit., p. 564. Romanian soldiers extended their genocide to non-Romanian Jews of the Soviet Ukraine as well. Raul Hilberg writes, "In that region the Romanians also killed around 150,000 indigenous Jews in the Odessa area and Golta. No country, besides Germany, was involved in massacres of Jews on such a scale." Raul Hilberg, op. cit., p. 759.

8 The estimated inmate population at Edinets was 10,000 on August 9. Raul Hilberg, op. cit., p. 771.

9 The confusion about crossing the Dniester was indeed caused by the Germans' own consternation at the numbers of Jews entering Transnistria. In the last week of July, local Romanian commanders began to force some 25,000 Jews from northern Bessarabia across the Dniester into what was still a German-controlled area. The Germans were alarmed at the spectre of hundreds of thousands of Jews driven across the Dniester into the rear of the 600 men of the *Einsatzgruppe D* who were attempting the staggering task of killing all the Jews of the southern Ukraine. The Germans told the Romanians "to proceed with the elimination of the Jewish element only in a systematic and slow manner." Raul Hilberg, op. cit., pp. 769-70.

10 "Among the Jews from the Edinets camp was one group originally evicted from the villages of Bukovina that had already endured a torment of two months' pointless wandering just to get there and then had to endure the Edinets camp regime itself." Radu Ioanid, *The Holocaust in Romania: The Destruction of Jews and Gypsies Under the Antonescu Regime, 1940-1944* (Chicago: Ivan R. Dee, 2000), p. 149.

11 According to Martin Gilbert, 70 to 100 people died at Edinets every day from mid-July to mid-September, 1941. Martin Gilbert, *Atlas of the Holocaust,* op. cit., p. 73.

12 A doctor who was present as we marched through Atachi from Edinets is quoted as follows: "Never shall I forget this scene. They are no longer human beings. Hungry, clad in rags, they drag themselves, tremble, moan, yell. In the bottom of their eyes is the fear of death, even as in the eyes of hunted animals fleeing before a pack of

hounds amid whining bullets. This herd of beaten men … march in a uniform, almost unconscious motion. The beasts permit no rest, driving them forward in the direction of the Dniester, the raft, the inferno. I hear for the first time: 'Whoever lags behind will be shot dead!'" S. Jagendorf, *Jagendorf's Foundry: A Memoir of the Romanian Holocaust, 1941-1944* (New York: HarperCollins, 1991), p. 23.

13 "As of November 28, three orphanages sheltered eight hundred. From April 1942 to May 1943, 356 children died there, mortality increasing especially during the last three months of 1942. Dr. Emanuel Faendrich depicted an apocalyptic situation on November 28, 1942:

The children live in large rooms that are not heated and that are badly ventilated, with fetid smells in some instances; during the day the children remain in dirty beds – they have no underwear, no bedding, nor the necessary clothing to leave their beds and walk around…. I found in one room 109 children…. I saw many children who suffered from boils, scabies, and other skin diseases." Radu Ioanid, op. cit., pp. 216–7.

14 The government had decided to exploit a large peat bog in the Tulcin district to manufacture heating briquettes. Jagendorf, op. cit., p. 159.

15 "On July 11, a gendarme caught thirteen Jewish escapees from Tulcin in the town of Jurkovca (Tulcin District); he killed twelve, one escaped." Radu Ioanid, op. cit., p. 192.

16 Jagendorf, who was in charge of the Mogilev ghetto, writes, "Only with great effort did we recover these people, who returned half dead from having to dig peat by hand." Jagendorf, op. cit., p. 160.

17 Several thousand Jews were incarcerated in Picziora (Peciora), a place in which hunger was so acute that inmates ate bark, leaves, grass, and dead human flesh. Raul Hilberg, op. cit., p. 779.

18 In 1941, an Order-in-Council authorizing one thousand Jewish orphans from Vichy France admission to Canada came to nothing. In February 1947, the Canadian Jewish Congress persuaded the government to reactivate this Order-in-Council; it was passed by cabinet on April 29, 1947. Irving Abella and Harold Troper, *None Is Too Many* (Toronto: Lester & Orpen Dennys, 1982), pp. 270-71

INDEX